HOAXED

EVERYTHING THEY TOLD YOU IS A LIE

MIKE CERNOVICH

Publishing services provided by 

ISBN-13: 978-0-9984901-1-3

CONTENTS

INTRODUCTION

When you're making a film, 90% of the best work gets left on the cutting room floor. You spend hundreds of hours interviewing dozens of interesting people, and each subject receives only a few minutes in a feature-length film.

Over the course of a year-and-a-half, I met some of the world's greatest media minds. I even interviewed Alex Jones, and asked him if he is a purveyor of fake fews.

For this book, we took several of the best interviews, edited them for clarity, and posted them for your enjoyment. Think of this *Hoaxed* book as a collection of interviews.

These interviews represent different viewpoints and I do not endorse anyone in particular or vouch for what they say, nor that they endorse me. You'll find that some of the interviewees are highly critical of my work, and they will challenge your views, whatever they may be.

I've also included some of my own original essays, and share my experience in dealing with fake news.

Be sure to update / synch this book in three weeks. It will be updated with exclusive images from *Hoaxed* and to improve any formatting issues. (There are always some glitches in the first version. We'll get any formatting issues and typos fixed immediately.)

Mike Cernovich
Orange County, California - 2018

P.S. If you pre-ordered *Hoaxed* before October 1st, email me a copy of your receipt to receive a free ticket to the film's Los Angeles premier on October 20th. Send this email to Backers@Cernovich.com

WHAT IT'S LIKE BEING LIED ABOUT

I'm an author, filmmaker, and journalist. You're reading this book, aren't you? And it's based on a major motion picture, which is a fancy way of saying movie. *Hoaxed* is my second film. My first film, *Silenced*, featured Alan Dershowitz, Candace Owens, and a diverse cast of rabbis, adherent Muslims, Christians, and offensive comedians and meme makers.

I enjoy talking to and about interesting people and interesting subjects, and don't really have "politics." Think about all of the profiles of me, and there have been thousands. None of them mention my actual political views, because my views are sort of boring.

My first book *Gorilla Mindset* has sold nearly 100,000 copies. The average book sells 1,000 copies in a lifetime, thus promoting multi-best-selling author Neil Strauss to say, "Selling 10,000 copies of a book is equivalent to a gold record. Selling 100,000 copies of a book is going platinum."

I'm currently involved in precedent-setting litigation in the Second Circuit Court of Appeals, after I sued to obtain records involving a convicted sexual predator. The Reporter's Committee for Freedom of the Press, a non-partisan organization devoted to journalism, filed a brief supporting my lawsuit. The Miami Herald also filed a lawsuit after mine was dismissed, claiming that my lawsuit was just and valid.

A member of Congress, John Conyers, resigned because of my reporting. And an A-List Hollywood actor was fired by Disney after my reporting surfaced some disturbing views he had. Chuck Todd asked the National Security Adviser of the United States of America about me on Meet the Press. That's the level of the game I play at, when I choose to.

As Muhammad Alisaid, "It's not bragging if you can back it up."

Yet if you Google me, you're be taken into an alternative universe called Wikiality, a term coined by left-wing comedian Stephen Colbert. According to the Urban dictionary, "Wikiality refers to the changing of reality or truth via a Wikipedia-like system, allowing the public to change facts as long as there are others that agree."

The Wikipedia entry on me describes me as an "alt-right conspiracy theorist."

I have a biracial family, so a "white ethnostate" isn't a desire of mine, and I don't like the alt-right guys. Countless articles from reputable sources explain that I'm not alt-right. It is simply inaccurate to describe me as alt-right, but accuracy doesn't matter to Wikipedia.

Some people with very disturbing Internet histories, in an effort to incite death threats against me, have taken over the Wikipedia entry on me. If you make a change to my Wikipedia page, the change will be reverted within 5 minutes. Whenever I'm in the news, the editors lock the page down to prevent anyone from editing it to reflect the truth about me.

I'm not the only victim of Wikiality. Nazism was the official political philosophy of the GOP, Google results showed. Whatever one thinks of the GOP (and I don't think highly of it), Nazism would be a bit too far. The Google result was disinformation.

Google refused to take personal responsibility for spreading disinformation. The fault was Wikipedia's, Google claimed.

Google prioritizes Wikipedia in its search result. The top search hit for nearly any subject will be Wikipedia. (Facebook, too, has integrated Wikipedia into its system, and when you share a link to a news article, and click for more information, the Wikipedia page shows up.)

The issue is that stalkers and harassers can take over a Wikipedia page. It only takes 3 people to collude against you, and your Wikipedia page will share whatever they want it to. There's nothing anyone can do to stop this.

When Wikipedia isn't outright fake, they exaggerate trivial stories.

Did you know, for example, that a member of Congress resigned because of me? John Conyers, Jr. settled a sexual harassment lawsuit against him. I obtained the settlement documents, which BuzzFeed published. Boom. He resigned. Don't take my word for it, the Washington Post wrote about my involvement in the Conyers story.

Susan Rice, former director of the National Security Agent, used her tremendous powers to spy on American people. The process, known as "unmasking," was the biggest spying scandal of 2017. Rice denied that she unmasked American citizens, and then was forced to admit it after I broke the story.

The Wikipedia page on me doesn't even mention the Susan Rice unmasking story, and it barely mentions my reporting on James Gunn. Gunn was fired from a billion-dollar film franchise after I uncovered disturbing Tweeted he had made, which he claimed were merely jokes about child molestation. James Gunn gets one line in the entry about me.

Five full paragraphs are devoted to a trivial internet beef I had with some guy whose name I can barely remember. Sometime a year or so ago, I found a Tweet by a mid-tier YouTube named Sam. His Tweet read: "Don't care re Polanski, but I hope if my daughter is ever raped it is by an older truly talented man w/ a great sense of mise en scene."

That Tweet was pretty creepy, to put it mildly, and I called MSNBC for comment. MSNBC cancelled Sam's contributor contract, although it quickly rehired him after Christopher Hayes came to Seder's rescue. Sam was only joking, Hayes claimed, and everyone needed to lighten up. What's a rape joke among friends?

In terms of my life, the Sam story wasn't a top 100. To the creeps who stalk my Wikipedia page, one trivial story takes on outsized importance. Five full paragraphs detailing every in-and-out to something I spent an hour on.

Meanwhile, my reporting on a member of Congress and A-list director receive a blur. How many journalists have forced a member of Congress to resign and reported a story leading to the director of a billion-dollar film franchise resign?

If Wikipedia were accurate, they'd describe me as an author, filmmaker, and sometimes journalist. They'd include in their entry that I've made multiple films and am involved in major free press litigation.

Wikipedia is a fake encyclopedia.

Do not trust anything you read in it.

JOURNALISTS DON'T READ BOOKS

My best-selling book *Gorilla Mindset* isn't remotely political, nor does it cover "how to be an alpha male." That doesn't stop so-called journalists from claiming *Gorilla Mindset* is everything from a wannabe guide to alphaness to a manual of the far right. Nonsense. My book has been read by all genders, religions, and races, and although it does have a strong male readership, 30% of Gorilla Mindset readers are women, and women attend all my seminars and other events.

What you'll learn about journalists is that they aren't particularly well-read. They sit on Twitter all day and Tweet snark at each other. They are obsessed with Twitter, and as much as I am mocking them, the truth is that I barely read actual books anymore. "Careful," Nietzsche said, "that when you fight illiterates, that you yourself do not become illiterate."

If journalists read, they'd know that Kindle has a feature that allows you to find the 10 most popular highlights of a book. *Gorilla Mindset*'s 10 most popular highlights include, "To get more out of life, you must get more out of yourself. You must take personal responsibility for your thoughts and emotions. You must stop blaming the system. Your days of looking outside of yourself for answers are gone."

How offensive, right?

Another popular passage from *Gorilla Mindset* reads, "Gorilla Mindset shift: Reframe the issues. Choose to focus on how the difficulty you're facing will make you stronger, more intelligent, more emotionally complex, or more resourceful." Totally triggering, isn't it?

Can you tolerate more shocking and outrageous words? Here's another paragraph: "Now, imagine you believe the world is abundant. The world is one of endless resources and unlimited potential. What you do matters. Your choices matter. You matter. Each day is a new day full of infinite possibilities." I must have been trolling when writing that passage, as it's a terrible word choice. Or something.

HACKED LIKE JOY REID

Far left-wing outlet MSNBC had found a new star in Joy Reid. Reid is everything you'd want in a news anchor - smart, charismatic, and aggressive. She's also a reformed Internet troll.

An anonymous whistle blower went through Reid's old blog posts. Using Twitter, this person began revealing some offensive content from Reid.

Reid's blog was loaded with 9/11 conspiracy theories, mean-spirited memes about John McCain, and even some homophobic jokes. I won't repeat what Reid said directly as it'd probably get his book flagged as hate speech by Amazon. You can run a Google search for Joy Reid's old blog posts for a laugh or dose of outrage.

Nothing Reid wrote offended me, but there was more than enough on her blog to get any conservative a lifetime ban from FoxNews.

When the first batch of offensive posts surfaced in December, 2017, Reid apologized. Everyone accepted her apology, because as you'll see throughout this book and film, there's a different set of standards that are applied to the far left. Reid moved on, just as Seder had moved on. Or so she thought.

In April, 2018, a new batch of shocking bigotry was released. What Reid said was as bad as anything wrong thinkers like me have said, and in many cases she said far worse than I allegedly have.

Rather than apologize once again, Reid outright lied. She claimed her blog had been hacked!

Time travelers, perhaps from Russia, planted offensive content on her blog. Yet her hacking tale quickly fell apart.

In life, your wins can be your losses. In Reid's case, the Library of Congress had made the decision to archive her blog years ago. This was a high honor, and also a back-up of her blog.

For Reid's story to be true, the Library of Congress would have had to have been hacked.

Reid claimed she filed a report with the FBI, although no one took this seriously, because while lying to the public isn't a crime, lying to the FBI most certainly is.

Joy Reid remains gainfully employed at NBC, despite posting bigoted content and then lying about being hacked.

When people claim I said something offensive in the past, I reply with, "No. I was hacked like Joy Reid."

That annoys a lot of journalists, and I don't care. Why do they hound me constantly about satire? Go talk to Joy Reid, Bill Clinton, Keith Ellision, or James Gunn.

And no one who is conservative should have to answer for any offensive words as long as Joy Reid remains on air. Double standards exist because we let them exist. It's time to stop playing by unfair and rigged rules.

When NBC fires Joy Reid, then Republicans should be willing to discuss whatever bad jokes they allegedly made. Until then, remember the Reid rule.

"I was hacked, like Joy Reid."

Post-script: Joy Reid was sued on September 25, 2018 for inciting a harassment hate mob on a woman. Reid posted a false accusation about the woman, leading to the innocent woman receiving death threats.

WHAT NO ONE TELLS YOU ABOUT SELECTIVE EDITING

Brett Kavanaugh learned a lesson about selective editing when Senator Kamala Harris shared a video where it appeared that Kavangaugh said that birth control was "abortion inducing." As people who watched the full hearings knew, Kanvuagh was paragraphing what someone else said in court. "They said," was how he began his segment.

I don't care what you think about Kavanaugh, as he's way above my social class. It's not my job to defend the man. But if you do care about the truth, it should matter to you that at sitting U.S. Senator is using edited videos to misrepresent what a Supreme Court nominee had said.

Selective editing is a nasty process which goes like this: Imagine you do a video where you say, "People call me a murder. Yes, totally, I murder people." You are being smug and dismissive, and maybe even laughing.

One day you get famous, and people start asking you questions about a video where you "confess" to murder. Confused, you listen to the video, hear what sounds like your voice, and can't figure out where the video came from.

At least once a day I get asked about audio of me saying some really nasty stuff. Because I've done several thousand hours of video, there is audio of me saying all sorts stuff that I never said.

There are even videos where I am quoting other people in the full video, but the part where I am quoting someone gets clipped off.

Once you become a public figure, you must become comfortable with people believing untrue stories about you.

But as a viewer and listener, be cautious. Most audio is clipped for a reason, and that's because there is other context that would explain it.

CENSORSHIP AS A FORM OF FAKE NEWS

You know that the entry about me on Wikipedia is fake because I'm able to prove to you that it's fake. This cannot be tolerated by the smear artists who, while living on trust funds, write for nasty blogs and work to destroy lives.

There's a concerted effort to ban influential public figures from social media and even from publishing books on Amazon. Literaly book burns are what we call "journalists" today.

There will be media efforts to ban this book you're reading, even though you're reading this book and won't see anything out of bounds. None of that matters. The truth doesn't matter.

Without social media, there's no way to fight back against fake news. There is no way to counter lies about WMDs in Iraq.

This is why journalist are attempting to censor and silence the people they write about. They want control over the narrative, so that they may lie and smear and destroy lives like their friends at Gawker did for almost a decade.

FAKE NEWS BODY COUNTS

If people really cared about stopping fake news, they'd ban the New York Times, CNN, and FoxNews from every platform. Let's look at body counts.

Cernovich - 0

New York Times – 50 million.

Yes that 50 million number is accurate. Walter Duranty of *The New York Times* won a Pulitzer Prize for his reporting on Stalin. According to Duranty, no one in the Ukraine or Soviet Union were starving. Reports about famines were fake news.

As we now know, Stalin starved tens of millions of people in the Ukraine and elsewhere. Duranty's lies emboldened Stalin and kept the U.S. from taking action to protect innocent lives.

The Times has not returned the Pulitizer Duranty won for his fake news about Stalin.

If Stalin's gulags are ancient history to you, consider the war in Iraq.

Every major media outlet reported, falsely, that there were weapons of mass destruction in Iraq. The number of dead in Iraq has been estimated at over 500,000.

The War in Iraq has also cost taxpayers trillions of dollars and created a refugee crisis. What could the U.S. have built with the $7 trillion spent in Iraq and Afghanistan?

Alex Jones of InfoWars speculated that the Sandy Hook massacre was a hoax. I find this insensitive, and have said so publicly. The emotional toll on the parents wasn't something Jones likely anticipated, as freaks called up the parents to call them "crisis actors." Imagine being a parent who lost a child, and having someone claim your child was alive?

Yet the worst Alex Jones did hasn't lead to any murders, let alone a number of deaths approaching those killed by Stalin, and more recently, those who died in Iraq. That's not to defend Jones, and indeed Jones has apologized to the Sandy Hook families several times for his error in judgment.

But let's keep it real. Whose errors and fake news have lead to the most deaths?

Fake news is deadly, and the mainstream media is responsible for most of the killings.

A RIGHT WING KFILE

The head of White House personnel doesn't live in Washington D.C. Residing in Brooklyn is the man with the final say so - Andrew Kaczynski, or KFILE for short. He has taken on a legend of his own, and and White House sources regularly call me to complain that another one of their friends was fired after he was able to dig up an old Tweet or radio hit.

What KFILE does is entirely legitimate, although it's fair to point out that he doesn't seem to find much dirt on liberals, and he should be vigilant to only "punch up" by using his resources to investigate the truly powerful rather than the merely annoying. (To his credit, KFILE wrote the first national news article on the credible domestic abuse allegations Keith Ellison's ex-girlfriend made against Ellison.)

According to Paul Farhi of the Washington Post, KFILE is the elephant who never forgets. In a glowing profile, Farhi lists the ghosts of White House staffers past, that is, people who lose their jobs after KFILE found some offensive social media posts. Farhi writes: "In each case, Kaczynski and cohorts dug up something damning about the nominee or appointee. And in each case, it wasn't some dark secret or sinister conspiracy from long ago. It was their own words."

I credit my methods to KFILE. It never occurred to me to listen to old podcasts or read old Tweets in order to do journalism, but after watching his methods and their effectiveness, I joined in.

James Gunn lost his job after I discovered some disgusting Tweets and blog posts. (More on Gunn, later.) Unlike KFILE, there was no glowing profile in the Washington Post for me.

Margaret Sullivan of the same Washington Post that gave a glowing profile to KFILE wrote about me. Here's what Sullivan said: "Much of the news media and most of polite society have little understanding of how these bad-faith attacks work. What is dug up is too often taken at face value, without crucial context about how tweets and other forms of expression are being turned into bludgeons in a cynical war against liberal values and individuals."

Does Sullivan have any self-awareness? Roseanne had been fired over a Tweet, which she didn't intend to be racist. No one defended her. KFILE regularly gets people fired for Tweets, and the Washington Post loves him. What are The Rules, Ms. Sullivan?

Jeer Heet of the New Republic, responding to my reporting about Gunn, wrote a blog entitled, "Weaponized Outrage Is a Threat to Free Speech." The Huffington Post was not amused that Gunn, who Tweeted out "jokes" about pre-pubescent girls, was fired due to my reporting. HuffPo's piece was entitled, "How Pizzagate Pusher Mike Cernovich Keeps Getting People Fired."

Let's be clear and state what Heet, Sullivan, HuffPO, and the rest of the journalists outraged at me are defending.

Here are some of James Gunns' Tweets:

- "The Expendables was so manly I f-cked the shit out of the little pussy boy next to me! The boys ARE back in town!"
- "I'm doing a big Hollywood film adaptation of The Giving Tree with a happy ending – the tree grows back and gives the kid a blowjob."

- "The Hardy Boys and the Mystery of What It Feels Like When Uncle Bernie Fists Me #SadChildrensBooks"
- "Watching Trapped in the Closet, R Kelly's second-best video after the one where he urinates on a child."

Should someone who work around children tell "jokes" like that? According to Sullivan and her colleagues at the Washington Post, I'm some sort of monster for reporting on what Gunn actually wrote. (And I have found much worse stuff about Gunn, which I'll be reporting later.)

There are several thousand news articles and blog posts about how awful it is that I find old Tweets and blog posts. When I report on these findings, the story isn't about what I found. The story is that I am "weaponizing outrage."

When the left finds bad Tweets from a conservative, that's journalism. When a conservative or someone on the right finds seemingly pedo Tweets from a Disney employee who directs children's movies, that's "bad faith" and "weaponized outrage."

My favorite part about finding really terrible things said by the left is when articles about my findings appear, and they all have this theme, "Ignore these Tweets Cernovich found, because here are some bad Tweets from him, which are totally real and super serious!"

Under the Reid Rule articulated earlier, I do not admit to have ever said anything offensive, and any bad Tweet allegedly uncovered was planted by the same people who hacked MSNBC anchor Joy Reid's blog.

SOMEONE CALL THE TWITTER POLICE

To understand the media requires you to set aside logic and reasoning. Embrace the double standard. For example, when far-left wing groups organize terrorist attacks online, they are engaging in activism. When a conservative organizes a peaceful boycott, he's engaged in harassment!

Journalists have become the Twitter police. If you post something they don't like, they'll immediately make a "media inquiry" to the powers that be. This is not activism, they will tell you, they are just asking questions. They thus badgered every social media company in existence for weeks to get Alex Jones banned. If you say their intent was to get Jones banned, they'll grimace. Oh no, they are hardworking journalists calling out bad behavior when they see it.

But what journalists won't do is report on far-left wing harassment against people they don't like.

I have a stalker who has send his followers to threaten my family. He made a fake video about my daughter, dubbing in audio to make her sound like she was saying something she wasn't. (My daughter is 21 months old.) This same stalker made a fake video that made it appear like my wife was abusing our daughter, and the stalker tagged in multiple child protective groups and his followers attempted to SWAT me.

For nearly two years, this stalker has told his followers to message and harass me, and he himself repeatedly emails and calls me despite being under a no-contact order.

Because this stalker has a verified account, I sent proof of the harassment (including a police report) to the same reporters who cover online harassment. I also showed them Tweets where the stalker doxed me.

Much to my surprise (not), they refuse to report on this harassment.

Among the journalists I showed the confirmed stalking to are those attended an event I threw in New York. Called A Night for Freedom, over 600 people met to party, listen to some talks, and goof off.

Later that night a 56-year-old Jewish man was leaving the party. He was attacked by a 30-year-old white man, who had protested outside the event. Part of ANTIFA, the attacker did what ANTIFA always does: He got violent.

The man was carried away in a stretcher.

This attack was planned and coordinated via social media.

Did the Twitter Police arrive, asking Twitter why they allow ANTIFA to threaten violence and organize attacks online? Surely, they did. Any honest journalism concerned with harassment would have reported on this article.

Surely, I jest.

Despite attending the event, journalists refused to report on the incident. They did, however, report that Chelsea Manning attended A Night for Freedom.

Yes, that's right, mean scary Mike Cernovich welcomes everyone, and Manning had a good time. At my events, we have a way of handling people you don't like. You either politely call people by their preferred pronouns, or you go into another room and do something else. You don't have to believe that transgenderism is legitimate, as your thoughts are your own. But you're not going to be a jerk at one of my events. Be nice to Manning or go talk to any of the other 600+ people in attendance.

The far left has a different set of rules. Far-left wing activists threatened Manning's life because she attended a "fascist" event. In a since-deleted Tweeting, Manning posted a picture of herself standing on a ledge, with the words, "I'm sorry."

Consider the implications of what happened. ANTIFA almost killed a 56-year-old Jewish man, and journalists said nothing. But they did have a lot to say about Manning attending my event, leading to her receiving death threats. If you enjoy irony, there's plenty of it to found in the left-wing media.

Don't believe media people when they claim to care about harassment. They don't care, or they would report on the bad behavior from their side. Harassment is a term they use when they want a conservative banned from social media.

KEITH ELLISON VS. BRETT KAVANAUGH

Think fast. Name the woman who accused Keith Ellison of beating her up.

Don't feel bad if you failed this pop quiz, as the media isn't interested in her story. A Google News search for "Karen Monahan" reveals just over 2,000 articles. Meanwhile, a Google News search for "Christine Blasey Ford" has over 1,200,00 results.

One might argue that Kavanaugh's accuser is more newsworthy because he's up for a lifetime Supreme Court appointments. But the news coverage differential isn't 10 to 1 or 100 to one. It's nearly 600 to one. (The number will exceed 1,000 to 1 by the time this book is published.)

Keith Ellison is a member of Congress. He's the deputy chair of the DNC. He is running for Attorney General of Minnesota, the state's highest law enforcement office. He has plans to run for the Senate.

And unlike Blasey Ford, Monahan made her accusation against Ellison immediately after the abuse is alleged to have occurred. Monahan has medical records. She has counselor's notes. She has made a stronger allegation against Ellison than Ford made against Kavanaugh. Yet if you watch the news, you see hardly any reporting on her.

This media blackout would of course come to no surprise to Juanita Broaddrick. Broaddrick claimed, quite credibly, that Bill Clinton raped her.

Bill Clinton went on a recent book tour and was not asked one time about Broaddrick's allegations.

The media does not care about violence against women. They care about accusations of violence that they can make against conservative men. Look at how long they covered up for Harvey Weinstein?

THE FACT CHECKS ARE FAKE

Can you spot the difference between these two statements?

> Statement 1: "African-American kids are unemployed or underemployed to the tune of 51 percent."
>
> Statement 2: "If you look at what's going on in this country, African-American youth is an example: 59 percent unemployment rate; 59 percent."

One of those statements was rated "Mostly True" by fact-checking website Politifact, whereas the other was rated as "Mostly false."

You might claim that 51% is smaller than 59%, and that would be a smart guess. But read the essay heading again. The fact checks are fake.

According to Politifact, the 59% unemployment claim is mostly false because, "The unemployment rate is a widely used term with a specific definition: It refers to the percentage of jobless people in the workforce who are actively seeking employment. In May, the unemployment rate for blacks ages 16 to 24 was 18.7 percent."

The 51% unemployment rate claim was mostly true because, "African-American and Hispanic youth have significantly worse prospects in the job market than whites do."

Do I need to tell you that the first statement was made by a Democrat, and the second was made by a Republican, or have you figured out the pattern by now?

Fact-checkers can manipulate outcomes in several ways. In the case above, they applied a literal meaning of the term "unemployment rate" when analyzing a Republican's statement. They applied a looser standard when analyzing a Democrat's claim.

Fact-checkers can also manipulate their results by refusing to rate claims made by their friends on the far left, thus giving the impression that mistakes are most often made by conservatives.

Or they can play other games, as a fact-checking website did to me.

In a since-forgotten school shooting in Santé Fe, the shooter wore a bunch of buttons and emblems, including a hammer-and-sickle logo. I made the uncontroversial statement that this logo was associated with ANTIFA. A fact-checking website that partners with Facebook and foreign governments said ANTIFA does not use the hammer-and-sickle logo.

According to the fact-checking blog, ANTIFA's official logo is two flags flying in tandem. Fair enough, except that I never said the hammer-and-sickle iconography was ANTIFA's official logo. My claim was that you'll see the hammer-and-sickle at every ANTIFA event.

Which is easy to confirm. Go into Google images and type, "ANTIFA HAMMER-AND-SICKLE." You'll see that ANTIFA always flies this flag.

The fact-checking website thus lied by claiming I stated a fact that I did not state.

Now some of you may think this is my griping and being sensitive, and it's not. I don't care about their lies, but Facebook does. Pages that have a bunch of negative fact-checks get demoted in the page rankings.

The upside to Facebook's partnership with fact-checking websites is this: Those sites can be sued for defamation. Defamation lawsuits are nearly impossible to win, because it's hard to show damages, especially if you're a public figure. If a fake-fact check leads to a loss of income, then someone could have a strong case against these institutions.

SNOPES COVERED UP A MASS SHOOTING

Floyd Lee Corkins had a plan. According to court documents, he wanted to "kill as many people as possible." Corkins took his gun and went into the Family Research Council building. The FRC had been identified as a "hate group" by the Southern Poverty Law Center because the FRC opposed gay marriage.

Corkins opened fired before being stopped by an armed guard. His plan to murder as many people as possible was stopped by a good guy with a gun.

Corkins plead guilty to committing acts of domestic terrorism, and his plea agreement said: "He identified the FRC as an anti-gay organization on the Southern Poverty Law Center Website...a subsequent search of Corkins's family computer revealed that on the [day of the shooting] Corkins used the computer to visit the [SPLC's] Website."

Corkins' plea agreement is a matter of public record and can be found using publicly available records search services. (Case Number 1:12-cr-00182-RWR, Document 15, page 18.)

Yet according to Snopes, the SPLC did not inspire the FRC shooting. Read Snope's article, "Is SPLC a 'Left-Wing Smear Group' That Encourages Violent Attacks? Partisan web sites have attempted to link Scalise shooter James Hodgkinson to the civil rights watchdog group Southern Poverty Law Center."

The claim that, "The Southern Poverty Law Center is a 'left-wing smear group' that incites hatred and violence against conservatives," was rated FALSE by Snopes.

Setting aside the fact that you can't rate an opinion as false, Snopes ignored official court records in clearing the SPLC of the FRC shooting.

According to Snopes, "the implication that the Southern Poverty Law Center inspired or encouraged these acts of violence has no discernible basis in fact."

In a stunning omission, Snopes ignored the Corkins plea agreement. According to documents filed with the plea agreement, "Consistent with his statement to the FBI, a subsequent search of Corkins's family computer revealed that on the afternoon of Sunday, August 12th, Corkins used the computer to visit the Southern Poverty Law Center's website."

Snopes could have argued that the SPLC wasn't responsible for every bad actor who reads their website. That would have been a fair argument to make. But that's not what Snopes did.

Snopes claimed, falsely, that "the implication that the Southern Poverty Law Center inspired or encouraged these acts of violence has no discernible basis in fact."

A transcript with the FBI interview with Corkins reads:

FBI Agent: And you, what was your intention when you went in there with the gun?

Corkins: Uh, it was to kill as many people as I could."

And as stated in the plea agreement, "[Corkins] was a political activist and considered the FRC a lobbying group. He committed the shooting for political reasons. He had identified the FRC as an anti-gay organization by the Southern Poverty Law Center."

Snopes is willing to lie even when publicly available court records exist. How can you trust them when it's impossible to fact-check them using public records?

THE SPLC AND PIZZAGATE SHOOTINGS

Snopes ignored public records implicating the SPLC in a mass shooting attempt for a strategic reason. The left wants to be able to blame conservatives for the bad acts of unaffiliated third parties while giving themselves a pass when their own actions directly inspire an attack. If Snopes had claimed that the SPLC shouldn't be blamed for mass shootings committed by "fans," then they'd have to similarly defend others who are blamed for the acts of third parties.

For example, I get blamed for the Pizzagate shooting, even though the shooter had never read my articles and was never aware of me. Journalists continue to repeat the line that I promulgated Pizzagate, while ignoring my actual words.

I believed then and believe now that Hollywood has a pedophile problem. It's not a coincidence that I thought to search James Gunn's social media accounts and blogs for "jokes" about abusing children. There's a pattern. Find a Hollywood star with an active social media account, and you'll find pedo jokes more often than not. That pattern means something to me, although the media claims we should all lighten up, at least when it comes to child abuse.

I posted to the hashtag #Pizzagate with stories about the Catholic Church, Jimmy Saville, and others. I never identified Comet Pizza as the source of any child sex trafficking ring. Even Rolling Stone, which is obsessed with me and hates me, didn't mention me in its massive Pizzagate wrap-up.

In a testament to the power of fake news, there is a video circulating on the Internet where it appears that I claim bad stuff is happening inside Comet Pizza. What happened? In January, 2017, I did a live stream about a planned terrorist attack where the conspirators met at Comet Pizza. Three members of a domestic terrorist group had planned to put acid into the ventilation system of the National Press Club, where I was holding an Inauguration event for over 1,000 people – including many moms.

Had the planned worked, over 1,000 people would have fled for the exits as poisonous gas filled the room. People would have died.

In a video discussing the planned I attack, I said, "They met a Comet Pizza!"

I wasn't talking about Pizzagate. I was talking about an actual terrorist plot, which the Washington Post reported about in an article entitled, "Protester pleads guilty to conspiring to disrupt DeploraBall for Trump supporters."

According to WaPo, "The video in which the alleged planned acid attack was discussed was recorded at Comet Ping Pong on Connecticut Avenue, the same pizza shop a gunman had entered weeks earlier to investigate fake news claims of an underground child-porn ring involving Democratic officials."

The video of me discussing this planned attack (for which three people pled guilty to crimes) was spliced with another video to make it appear that I suggested that Comet Pizza was at the center of a sex trafficking ring.

The facts of Pizzagate are clear. I was never threatened with any lawsuit by anyone, as I simply did not blame Comet Pizza or any illicit activity. To the contrary, I advised people against singling out any private figure. I posted to a hashtag about the serious problem of Hollywood pedophiles and media sexual predators.

Unlike the SPLC, I have never inspired a mass shooting.

And let me be clear here yet again: I disavow any political violence, and in fact held a rally against political violence. This rally happened before the fateful Scalise shooting. The Scalise shooting, you'll recall, was a far-left wing terrorist attack on a Republican congressman.

WHAT IT'S LIKE BEING AN INFLUENTIAL MEDIA FIGURE

Do you want to have angry people yell at you all day, and have people bombard you with trivial concerns? Oh and those are your fans!

If so, then welcome to my exciting life as a media and political influencer.

Here is what you can look forward to:

You'll be told every day that you need to be doing more. The people telling you this will never offer you resources to accomplish more. And their own lives are a mess. But they know what YOU should be doing, and they will tell you every day.

Your emails and DMs will be filled with ways for you to promote people for free. Usually these are a copy-and-pasted link to a Tweet. Not even a pitch. Just a DM of a Tweet. Several times a day.

You will get business "pitches." These "pitches" will be walls of texts and "ideas" rather than fully-formed businesses.

Because you get 1,000's of messages every day, people will accuse you of ignoring them.

When you block people for annoying you, they'll message you on other social media platforms demanding you unblock them.

People will get angry that you aren't "spending enough time with them," which doesn't make any sense but trust me people will expect you to listen to them talk about their "life problem" for hours.

Journalists will see your large platform and believe they should be as popular as you are. They'll stalk your every move and lie about you.

The same journalists jealous about your fame will also call Twitter a "hell site" and whine all day about how bad social media is. Like most people, journalists don't know what they want, and assume they want what you have. (Read Rene Girard and his theory of mimetics.)

People will assume you make millions of dollars from social media. You won't.

You'll meet people you'd never have met.

You'll have some stories for life that you can never tell, and besides, no one would believe those stories.

You'll have a backstage pass to the underbelly of humanity.

I love my job, although you might not like it much.

For someone with options in life, the question is: Is it worth it?

Most people go into politics because they couldn't make it in business, cut it as a real writer, or invent anything in tech. Why do you think tech journalists are nasty? When you have an IQ of 115, the Dunning–Kruger effect kicks in. You're smart enough to think you understand a company like Uber, but you'd never have had the vision, aggression, or focus to start such a company.

You soon begin to believe that those entitled tech bros have something that you deserve. (Again, read your Girard.)

This effect also explains why journalists are always attacking social media companies. Garden variety, conventional thinkers believe they should run a company like Twitter or Facebook. They lash out at their betters.

I'm a mindset guy who enjoys going to the gym. I got into politics and media as a hobby, and soon it took over my life.

"CREDIBLY ACCUSED"

Journalists like to claim that they are very independent thinkers who exist independent of the Democrat party establishment. Proving otherwise was hard before social media. Today it's much easier, as Twitter's search function gives you real-time insight into media narratives.

When news broke of an accusation of misconduct made against Supreme Court nominee Brett Kavanaugh, so-called journalists all seemed to use the same language patterns and talking points.

- "So, to summarize, a confessed serial sexual predator nominated a man who is credibly accused of attempted rape to be the key vote to strip women of reproductive freedom." - Ian Millhiser, Think Progress.
- "It is worth pondering that if this doesn't make a difference—and good money says it won't—2 of the 9 justices of the US Supreme Court will have been credibly accused of serious sexual misconduct and confirmed anyway. That is quite a statement to the women of this county." - Susan Hennessey, Brookings.
- "Once upon a time, catching a Supreme Court nominee in a pretty obvious lie, at the same time he's being credibly accused of other deceptions, would probably have been disqualifying

and certainly led to a pause. But this is the modern GOP." - Paul Krugman, NY Times.

- "If Brett Kavanaugh is confirmed, a full third of the male justices on the Supreme Court will have been credibly accused of doing serious harm to women and given lifetime appointments anyway." - NY Magazine's Twitter account.
- "I get Republicans are frustrated this is coming up now, but it also feels like in focusing on the timing, they're overlooking the fact their Supreme Court nominee is credibly accused of attempted rape." - Amber Phillips, the Washington Post.

You can find thousands of instances where this same talking point is repeated over and over again.

Can I credibly accuse the media of colluding with each other to get their talking points in order?

CNN OR CERNOVICH: WHO CAN YOU TRUST MORE?

Although my record isn't perfect, I'm happy to compare my track record with CNN's. Let's look at some major stories that they blew.

- Jake Tapper reported that fired FBI director James Comey would testify that he never told Trump he was under investigation. After Comey testified, Tapper's article was updated to include this disclaimer, "The article and headline have been corrected to reflect that Comey does not directly dispute that Trump was told multiple times he was not under investigation in his prepared testimony released after this story was published.
- Jim Acosta claimed Trump did not visit Steve Scalise after the tragic mass shooting committed by a far-left wing terrorist.
- CNN had to retract a story about Anthony Scarmucci after it was revealed to be fake news.
- CNN White House Reporter Jeremy Diamond claimed Trump was first President since George H.W. Bush to not take questions at a press conference held in China. Jake Tapper himself RT'ed Diamond. This claim was false.
- CNN claimed that Trump committed a faux pas during a fish feeding ceremony held in Japan.

- White House reporter Manu Raju claimed Donald Trump Jr. had advanced knowledge of the WikiLeaks release of the Podesta emails. This story was confirmed by two sources, and it was fake news. To this day, Raju refuses to burn the sources who fed him a fake story.

Those stories are only a sampling of the many errors made by CNN, and those errors are from CNN's biggest names. Jake Tapper is the gold standard of objective journalism, and he blew his only real story of the year. Acosta is CNN's White House correspondent. Raju is CNN's top man covering Congress. These weren't trivial mistakes made by the random intern who gets people coffee. These were mistakes made by those who should be at the top of the industry.

IS DEEP STATE REAL?

A reporter asked me a series of questions about "deep state." His questions are in italics.

Although you didn't specifically pose this question, one detail about the "deep state" debate has perplexed me. Everyone speaks of the intelligence community. Senator Schumer said on Maddow (1/3/2017) "Let me tell you, you take on the intelligence community, they have six ways from Sunday at getting back at you."

The State Department had what was known as the Seventh Floor Group, and was spoken of by the FBI as a "shadow government."

Why is the IC and thing, and the 7th Floor Group a thing, but "deep state" is a conspiracy theory? We all have a sense for The Bureaucracy, and know that if you want a zoning permit, some random clerk may have more power than the mayor. Yet for purposes of discussing "deep state," we suspend our disbelief and ignore our prior understanding of the world to dismiss it as a baseless conspiracy theory.

Anyone who has worked in a corporate environment has experienced the power of cliques, and knows a few rogue employees can sabotage managers and passively-aggressively disrupt work processes. Why are government employees immune from office politics, which result from the human desire to form tribes?

As to your specific questions...

1) *Some tension typically exists between presidents and agencies. Experts say this is good. An overly acquiescent executive branch could indicate the president is missing out on valuable input. On the other hand, extreme conflict could be undemocratic. The point the experts miss is this: Input and dissent are welcome in the planning phase.*

During the execution phase, you follow orders. Every military person knows this. When the higher-ups ask for advice, give it. Be candid. When the orders come down, you perform the mission pursuant to the commander's intent and chain of command.

a) *Do you think the dynamic between Trump and his subordinates — especially in law enforcement, national security and the intelligence community — is healthy or unhealthy?*

I think it's ironic that MAGA, which is pro law enforcement, distrusts the FBI more than civil libertarians do. This "switch" has been peculiar to watch and more evidence that tribalism robs humans of independent thought. "Black Lives Matter," the left says before giving massive amounts of money to Andrew McCabe, a man who lied under oath. When McCabe was in the FBI, how would he have treated an African American who lied to him during an interview? According to the IG Report, McCabe lied under oath, and as of now hasn't faced any sort of prosecution. Is this white privilege? Fed privilege? Or something else? It's worth talking about, but no one is talking. Meanwhile MAGA criticizes kneelers for protesting police misconduct. If the "deep state" is real, then perhaps black men sometimes feel the brunt of these forces? Maybe have a conversation with each other? It's absolute lunacy and thoughtlessness on both sides.

b) *Are there instances where a line was crossed during the Trump presidency?*

The chatter I've heard from sources is that most of what "deep state" does to Trump is the sort of passive-aggressive sabotage you'd see in any corporate environment, although to a higher degree. I haven't seen any "treason," and certainly don't consider the NY Times op-ed by Anonymous to be treasonous.

2) *The Deep State label has been applied to, among others: the Justice Department, FBI and Special Counsel Robert Mueller; Hillary Clinton, Fusion GPS, Huma Abedin; the Obama administration, John Brennan and the press.*

Ken Dilanian was fired from the LA Times for acting as what is best described as being a spokesman for the CIA. The Intercept referred to Dilanian as the CIA's "mop-up man."

Now the hard question is this: Do reporters conspire with the deep state, or are they simply giving too favorable coverage or offering spin in order to keep a source? Those are hard questions, but again, no one is having them in public! And my experience dealing with reporters is that 99% of them aren't part of deep state, and most don't even have source access to the highest levels of the intelligence community. However here is the Guardian in 2014 agitating for John Brennan to be fired because he lied under oath about a spying program.

The coverage of Brennan has changed considerably, to put it mildly, and he's become sort of a Resistance folk her on social media. The way the press has rehabilitated perjurers and war criminals is certainly worthy of discussing, although tribalism rather than conspiracy is the more likely explanation.

Anthony Weiner had access to Huma Abedin's laptop, which contained classified information. That would have got anyone else caught up. Yet she received a pass. When you look at the crimes committed, which in many such as Brennan's aren't debatable, and the way people are treated, you start to wonder why they received a pass.

a) One risk of such theories is they can become ever-expanding and unfalsifiable (how would you disprove Huma Abedin is a Deep State member, for e.g.?). In general, what are the limits of the Deep State theory? Or is it potentially limitless?

The limits of deep state, like the limits of the racism slur, are limited by the human capacity to draw lines. With Abedin, you observe the following: She was Hillary Clinton's right-hand woman, she allowed her husband to access her laptop, which contained classified information, and she received a pass. Someone made that decision to protect her.

b) Some argue the Deep State label is nothing more than an all-purpose partisan smear used to deflect criticism away from the Trump administration. What do you make of this?

Like "racism," "socialism," and "fascism," the term "deep state" is losing its meaning due to overuse. George Orwell wrote about these issues decades ago, noting, "The word Fascism has now no meaning except in so far as it signifies 'something not desirable'."

I use deep state in one of two ways: (a) As a meme. "My car wouldn't start. Deep state obviously got to it." Once my laptop was acting buggy and I blamed deep state as a joke. People pretended I wasn't joking, so now I can't have fun with it anymore other than in smaller groups. (b) As a reference to the true power base within the government. All of us abuse language, which is why Orwell's essays hold up well. If I plagiarized *Politics and the English Language*, people who had never read it would think it was the timeliest essay of the day.

IT'S NOT OK TO SPREAD FAKE NEWS

The OK gesture is made by joining your thumb and forefinger. It's a common gesture used by celebrities. It's also, according to fake news journalist Emma Roller, a "white power" sign.

When I reported from the White House with Cassandra Fairbanks, we went onto the pedestal and snapped a picture of us doing the OK sign. I had begun using the OK sign years ago as a joke about the Illuminati. According to an online conspiracy theory, Jay-Z and Beyoncé are part of the Illuminati, and the OK gesture was their symbol.

Unbeknownst to me, some trolls at 4Chan had a plan. They wanted to prove that journalists are stupid enough to fall for anything, and thus they shared memes purporting to be the ADL. According to these informational flyers, the OK sign secretly met "white power."

Proving them right, Roller wrote a story for the Independent about Fairbanks and I making the OK sign. The ADL debunked Roller's reporting, but that didn't stop her story from being on the front page of Yahoo! News.

Fairbanks sued Roller for libel. The judge dismissed the case, because it's nearly impossible for a public figure to win a defamation lawsuit. In the United States, to win a defamation lawsuit you must prove what's known as "actual malice." Actual malice doesn't mean the speaker or writer had malicious heart. Actual malice is a legal term of art meaning that the person spoke with reckless disregard of truth or falsity, and you must show this by clear and convincing evidence. How can you prove to a court that the person really didn't believe what he or she said?

Although I laughed off the fake news article about me, Roller could have gotten me killed. What if a Floyd Lee Corkins type had seen her story and then went on a mass shooting?

Fake news has deadly consequences.

SCOTT ADAMS INTERVIEW

OK. Who are you and what are you about?

I am Scott Adams. I'm the creator of the Dilbert comic strip and, for the last two years, I've been writing a lot about President Trump's powers of persuasion. I'm a trained hypnotist and have studied persuasion for decades for my work, and in him I noticed a special set of tools that I've been writing about.

It's interesting you call yourself, "the creator of Dilbert," because I read your book — it's a long title, *How To Fail At Nearly Everything In Life And Still Win Big* — and I've been familiar with Dilbert, so when I think of you, I think of you as more of a mindset guy or something else outside of Dilbert.

My brand has changed a little bit, because as I write more about persuasion — and, in particular, as it applies to President Trump — people are starting to know me from that part of my writing and less about the cartoon.

Yes, because I actually recommended — when I read your book on life, essentially — how you really systematized a lot of things that I've intuitively sort of recognized and noticed in people. That book kind of took off in the last couple of years.

Yeah. So my book, *How To Fail At Almost Everything And Still Win Big*, is about persuasion, in a sense. It's about how to persuade yourself. It's about how to reprogram yourself to be more effective. So that was my introduction to the world of persuasion, in terms of the audience's perception of me.

Yeah, that's an interesting point...which is that, for example, you talk about mantras in your book. And a mantra is ultimately convincing yourself to believe in yourself.

Affirmations, yeah.

Affirmations are persuasion. So I guess we would say that fake-, of course, humorous persuasion, too, so making somebody laugh-, I read your article from years ago on what the six elements of humor...

Yeah. So persuasion is in everything. So if you're communicating, you're persuading — even if the only thing you're trying to persuade is that you're smart, or you want somebody to like you, or think you're competent. So persuasion is just-, it's around everything, it's in everything. And if you don't recognize it for what it is, you're missing a big dimension of your-, of your experience.

Now, when you break up persuasion, it seems like a lot of people have weird superstitions about it. Maybe talk about that.

Well, persuasion is scary to people — especially if they think it's the same as manipulation. Now, I try to-, I try to have a distinction between manipulation and just persuasion based on intent. If your intention is to do something that's good for you, and bad for someone else, that's probably manipulation. If it's in a business context, then both sides are doing it, and you both have commercial grade negotiating skills — well, that's a little bit fair, because you both know what the game is and you're both playing. But you certainly wouldn't want to use persuasion to just do something evil. It's a tool — and you could do good things with it or evil — just like any other tool.

Is the media trying to persuade us when they share the news?

The media's persuasion comes in a lot of different forms. One of them is visual. The most persuasive thing is visual. Our visual sense overpowers everything else. So what they choose to show as an image is the message, no matter what the "yak-yak-yak" is that comes over it...no matter what the other words on the screen say. What you remember is what you saw. So if you see the president — let's say, working with minorities and, you know, them liking him and touching him and and all, being happy — that's the image that sticks with you. And if you see an image of Melania Trump wearing high heels on the way to a hurricane disaster — of course, it was only the first few steps to the helicopter she wore those heels — but it doesn't matter what the explanation is. What's-, what sticks in your head is the picture of the *heels*. That's why it was such a big story is there was a picture involved. You take the picture away and there's no story.

So, with the media, by choosing what image to use, are trying to persuade people about something.

The media is persuading both by visual images, but also by what topics they cover and what they don't: Who is talking about it, how credible they are, how many times you ask the same question over and over. So you could watch, let's say, CNN, and then switch back-and-forth between FOX and CNN and you would see the same news. Meaning that the facts would be reported, essentially, the same, but the amount of time they spend talking about one fact, versus the other fact, is completely different. And that's where all the persuasion is.

Yeah I read a book — I think it's called, *How To [Watch] TV News*, or something — by Neil Postman, and a journalist had confessed — this is, I think, a hundred years ago — that if you want to manufacture a crime wave, all you do is start reporting on the crimes that occur every day in any big city.

Yeah, you can-, you can cause some amount of the public to be influenced by just about anything, if you give them enough messages. So, most people are not that influenced by just watching the news, right? They're already set in their ways and it's not going to change. But if you're working on a big population of people over time, and you're very consistent in your message, you can get five percent of the people to believe anything.

Maybe more than five percent of the people.

Yeah, depending-, depending how good you are — how long you take them and where they started from — you could get more than five percent.

And I think the more interesting point, in terms of focusing on, how by selectively focusing on something that was already, you make people think that there is something bigger than it really is. So, for example: Right now, in San Francisco, I'm sure somebody is being mugged, right? On just any given day — and nobody writes about it. But when you say, "On Saturday, there was a mugging... on Sunday, there was yet another mugging...on Monday...*Oh, my*

***God! Three days in a row of mugging!"* so, then people think there is an *epidemic* of muggings. Maybe talk about the role of focusing on any given subject in manufacturing a media narrative.**

So, the things that people consider important are not the things that *are* important. They're the things they're thinking about. So, whatever you're thinking about just seems like that's the *big thing* because your brain can't handle everything. You've got to-, you've got to, you know, filter out the small stuff and decide what you're focusing on. So, if the media makes you focus on one thing, you're going to think that's important, eventually. Even if it isn't.

Is the media trying to get people to focus on one given subject?

Well, the media right now is sort of split down the middle. People who were sort of left-focused media were anti-Trumpers at this moment than the people who are more pro-Trump. And my observation is that the team that's out-of-power gets the craziest and has to try the hardest to persuade, because they're starting from a hole and they've got to punch hard. The-, the group that has their person in the White House feels like "business as usual", and just reports the facts, and that is going to get them further. You know, they're all, of course, biased on both sides. But the out-of-power side is always going to be the crazy one until the power changes.

One thing I've noticed, in media coverage, is that if you have a hundred people — say, at a Trump event — and ninety-nine of them are nice, all the cameras go to one person who maybe isn't so nice.

The news only cares about the stuff that is visual, that's violent, is provocative. It's-it's the thing that you don't see. So, there's no such thing as news about somebody who did the thing that they always do — that they did a little bit better. That's not news. Somebody's gotta, you know, break the mold, and the people doing that are the minority. Meaning, if there are a hundred people, one of them might be breaking the law, but they're going to get all the-, all the camera time.

Do you think that the media created a certain narrative about Trump supporters that maybe wasn't fair?

I think both sides in the political realm create a cartoon version of the other and try to brand all the people on the other side by that, by the worst few people. So, on the right, the right got branded as a bunch of "KKK racists," when, in fact, the average Republican is nothing like that. The left is branded as: "You Antifa crazy people with masks," and, you know, they want to open borders and, you know, get rid of the government. There are very few people on the left who actually would embrace all of that stuff. So it's really cartoon characters on *both* sides.

Yeah, I sometimes feel like we're-, we don't talk to each other. We talk to the caricature of you that I'm [believing] you really are.

Communication depends primarily — and this is probably the first rule of communication — that it doesn't matter what someone says. It only matters what you think they were thinking. And if you think somebody is evil, whatever comes out of their mouth is going to sound pretty evil. And if you-, if you think that person is on your side, even if they say something that sounds a little bit evil, you're going to say, "Uhh, that's Bob — he doesn't mean that."

So [through] our expectations — based, really, on magical thinking in many cases — we imagine we can see what's in the soul of other people. That's the most classic mistake you could make, because we're really terrible at that. I mean, if you've ever been in a relationship of any kind, you know that a lot of it is: "Well, I thought you were thinking this, and I figured you were mad, but I couldn't tell." You can't even tell with your loved ones.

We certainly can't tell with strangers that we've never met, [that] we've seen on television: "Well, that person has evil in his or her soul and, therefore, I look at their message that way." So, probably the biggest flaw in our perceptions about other people is that we imagine that we have this clear insight into their soul. You know, they're, uh, good or bad. And, weirdly, we imagine that these normal people — who would be our friends in any other context — are actually like monsters on the inside. And it's pretty rare that anybody is actually a monster on the inside.

Yeah, one of the things I actually tell people with my mindset thing is what I call the "STS" method, which is: Stop Telling Stories. Which is, you go to meet somebody, like, "Oh, look at that guy. Oh, but he's dressed a certain way. Therefore I know what he believes," and your whole entire interaction is based on this story that you've told yourself about this person that you've never even met. And the story that people have told about Trump supporters is that they're all Neo-Nazis, KKK, evil people. They want to destroy America.

There are a couple of things happening with the "branding," if you will, of Trump supporters. One is that it's just a normal political process that both sides, you know, brand each other negatively. But, on top of that, we had that surprise election outcome, which was this enormous trigger for cognitive dissonance. It was one-half of the country found out that they weren't smart. They didn't understand the world they were living in. They weren't as clever as they imagined they were. They were just wrong about so much and they found it out, sort of, at the same time, you know, on election night. And that triggers people.

If people have normal brains — so this is not a-, not an *insult* to any of these people — the normal way the brain works is that when your worldview gets shook like that, you have to rewrite the script in your head to make it make sense. And a lot of people rewrote the script so that they would still be right. And the way they would still be right is, "Ah-ha! Maybe we were wrong about who got elected. We were certainly right that he is a monster and he must be a racist and he will ruin the world." And then they watch for the evidence of that. And amazingly, they see it, but only they can see it. The other half, they got what they expected, which was President Trump — they voted for him, they wanted him. That's just what we expected to happen. We were glad they did. They-, they're more likely to see an unbiased view. Of course, everybody's biased. There's no such thing as *unbiased* in our world.

But, the Trump supporters didn't get triggered in such a violent way as the people who said, "This man could never be president." So they really had to rewrite their movie in their heads to make it make sense. And the best way they can do it is to say, "Yeah, we were right — he's a monster — you'll see any minute now." And we wait, and we don't see it.

Since you were one of the first — if not *the* first — people who predicted Trump to win, your phone must have been blowing off the hook with the media trying to get you to come explain this, right?

I became suddenly very popular when my prediction of a Trump win happened, because I was one of the-, one of the first people who predicted it. Now, I'm pretty sure a guy named Mike Cernovich predicted that about the same time, or earlier than I did. But, yeah, I became quite popular for getting it right. Now, of course, at the same time, I have to say *somebody* was going to get it right if it-, if we're being completely objective. A lot of people had their pet ideas about what would happen and what wouldn't happen and somebody was going to be right. And this-, and this time I was on the side that was right.

I'd like to think there was a reason for my being right, but I can't know.

One thing I noticed, though, is that when people go, "Oh, I bet you the media's calling Scott Adams," saying, "Come on and explain why Trump really won!" and I didn't see that latter part happening.

After Trump won, I saw an article on CNN's website in which they listed — I believe it was twenty-four different reasons, from different publications — that said, "Well here's the reason this result was a surprise." And I don't think any of those results included my best explanation which is: He's just really *persuasive*. And he knows the tools and he works the tools well. He understood the public and connected with them.

And I thought that a lot more people would invite me on and say, "Can you explain your theory?" But, as soon as the election was over, people sort of retreated back to the idea that they were smart all along, and that there really was a reason that they were right all along — even though they were totally *wrong*.

So I did expect a little more attention for being that right for that long. But you know the media has its own-, its own agenda.

Well, that's why I asked it, because it kind of segues into the whole subject of Fake News, where, if you were real news, you would say, "Wow, son of a gun, this guy had it right so early. Why don't we have him come on? Maybe his explanation is a good one. Maybe we should have him on our panels." You wouldn't think that you would be-, CNN would really want to know the truth and get you to come on and share your version of the truth.

Well, I have been invited on CNN and Fox News, and I'll probably do a lot of other things in conjunction with a book tour — my book, *Win Bigly*. But it took awhile. And we've-, we've lived with our new president for awhile. And so I'll give my explanation of how it happened. But it's competing with — maybe, by now — twenty, thirty, fifty different explanations of why it happened the way it did.

I find it fascinating that the people who are wrong on election season are still the people explaining what is happening in the world and what really is going on in Trumpland.

One of the most interesting results of the election was that the people who were wrong about everything from the very beginning — I mean as wrong as you could possibly be — are still on television and acting like, "Well, this time we got it right." And I think the viewers can't really tell the difference, because they sounded smart before and they sound smart now. And maybe they figure, "Well, this time they got it right."

Yeah I've seen research that says that people respect certainty more than truth, and they'll forgive you for being wrong, but they won't forgive you for being nuanced and being uncertain.

One of the-, one of the elements of persuasion is that a simple explanation is powerful. So, anybody who has a simple explanation usually is the winner of the persuasion contest. So, if you're certain and you're simple and you can communicate it easily, and especially if there's a visual element to it — that always helps — that's going to be your most persuasive package.

Maybe that's why people decided on the whole "Russia hacked the election" theme?

The Russia hacking the election story — we're still waiting for the details to come out. But, as of this moment, it looks like it's dissolving. And one of the interesting things about that, for me, is that it would be the next time that all the people who were wrong about everything are wrong again. And, once again, an enormous question in which they have to notice that half the country wasn't wrong. Half the country has been right all the way through the process. And I don't know how you could ignore that forever — if you're always on the wrong side of these things — and the other-, the other side is not. And you can measure it, you know. Trump got elected...or he didn't. You know, it-, it's measurable.

So, it's hard for them to be credible going forward, unless they get a few right.

Or people just forget. One of my sort of "awakening" moments in life was when the financial crisis hit. I thought, well surely everybody in the media who said housing can never go down, and there's no bubble, and Bear Stearns is fine...surely all those people are going to be fired. And not only were they not fired, but nobody even held them accountable and said, "You guys got it all wrong."

Yeah, it turns out that being wrong is not a big problem...if you're-, if you're a talking head pundit, or any kind of a public figure. People are so wrong, so often, that if you started holding it against people every time they were wrong, you just couldn't-, you couldn't deal with people at all, because everybody is wrong — a lot. I'm a little more forgiving about the people who were wrong, because I figured it could be *me* next time. And I'm also-, I have a little bit of humility about all the times I've been wrong in the past, and I try to hold that in my head when I'm looking at a current topic, and say, "Okay..." — for something that looks like this, you know, roughly speaking — "...how many times have I been wrong in the past?" And there's almost always-, there's some example that I can say, "Okay, I've been wrong about this sort of thing before." So, I try to use that to help my bias. But, you know, we are biased humans and you can't-, you can't be unbiased entirely.

Or there is a thing where, if you have any kind of platform, people say, "What's your opinion on this?" And I'll say, "Well I don't have one." "What do you mean? How can you not have an opinion on..." whatever. "Because I've never looked at it." Why would I know about Saudi Arabia and Qatar, for example, and the relationship between that — two heads of state? I had no idea.

When people are asking me for my opinion on the big, complicated world affairs like, "What do we do with trade deals and how do we solve North Korea," and, you know, "What do we do with ISIS? And what about tax rates?" I always have the same answer, which is: I have no idea what is the right answer for those things, but one thing I'm sure of is that the person I'm talking to — they don't have any idea either. They might have a strong preference. But these things are, by their nature, big and complicated, and our brains are really not designed for it to get the right answer on that stuff all the time. So, I usually default to, "Well, let's see what the experts say. Make sure it makes a little bit of sense." But it's really hard for me to get ahead of any of those big, complicated issues and say, "Here's the answer. This is simple." That's just a huge illusion, that people have any kind of power to-, to know what's right in complex situations.

How, then, would we know if the media or the news that we're watching is *true*?

I probably have less belief in the news than the average person, because my experience is being part of the news. In other words, being a *subject* of the news. So, during the past couple of years — especially over the course of the election — there were a number of articles about me. So they were about me, personally, or about my views, and I could look at them and I could see that they're just completely *wrong*. Now, often you don't have that opportunity. You can't look at the news about a world event and say, "Well that's wrong. That news is just wrong." But what is about *you*, and it's about your inner thoughts, and somebody is reporting what I'm thinking, or even what I'm saying — incorrectly — I *know* that's wrong. And when you see how often that happens — really, any feature article about me will have maybe a handful to more complete factual inaccuracies — the regular public never sees how many factual errors there are in ordinary reporting. And I'm an easy story. If you want to know anything about me, just ask, and I will give the-, probably the correct answer, because it's *about* me. But even those stories are just riddled with factual errors and, in many cases, fairly obvious bias built into the story to create a narrative around something. So, it's hard to trust the news when you're part of the news, and when you see it from the ugly side.

Yeah, there's even the Geller-Mann Effect, which is: You're reading the newspaper. You read an article you know something about, and you go, "This is completely wrong." They got cause-and-effect backwards. And then you turn the page, and now you're reading something else, and go, "Well, that *must* be true, though." And you forget that they completely got something that you understand *wrong*. Why would you believe the *next* story you're reading?

I've lost faith in any kind of story that has anything to do with science, because you know that the illusion is that I — the non-scientist — am somehow judging the quality of the science. And I'm not doing that. I'm judging the credibility of the reporting about the science, which is an entirely different thing, and the reporting tends to be terrible. They get cause-and-effect backwards, et cetera. But my favorite example of this-, I want-, let's call it a "prediction": For years, we've been seeing stories that drinking a small amount of wine is actually good for you. Maybe that's true. I'm gonna give that a big, "Maybe that could be true." In my opinion, there's almost no chance that's true. That has "fake news" written all over it. It's probably something like, the people who can drink moderately at all probably have friends, that's why they're drinking moderately. If you can do anything moderately, you're probably a person who's got your life under control. So there are all these different variables. But no, I don't believe for a moment that putting alcohol into your body — which is effectively *poison* — that a little bit of it is good for you. So when I see any other story about a scientific breakthrough or a new scientific correlation, just a big red flag goes up and says, "Probably not...probably not."

There are multiple layers, too. One is that the scientist doesn't have an agenda. Even though a few of them have been caught hyping studies in their press releases, and then the press release becomes a basis for a story in scientific reporting.

Yeah, you've got so much bias. First, from the scientists themselves, because they're humans. You know, one of the things that drives me crazy is when people say the scientific method has, you know, driven out the bias, because we get your peer review and you need to repeat the studies. Yes, that's true. But all the people doing this stuff are all humans and there's no process that can get rid of all the bias in humans. You know, science is great. I'm a big fan. It does move truth in the right direction over time. But how do you ever know, in this journey of science on any topic, how do you know when it's at the end, where they actually got the right answer, and that will never change...or you're halfway there and you've got the wrong answer, and someday it will change? You can't tell, because when you're in it, it looks the same.

And there's actually a scientific method to try to control our biases. With journalism, there isn't even a method.

At least science has a process. You know the scientific method is going to get you closer to truth than maybe anything that humans have invented yet. So, it's the best we've got. Journalists don't really have anything like that. There's no-, there's no big penalty for being wrong about stuff. You know, you can keep your job. And without that standard, people are putting the same amount of credibility on science as they do on somebody reporting a story. Like, to the average person, a person reporting a story is just as credible as the consensus of science, and they should not be.

Have you ever been — and I know you don't consider yourself a 'victim' — but, in the colloquial understanding of the word, have you ever been a victim of Fake News?

I've had quite a bit of Fake News lobbed at me, and almost all of it takes the form of assuming that my inner soul is dark and broken and that, you know, I'm sitting in my secret lair, and thinking bad things about women and minorities. The truth, for anyone who knows me personally, could not be further from any of that stuff. So, to actually see the Fake News about yourself, and have it actually affect your life, affect your career, affect what people — [DOG YIPS][Laughter] — apparently, this is a very boring answer. My dog fell asleep in the middle of the interview —

— What was I saying?

To have Fake News written about you and how it impacts you.

It's really quite an experience to have Fake News written about you, personally, and it's happened to me a number of times, usually in the form of somebody is imagining what's in my dark soul, and they imagine I hate something, or I'm really biased against something, or something happened in my childhood that made me this way. Almost always, that's completely off-base. And until it happens to you, and you see it repeatedly, you can't really understand how powerful the Fake News is — how much it changes, you know, real people's lives and how widespread it is.

What are some of the consequences that you had as a result of Fake News?

The Dilbert audience probably went from something like sixty percent male/forty percent female in the early days, to — after a number of Fake News stories about me — probably ninety-four percent male now. So, women just read things that simply weren't true — were taken out of context — and said, "Hey, this guy said something bad about us." In every case that I'm aware of, [it] was taken out of context, or it wasn't what I actually said, or was some misinterpretation of what I said. But those are real life consequences. So, probably took, I don't know, thirty percent of my income right off the top — Fake News did.

What was the Fake News?

Well, the Fake News was that I had said negative things about women — which, if you saw them in context, you would understand that they weren't. But, out of context — whoa! — they sounded terrible. If I had-, if I thought somebody actually thought the things that people *said* I thought, I would not like that person. But, of course, I didn't say those things. Or, certainly, I didn't *mean* those things. The words are easily taken out of context.

So, in other words, media still has mass influence over people.

People, like me, who live and die by the attention of the public, you know, that's-, that's my business model, is I have to make the public happy. But there are other people whose business model involves smearing other people who are in the public eye.

So, every once in a while, I pop up on somebody's radar screen. Some complete stranger will write a detailed, long piece about me, and I won't know about it until I read it, and it'll just be riddled with errors, and I would certainly understand if somebody was learning about me for the first time by one of these articles, that they would have an entirely wrong opinion about what's going on.

Is that maybe a testament to the influence and the responsibility that journalism should have? It should be more responsible?

That's sort of like "air is good". Everybody should be responsible. I don't know how to answer that question.

Wellit's a massive obligation. You know that if you get published in *The New York Times*, you know that you could pretty much ruin a person's life. That's a little bit-, we should all be responsible, nice. If I'm rude to the barista at Starbucks, that's a bad thing — a bad human — but that person's life is going to go on. But if I write an article about that person, especially in a large publication, that person's life is never going to be the same.

So that-, the media, and especially the Fake News, can ruin lives fairly easily. And, obviously, the-, the news organizations, they have some responsibility not to do that. But there are-, there is a legitimate case to be made that a lot of the errors are probably accidental or, in many cases, the bias that they put into the articles are based on their own misconceptions. In other words, they-, they have a starting bias and then-, then that's how they see the world. Confirmation bias kicks in and that's all they can say. So, some of it is probably honest. You know the result is Fake News. But I think, in a lot of cases, the people writing it don't know it's fake. They're seeing what they see.

I think the only way you can deal with that is — and I'd love to say this — is that whenever there's an article in which humans are mentioned, like *real* people, whose lives can be influenced, that there should be some obligation for a response that maybe they wait a day or two. You know, you can't do everything at the same time, but just give them a dedicated little box at the bottom to say, "What do you think of this article?" that is linked to some of these blogs that they can respond. And I think you'd have a different picture of people if you let them respond to this sort of fake-newsy, biased reporting.

One of the challenges about describing Fake News is the issue that you've raised, which is: I've talked to people who genuinely believe the things they're doing. They're not trying to spread lies; it's more of a perceptual error, or a bias error. So maybe talk about how your "two movies" kind of metaphor would relate to Fake News. So, in other words, they don't think it's Fake News — they actually think it's true news.

A lot of what we see as Fake News is stuff that's wrong. But the person who is writing it thinks it's true. And I refer to this as the "two movies playing on one screen." So if you took a bunch of anti-Trumpers, and a bunch of Trump supporters, and put them in the same theater and said, "Watch this movie," and when they left, if that movie was about Trump, they would come out with completely different ideas of what they had just watched, even though they'd watched exactly the same thing. And unless you study persuasion — and it helps to actually be a trained hypnotist, as I am — you don't realize how powerful is the ability to change somebody's perception of something they're looking at with their own eyes, listening to with their own ears, in real time. My best example of this is — to give you an idea of how the "two movie" thing can be real — is there's something called the "McGurk Effect." And until you see it — and you could just Google this, just Google "McGurk Effect", and it will blow your mind, it's a real short clip — and it shows a person saying, "Bah bah bah" — just B-A-H — "Bah bah bah." And then they have the person fake their lips like they're saying the letter "F," and your ears start hearing "Fah." And it's *not* what's happening.

So, right in the moment, you can watch your own powers of perception completely rewritten in real time, and you can do it a hundred times and you'll get the same effect. In other words, you can't even get over it. Even knowing how it's done doesn't help a bit. And so, when you see how powerful is our ability to rewrite or to create a movie in our head, and then live with that movie, you never see the world the same again.

So Fake News is, probably most of it anyway, people who are just living in a different movie and seeing different things and then confirmation bias makes them say, "Yeah, there's another piece of evidence for my side...yeah, there's another one...," even though other people could look at it and just say, "What the hell are you talking about?" You know, "I don't see it."

Is there a way to solve the problem of Fake News?

I don't think there's any way to solve Fake News in the sense that there will always be people writing things and putting their spin on it. Sometimes they would be bad actors who are doing it intentionally and sometimes they'll just be under the wrong impression. But neither of those things is easy to fix. The best thing you can do is make sure that the response is connected. You know, on the Internet, there's no excuse to have the response disconnected from the original article. That should be basic journalism rule. You know, there should be a rule as clear and universal as, you know, "Are you speaking on the record, or off the record?" You know, some kind of rule that says, "If I write an article and you're the subject of it, we're going to give you a link at the bottom to your rebuttal." That would be-, that would be probably as good as you can get.

How do we as humans find out what is true?

I wonder sometimes if there is a truth that is accessible to us, without getting too deep. Let me just make a general statement that I don't think humans evolved to understand truth and to perceive the reality accurately. Evolution only cared that you reproduced. So, as long as you could reproduce, evolution was happy. Right? That was all you needed to do.

So you could believe that you reincarnated from a seventeenth century monk. I could believe that my prophet flew to heaven on a winged horse. But we both go to the grocery store. We're standing next to each other. We buy food. We eat. The fact that we're living in different realities doesn't matter as much as you'd imagine. And so-, and so when I think, "How do people find truth," you know, "How did they really know what is really true?" The first thing I have to say is, "I don't know if it's a thing." Like, I don't know if we can ever know it's true. We're just not designed-, we're not the right instrument for that. Humans are the wrong tool for finding truth. Now, you probably say, "Well, science makes up for that." And within the limited realm of science — which isn't most of our experience, you know — you can get closer to the truth over time for sure. But you can never really know if you're all the way there.

And I think that leads to a misconception a lot of people have about you, which is that, when you say that it isn't necessarily what is true, but it's what people believe, that doesn't mean you advocate lying.

When I talk about persuasion, I talk about it as a tool. Now, a tool can either be good or bad — it just depends how you're using it. People often say, "Well, then, you're in favor of manipulation and evil and you don't care about what's true and what's not true." And, of course, that's not the case. I care what's true, because if you walk into-, if you walk in front of a truck, that's the *truth* and it's going to *kill* you. Right? But in terms of decision-making, people don't use the truth the way you imagine they would or should. So, that's the point. In decision-making, we ignore it. It would be great if we didn't. If you want my opinion, I'd love if only the truth was, you know, the thing that we knew and cared about and that was driving our decisions. It's just an observation that we don't.

And we're more concerned with how we feel than what's actually true.

I think people decide what is true based largely on how they feel. So, if you feel something is true, it's hard to talk you out of it. And once you have a feelings-based reality, it's going to take a lot of persuasion to get somebody off of that.

'Cause you once said that how we would define ourselves as people would be our preferences.

I've said that if you're trying to figure out what a human is, you know, it's not your arms or legs, because you can lose those and still be the person. It's not even how you used to think. It's not even your DNA, except in a scientific sense. But what kind of defines a person is your-, is your preferences, at the moment. So, the things you would prefer to do, the way you would handle things, the way you see it — that's sort of who you are.

You were talking about journalists and media, and whether they're acting in good faith, or why they have a particular bias. How can we tell when someone isn't acting in good faith, and they are deliberately lying or trying to mislead? Where are the "tells" of someone acting in that way?

It's always going to be hard to figure out which people in the media are intentionally telling an untruth, or intentionally biased, versus someone who just can't tell the difference. If you're looking for clues, one thing I'd look for is to see if they've ever crossed to the other side. Have they ever taken the other-, the other position and said, "Well, I'm usually, you know, agreeing with Republicans, but on this, you know, I'm pretty hard on the left." So, if you don't see somebody at least *occasionally* crossing over, you're going to have to ask yourself, "Why is that?" I mean, you know, that's kind of rare that you don't at least find something on the other side that is useful. So, that's probably the biggest "tell." You know, can somebody cross over and feel okay about it and make a case on the other side, or were they just always on one side?

Do you think that "Who's financing who?" that that has any influence on what kind of stories are being told?

You certainly have to know who's paying the people who are writing, or else you don't know the full story. So, if you know that the organization paying them has an agenda, you could probably reduce what credibility you would put on the writer, because, you know, it's the money that's going to be tarnishing everything. I would say, "Follow the money," and look for signs that the person has ever done anything that leaves their brand-, and leaves the-, leaves the singular message that they've been trying to create. Do they ever-, do they ever have an opinion outside of that?

Could you talk about framing the narrative, and what that means, and how important that is for persuasion?

In persuasion, there's a thing called, "framing." So, it's-, it's how you think about a situation — and people can frame things very differently — and skilled persuaders are especially good at it. So, it's something I'm trained to do, which is, especially, if you're new to like a new story. Whoever gets there first and says, "Well, here's my interpretation," they framed it. They've given you a way to think about it. It's tough to get that out of your head. So, your first impression of how to think about a story is really super sticky. So, going first makes a big difference. I started doing a lot of live streaming on Periscope and, when there's a big story, I can be live to the world within minutes. I just pick up my phone and I'm on live to the world, and the framing that I put on things — I'm quite aware of the fact that because I'm both persuasive by training and I'm first, that my framing is exceptionally sticky — and I see it sometimes expressed on TV, and I think to myself, "That looks like something I said," but you can never be sure where influence is carried.

If you were making a documentary on Fake News, and you wanted to persuade people that the mainstream media has engaged in a fair amount of lies and deception and unconscious bias, how would you frame the narrative of the documentary?

One of the things I don't think you need to convince anybody anymore is that the media is biased. I think there used to be a day, maybe when I was a kid, when people said, "Well, the news is at least trying not to be biased — they're at least *trying*." But now, nobody believes that. What they do believe — which is weirder and maybe worse — is that they believe that only the other side is biased. And that's a tough one to crack. So, how do you convince somebody that their own side is feeding them garbage and has for a long time? I found that you can even — [DOG COUGHS] — sorry, Fake News does this to my dog.

As soon as I say, "CNN," she starts coughing. I don't think that's a coincidence.

But, it's really hard to get people off of their belief that their side is the "right" side. They can certainly see all the bias on the other side. That's just big and glowing. What I like to do is literally switch back and forth between the major networks. So, going between Fox News and CNN, when there's breaking news, and watching what they say about it. Now, the facts will be the same. They pretty much have the *same* facts — but watch what they decide to talk about, what emphasis they put — and watching that is just mind-boggling. If you-, if you rapidly switch back-and-forth, when there's breaking news, that's the best time to do it.

Do you think there's any danger that, now that there's so many — for instance, you just being able to pop onto Periscope and reach thousands of people — that that will encourage demagoguery and people that will, you know, not be in good faith, but they're outside the mainstream, you know, gaining a lot of power...do you think there's a danger?

One of the most important and underreported shifts in much of the world, and especially in the United States, is that we started as a republic. You know, that's the way we were formed — in which we would elect some smart people, send them off to Washington on their horse, they'd make some good decisions, and then we'd all be happy. But today, social media is the government — we don't recognize as such — but it's very unusual now for our elected officials to do something that the majority doesn't favor, and the majority is expressed through social media. That's how the majority gets formed. So, today, I think the government is the best persuaders. I mean, the people who know how to use persuasion and are invested in the topic.

If they do a good job persuading, the idea itself travels. So, the politicians end up being recipients of what social media told them is okay to say. And if they get out of that box, they can't get re-elected, because the whole deal is: you've got to be popular. I think in the old days, they could get away with saying, "Well, I know some people don't like it. But I made a good decision on your behalf." I don't think that works anymore. I think social media decides that the consensus — the majority — needs to get what it wants. And so, that's a big change, and it puts the power in the hands of the people who are persuasive.

Would you offer any critiques of what's called the "New Media?" So people-, like, people on the left and right, so people like Mike, people like the Young Turks, you know, alternative media outlets... do you think, you know...what kind of critiques would you offer?

Well, today, almost anybody can be in the news business just by turning on their phone or their iPad and live streaming. It doesn't take much to set up a podcast, so it puts a lot of people in the position of looking like news, but they don't have necessarily the same sources — the same resources, for the most part — they're talking about the news that they saw somewhere else. There are some exceptions where a lot of the new media now actually has better sources than the mainstream media. But that's still the exception.

So, I think the problem is that if you've-, you've got a podcast, and you're trying to fill minutes, and you don't have access to the base source information and you've got to talk about something — you're going to get really speculative. Because you've got to fill the time. So, I think that's the danger — is the speculation — because the speculation starts to look real to the audience if you speculate enough.

Good example is all that Russian stuff with Trump. Most of that, that the audience sees, is a lot of speculation. But there's so much of it that people literally say — and it makes me laugh when you hear it — "Well, there's so much smoke. There *must* be fire." But the people saying that are making the smoke and they don't see the fire. So, you know, speculation is...there's a danger in [that] the new media probably brings more speculation than you would see otherwise.

What do you think about 'Pizzagate?' — about how that was an example of mass hysteria?

Pizzagate's a pretty good example of mass hysteria. I've used that example a lot. The amazing thing about Pizzagate is that if you are looking into the evidence for it, it's really compelling — meaning that it's hard to imagine that all of that evidence doesn't mean what the Pizzagate, you know, conspiracy people thought it meant. But it's also classic confirmation bias. So, someone like me — who comes to it with a background in knowing about confirmation bias, and how frequently it occurs, and how easy it would be for it to happen in this situation — so when I looked at Pizzagate, my first impression was, "Yeah, this is really compelling. Probably **not true**." Right? So the fact that the evidence was really, really good didn't mean anything to me, because that's a *wait and see*. And then we waited, and we didn't see the-, you know, the proof in a hard form and that conspiracy theory started to fade away.

Could you talk about the way in which, if you sat down for an interview — well, *this* interview is going to be edited — sat down for a mainstream media interview, and you're interviewed for two, three, four hours and they cut it down to, like, thirty seconds, a minute, five minutes...that experience versus, you know, going on a Periscope with somebody like Mike and interviewing for an hour and it's all out there immediately and there's no filter.

One of the biggest, best, most positive things that's happening in the world is that when you take the news media out of the, you know, "I've got a half an hour to do this," or, "...five minutes to do this," and you put it into the world of podcasts and live streaming — where there's no end, you can just talk as long as you want — you start to break free from the power of the editors to take something you've said, carve it up and take it into context and change its meaning. But most of that change happens because of just editing choices — they just want to make it smaller — and it just changes the meaning when you take out the nuance. Some of it probably is just bad actors doing bad things, but I would say for the bigger-, bigger outlets, that's probably more that they're just trying to make it fit the time. But it does change the meaning of what the person said. It can make you go from looking smart to stupid, because the thing you said that they put on the air doesn't make sense without the part that they cut out. That is a big problem. But the new media's solving that by not having an end to any of their segments. We'll talk until we've told the whole story.

With social media, there's been a lot of stories about how they censor these new voices that are on the right, especially, and how that maybe ties into the mainstream, who seem to also favor a side. It seems to favor the left side more, right? Maybe that's a confirmation bias thing as well, but maybe you can speak to that a little bit.

So, the good news is that anybody can have a voice and, if they do a good job, they can build an audience on social media and get their version of the truth out. On the bad side, the people who own the various social media companies tend to be left-leaning, and it's at least the impression of the people on the right — and I'll be careful with my words — it's their impression that they're being 'shadowbanned,' as it's called. In other words, that their tweets don't show up where they should. People who are following them become automatically unfollowed. The other story doesn't show very high up in the feed, and that sort of thing. Now, depending who you talk to, that phenomenon has either been not demonstrated to be true, or totally demonstrated to be true. Right? I will just tell you that my own brother follows me on Twitter, and *only* me. He has an account that only does that, and he got automatically unfollowed from my account — and also on Periscope — at the *same time*. Now that-, that wasn't an accident. So, I don't know what Twitter's *official* explanation for that is, but, you know, I'm pretty sure that something's happening there. Whether Twitter management is behind it, or it's something happening in the bowels of the organization — or if it's just some kind of weird glitch in the algorithm — it does seem to be happening. Now, what I don't know is if there's somebody on the left who got unfollowed too, like, I don't see that. So, I gotta be careful. I have to be careful in saying that I can only see the stuff I can see. That's the stuff I know, but I don't want to over-interpret it now.

If it's true that the right is being consistently shadowbanned, and their messages are being diminished, the funny thing about that is that the most persuasive, powerful, best communicators are also all on the right. So, there's this weird coincidental balance, where the best persuaders are on the right, and the people who can shadowban them — if it's happening — are on the left. So, there is a little bit of a balance there, and maybe that's good. You know, maybe the world is better with a little bit of balance. I think we're rapidly heading toward a place where the big social media companies will just have to be regulated, because the public will-, will simply rely on them too much. They'll be too important to the outcomes of society. And if society doesn't trust them, that's a big problem. So I don't think you want to regulate totally in that way. But here's my prediction: I think that at least-, at least the algorithm — the code that says what is displayed where — probably will have to get audited by the government on a regular basis, or somebody that they, you know, select to do that. I think that has to happen, actually.

Why do you call people on the right better at persuasion? What makes them better at persuasion? How would you rate the mainstream media's ability to persuade?

For some reason, the people on the right are better Persuaders. And if-, if you ask me, "Why is that?" I actually don't know. It's actually sort of a question that-, it's an open question to me. It's simply an observation that — at least during the entire Trump cycle — the people who understood persuasion, they knew its ways, they-, they tended to be on the right. Now, could be that because Trump is so persuasive himself, that he attracted voices that understood that, and that those voices were more credible, because they kept being right and that probably raised your profile. So, there's probably an observational thing to it — meaning that I may notice the voices on the right *because* of Trump, and because they got more attention. But during the campaign, the Clinton campaign was absolutely terrible at persuasion until the final summer before the election — when Bernie dropped out — and then, suddenly — and I'm guessing that probably there were some advisers working for Bernie who went over to the Clinton team then — they went full weapons-grade after that, and their persuasion got first-rate. So, until then, the right just owned the persuasion. But, by the summer of 2016, the left was full weapons-grade.

How much do you think facts matter when it comes to persuasion?

A lot of people ask me how important facts are when it comes to persuasion. Now, if you have the facts, and they can be verified and people can check, they're very persuasive. But it turns out that, in many cases, we don't have the facts and, in many more cases, the facts are less persuasive than a well-crafted non-fact. Now, I want to be very careful: I'm not in favor of *lying*. I love a world where people don't have to lie — that it's not necessary. I'm simply making a statement that people can lie and still be persuasive.

Now, how ethical that is has a lot to do with, you know, what's the-, what's the outcome, and do the ends justify the means? I would say in some cases, yes, I would lie to a terrorist to save your life. But I wouldn't lie to my best friend to save a dollar. Right? So, it really does matter what is the topic. And if they're on the extremes. I think you could go either way.

Do you consider spinning-, do you think that's lying? Would you distinguish those?

I think there's a difference between being "factually inaccurate" and "spinning." But the outcome can be very similar. In other words, in both cases you may have influenced toward an outcome. So, I'm not sure that spinning is more honest or ethical, or honorable. But they're different. That's the only thing you can say about them.

Going back to the "two movies/one screen" analogy...I don't know what we can do to make people look at the same movie and come out and, "Oh, everyone's talking about the same movie," but how do we get them to at least come out of the theater and talk to each other about what they saw and not hate each other?

It's really hard to solve for the fact that people are in the same theater, but watching two movies on the same screen, because they're so invested in their movie that even if you showed them solid evidence that their movie was wrong, they would say, "Well, your evidence is wrong." Or, "Well, I'll change my movie a little bit, but it's still basically the same movie."

So, the only thing you can do is work on them over time with lots of evidence. So, if somebody thinks, "Hey, this Russia thing is real!" all you need is a bunch of outcomes that show it's not. One probably isn't enough. Several is probably good. But, beyond that, sometimes you need what I call a "fake because" — in other words, people sometimes just need a reason to go to the other side. A reason to change their mind. And the reason — and this is the weird part, and this is well understood in the field of persuasion — the reason doesn't have to be *real*. Sometimes people are just ready. You know, it's the weight of things that have happened before, but they still need a trigger. They need a thing to tell their siblings. It's like, "Here's why I changed my mind. It was *this* thing."

Hurricane Harvey might be that thing, because it just took us all out of our old movies and said, "All right. I don't care what the movie was on your screen or mine. Right now we're worried about the people, you know, who are damaged by Harvey. We're on the same side. We don't care about race or anything — we don't care. We're just-, we're on the same team." So, something like that can just shake what you were thinking. It just gives you an excuse to say, "Well, you know, I thought maybe Trump was a monster, but he handled that Harvey thing well. He had enough empathy." I'm just saying that hypothetically, this can happen. And that might be the "because" that they needed to switch.

How do we as human beings develop confirmation bias, and is that something that is maybe understood by mainstream forces, and maybe they use that to get an early [in] with people?

So, when I talk about confirmation bias, I think people reflexively say, "How can I get rid of that? How can I have less of that?" The bad news is that I don't think confirmation bias is a bug in our software. Confirmation bias *is* the software. We're designed by evolution that way. And what I mean by "designed" is that: Imagine if your brain had to reinterpret your whole environment every time you get new information. It's just more efficient to say, "Well, I was right before. I'm still right," because you don't want to re-, you know, re-juggle your entire world view every few minutes — as new information is coming in — and people like to stick with what they got. It's just easier to use less-, less resources, you know, fewer resources. It's probably just how we evolved. And so, I don't think you can get rid of it. You can, however, learn to notice if there's a trigger. So, if you're in a situation where somebody has a trigger, and you *don't,* the odds are — if you've identified the trigger correctly — that you're more likely closer to the *truth*. But, you can never know.

But why is one person-, why do they grow up, you know...one person may be liberal, one person may be more libertarian, or something like that. Where does that begin? How does it develop?

There's some science that suggests there might be some kind of genetic bias toward being conservative or liberal, and I'm going to say that sounds right to me. So without-, without blessing the science, I'll just say that it "smells right to me." But, beyond that, you've got the social pressure. You've got the, "How old are you?" that probably makes a big difference. And you've got, "What are your friends saying?", you know, "What are you seeing on social media?" So, it's a whole bunch of things. But, I think, a little bit genetic, and a whole bunch of social.

We're asking this, you know, before you go on your book tour. So, I was just gonna ask what you anticipate the media's response and reaction to you will be as you go on that tour?

So, when I go on my book tour for *Win Bigly*, I can tell you with fair certainty what's going to happen: The people who are inclined to like me are going to say, "This is the *best* book you've ever written, Scott." The people who are pretty sure they hate me, because I've said things that they didn't like in politics — or any other thing I've said — are going to interpret the book as something I didn't mean and didn't say. So, in other words, most of the criticisms will not be about what's in the book. I would say — I'll go even further: Close to one hundred percent, but at least ninety percent, of the criticisms which I will inevitably get, will be based on somebody's belief of what's in my soul — that they imagine they could read my mind — or something I didn't say that they think is implied. Or some weight they think I've given to something that I really haven't — maybe I just didn't *talk* about it — so, almost all of the critics will be criticizing, essentially, a hallucination of what they think they saw. And I say something like that, and I'm completely aware that anybody who is not trained in persuasion hearing this will say, "Oh *that's* convenient, you *author*, you, that's sort of an *author* thing to say, you know, to protect you when you get criticized." And I have no defense against that. I'm just telling you that any person trained in persuasion would agree that if they can't find something wrong with it, they will *imagine* there's something wrong with it. And that will be good enough.

There's a thing on Twitter that people say, and they'll quote a tweet and say "the mask slips" when someone tweets something inflammatory. How do we know when it's "someone's mask is slipping" or whether, perhaps, they just do something out of character, for instance? Is there persuasion or confirmation bias coming into play with that?

Well, sometimes it's hard to know if you're seeing somebody acting out of character or they have, you know, let the "mask slip" and you're peering into their soul. My caution to that is: You're not good at peering into souls. You just *think* you are. Everybody thinks they're good at it. Everybody's *wrong*. We're all terrible at it. So, until you've seen, like, a body of evidence that somebody has changed their view in some way, or it is revealing a new view, you need to wait for a few data points. You know, the first data point that looks like it's out-of-bounds is almost certainly *nothing*. You know, you need a few.

GAVIN MCINNIS INTERVIEW

Okay. My name is Gavin McInnes. I do a TV show on CRTV.com called, "Get Off My Lawn!" I've got a big history in media that goes back to the early '90s of being a "bad boy." And I am, as Roger Stone says of himself, an "agent provocateur."

CRTV — what's that?

CRTV is *Conservative Review Television*. I quit *Compound Media*, *TakiMag*, and *Rebel*. And I think that they have a long-term plan that really interests me, and it sort of feels like Fox in the late '90s — Fox News. It feels like "the sky is the limit." And I sound like I'm shilling my own brand, my own company, my own employer, and I am — but I'm rich. So I wouldn't go there if I didn't believe in it. And what I think is happening is: I think the investors , I'm sure they're right-wing. But I don't think that's really what pushes them. I think it's just "don't pull" in the market. Right now, you have eighty percent of the media is left-wing and, always, the country is going to be about fifty-fifty. So that's just *dumb*. That's too many fast-food joints, too many burger joints, not enough pizza stands. So they're saying, "All right, well, let's move this over because there's-, there's a huge hole." And I don't think Fox News has a bright future. I think the Murdochs are trying to water it down because they want to sell it with Sky News. I believe Sky News is worth about twenty billion dollars — I think Fox is only worth about three-and-a-half/four billion. And you can't sell a contentious media entity in Britain. I forget the rule. So they want to-, the Murdoch boys — who are just as left-wing as *the* Pinch Sulzberger — they're rich kids, they want to dilute it down to nothing so it's nice and marketable, and sell that — and then Fox is gone. We lose *Hannity* and we lose everything else. So there's going to be an even bigger hole soon. But, right now, all you have is Fox News. Every other mainstream media is left-wing and, as far as print goes, it's a similar story. We only really have *Breitbart* online, fighting the good fight, and no matter how you feel about politics, as an angel investor coming in from outer space, you must go, "Wait a minute. Ninety percent of the coverage of Trump this summer was negative. That's not indicative of a balanced media, that's indicative of a nine-out-of-ten reporters with an ax to grind. How about we have four-out-of-ten reporters who don't have an ax to grind and are at least [representing] the right, and we can take advantage of that hole in the market?"

So I'm excited to be on CRTV and to do my show *Get Off My Lawn!* for a number of reasons, including: I want to get the family back. I kind of regret, in a way, with *Vice* promoting this endless hedonism. It was really fun, but I created a monster in a sense that a lot of these women think they can just have sex for the rest of their lives and there'll be no comeuppance, that their ovaries won't dry up. And a lot of these guys go, "Oh, just keep getting laid. Women don't want a ring on it. And I can just play video games all day and then 'Netflix and chill' every time I'm horny." So, I've sort of made this wrinkled teenager this perpetual adolescent that I want to dial back and say "Hold on...hold on...hold on!" And this was in my book, *Death of Cool:* "Have your party years. That's great, guys." But then there's a new chapter called, "Kids." And if you're a forty-seven-year-old dad, like me, you're an *old* dad. It's hard to chase my four-year-old around the house. I'm exhausted, let alone the other-, the ten-year-old, the nine-year-old... So, that's a big part of my agenda, too, is promoting the family and getting sort of the mainstream young people to be entrepreneurs and to understand that being a housewife is *cool.* And to understand that having kids is *fun.*

But overall, the big business plan, I think-, I can't believe that we live in a society like America where the media is so wildly biased to the left. It just doesn't make business sense. It doesn't-, it doesn't add up to service.

Yeah, liberals think that conservatives just take as a given that the media's biased. But why do you think that they can't see their *own* bias?

Well, actually, the guy-, the *Republican Like Me* — the CEO, Ken Stern/Stein? — the guy who wrote that book and traveled the country, he goes, "I didn't realize what a bubble I was in." I think it's unnatural to want to confront people all the time. Now I'm Scottish, and our culture's *booze*, so we like a good fight — even a physical fistfight can be fun — but I think, you know, a lot of the mid-westerners — a lot of middle-class and upper-middle-class people — they've never been in a fight. They don't really understand the joys of conflict. So they just take their spoon-fed media and they go, "Trump is Hitler. He's the most dangerous president ever. We have white supremacists in the White House." I've read that in at least five different places. Ergo, "I'm a well-informed person and that's a fact." And, you know, it splits families up. Like you have aunts who don't go to their niece's birthday party, because there's a rumor that the dad is a pro-Trump guy and that must mean, "He's a Nazi." They don't want their daughter around Klansmen and swastikas. So these lies have deep-seated effects, that affect people's personal lives. It's sick and depraved. You know, they call-, they say, "Oh, the conservatives are homophobes." I don't even like the term, "conservative." We're just *not liberals*. We just don't follow their stupid dogma, but our side includes libertarians who hate Neo-Cons, who hate Paleo-Cons, who hate Anarcho-Capitalists, who hate Hotep, you know, who hate the alt-light, [who] hate the alt-right, [who] hate the new right. There's-, there's a whole cornucopia of people out here. The only thing we all have in common is we don't imbue the government with any kind of authority. That sounds very healthy to me. Also sounds kind of cool, which is probably why millennials are joining our side more than ever. But, anyway, the concept with conservatives just seems to be — besides smaller government — it's also like, "Come on in! Let's hash it out...let's discuss it." Free speech, you know, say what's on your mind.

You can insult me. I can take it...no...insults — if you call me "fat" and say I'm "unhealthy," [or] I actually "secretly want supremacy and colonialism" — you know what? You should just leave. Just go. I know I'm contradicting myself, but sometimes, you know, when we give them the time of day, they just tell you, "It's a-million o'clock." It gets tiring.

Tell us how you started *Vice* and how you got into media...all that stuff.

I got into media by accident, really. I was a cartoonist...uh, there was a new magazine started out that eventually became *Vice Media* and writers were just so bad at their jobs. I mean, they were so affected, and they wanted to be Hunter Thompson, or something. So why isn't anyone writing the way they talk in bars? So I started doing that and that sort of became the *brand.* And then, after I left there, that sort of became my media brand when I would do Fox News and other things...just speak normally, you know. And Coulter seems so controversial. But if you were talking to her in a bar, you'd go, "That's not controversial — that's just 'raunchy.'" And that is a truly "American" thing.

But we strayed from that, so...I've been doing this since the early '90s, but it's only since Trump it's become an "unthinkable taboo." And that says a lot, too, about-, about the culture, I think-, I think you'll notice that even if you keep your views the same — I mean I still have the same sort of "punk rock anarchist" views I had when I was a teenager, which was: "don't listen to other people, I hate authority. I want individuals to have all the rights that-, that belong to them without anyone else getting involved."

You know, I'm an anarchist and that goes from being called a "Nazi", to a "racist," or "communist," depending on the time. It used to be "radical," you know, in the '80s to say, "I want to abolish the government." Now it's become "racist."

What is "fake news" — how would you describe fake news?

I don't like the term "fake news" anymore, because fake news is just...fake news is: "Donald Trump doesn't *really* board his helicopter. It's a double that does it. And he takes the train because he's scared of flying." That's just a *lie*. That's fake. This is *different*. What we're seeing now — we're seeing "mentally ill news," which is this myopic obsession with *one* thing and it's-, you feel like you're working in a lunatic asylum.

Say you're working in a loony bin, and there was this one guy going, "The Khmer Rouge!" or "Coming the Khmer Rouge!" or "Coming Pol Pot is upstairs!...the Khmer Rouge were going to invade Iraq. We've got to stop the communists in Cambodia!" And you go, "All right, Mr. McGillicuddy, that's okay..." And you lead him to his room and you go, "He was a-bitchin' about the 'Khmer Rouge' again." That's the way the media is with "Nazis." They see Nazis in their soup. They're *everywhere*.

I actually call it "not-see glasses," because they don't see Islam. They don't see the Pulse shooting. They don't see in San Bernardino. They'll just *see* Charlottesville. They'll see one example of a "white supremacist killing" and that's *all* they'll see, and then we'll start Crow-barring other things in there like Dylann Roof, or any lunatic who happened to say something "racist" once.

It's a bizarre obsession that's not fake. It's mentally ill. And we have to treat these people that way. They're not-, they're not there to debate or get to the answers. You know, when two people-, when two people debate their mutual goals: I want to present my argument in a-, in a *convincing* way. I want to present my argument and convincing way and, if they're both intelligent, the loser will be happy with losing, because he's smarter now. And that's been the history of debates since the beginning of civilization till five years ago. And now liberals, they don't want to debate, because they don't want the same thing as you. They don't want to convey ideas. They want power and they want you to go away because you heard their narrative. So is that "fake?" No, not really. And I thought, *When Cernovich was on 60 Minutes, that was a great example of the myth of fake news.* What's his name? — Scott Pellegrino? — Scott Pelley brought up these weird sites that no one had ever heard of, like The Daily Amazonian, Las Vegas Herald...and you go, *I've never heard of this.*

And then he shows some articles that have just been made up for clickbait. Everyone knows those. You know what they say, "Stars who have aged badly," or "Stars embarrassed by their kids," and have a kid with facial tattoos. You *know* that's not Michael Douglas' son. You know it's clickbait. You can tell — *everyone* can tell — it's like the difference between pornography and eroticism: it's glaringly obvious.

And Scott Pelley wasn't *really* talking about those sites. Those were just examples he had to use to prove this lie — that there's a fake news problem — and he's talking about it. The irony is: he *was* the fake news...the fake news is *60 Minutes* denigrating anyone who's remotely curious...anyone that does their job the way they talk about entrepreneurs — you got to check on this group, on the feature they did where they just talked about his social tics because they don't like entrepreneurs. But, the real narrative that *60 Minutes* pushes is this idea that Hillary was "hard-done by" and that Republicans are "racist." That's the true "fake news" that's going on, not these made-up, innocuous websites...and that fake news is "mentally ill news," because it is obsessed with the myth of "Nazis" and "white supremacists" and blah blah blah.

Now how did they get there? I think they got there because they're the bourgeoisie now. They're the "new elite." And these guys went to private school...when they traveled, they would have, you know, the finest foods. Pinch Sulzberger — from the New York Times — he *loves* Indonesia, because when he thinks of Indonesia, he thinks of the delicious little delicacies he'd have.

These strange little deep-fried insects, or whatever they eat over there. And so that becomes his idea of "multiculturalism."

So when these guys see working-class Americans, whom they've never spoken to, they go, "Well that's *clearly* someone in the Klan, if they don't like diversity, and they don't like open borders, because open borders mean, 'My nanny is good to my kid and my lawn is spotless.' And 'diversity' means a bunch of different restaurants, and gay marriage means 'two gay dudes that are rich that I was at their wedding this summer and it was beautiful.' And if you're against *that*, then you're against *beauty*, so you're a dumb redneck jerk!"

And that is a strange little — what are those little things? — those snow globes? That's a strange "snow globe" version of America. And they're not open to debate...they're not open to questioning...they just shake it up, look at that, and go, "Who could have a problem with that? It's beautiful. Santa's there." And you go, "Well that's not what it is." You know, gay marriage sounded like gay marriage when it first came out. It turns out it's a lot about sabotaging Catholicism, sabotaging Christianity, penalizing bakers, penalizing people that don't follow that dogma. It turns out open borders is brutal on the working class. It's a real strain on our social systems...it's expensive...they don't put in more than they take out. It's also a drain just in how much money they send out. It also murders the cities these Mexicans come from, because they lose their fathers.

And as far as diversity goes: Yeah, well your diversity used to include people who admired the West, admired liberty — Sikhs, Hindus, people who were excited to be here and wanted to assimilate. Now you're-, you're pulling in Islam and you're pulling in people who want to set up Fifth columns who don't appreciate liberty or democracy, and they don't like homosexuals. The guy who shot up Pulse Nightclub chose Pulse Nightclub *on purpose*. He chose a place replete with ho-, unarmed homosexuals. So your lack of rigor in your routine, your lack of back-and-forth has allowed you to live in a bubble. And what was his name? Ken Stern, I think? The old CEO of NPR? He just wrote a book about this. I think it's called, "A Republican in the Wild," or *Republican Like Me*...that's what it's called. And he went and met these people and he realized: "I didn't know anything." For example, it didn't occur to him that just having a gun in the area prevents crime. If you're in an area where a lot of women tend to have a gun in their purse, those women don't get raped. *Not* because they pulled the gun, but because it's generally known that women are armed in that area — and thieves and rapists and murderers, they have self-preservation still intact in their twisted minds, and they get deterred by gun ownership.

So do you think its just kind of a myopia in class difference, or is there something more nefarious? Is there more intentionality behind pushing the narratives?

Well that's the trillion dollar question.

Are these just naive rich people in media? *60 Minutes*, *[The] New York Times*...are they just the bourgeoisie saying, "Let them eat cake!"? Or is this a globalist plot to shut down Western society? And George Soros has been very open about how much money he's donated to these companies. You look at the way CNN treats Antifa and CNN treats *any* patriotic group. It's the "KKK versus Che Guevara" as far as they're concerned. So it is very suspicious.

I don't know. I don't have the resources to-, to find out. But I can sit there on the front lines and constantly be beating these people back. And I do — I would say every day this month, on average — some days, three-a-day, some days, zero-a-day...I'm sending out legal letters to these people going, "I'm not a Nazi." "The Proud Boys aren't Nazis" — that's a men's club I run — "You've got it all wrong...please issue a retraction"...blah blah blah. I get in their face. Argue with them. I expose them and they don't like that, because they're used to just being able to crap on people and run away giggling. So I don't know if this-, where this links to globalism and some sort of sinister plot. I don't really care because, at the end of the day, my job is to expose these people for lying. And that's what I'm doing.

Could you talk a little bit more about your experiences with the media in terms of them lying about you and spreading falsehoods about you?

Oh, my God. Falsehoods about me is endless. Endless. They've got Ben Shapiro with a yarmulke on. Alan Dershowitz, who wrote *The Case For Israel.* The both of them are seen as "Nazis." They're spending all their time trying to find evidence there, while chaos goes on around them with Islam and the alt-left.

But yeah, with me, they say I'm a Nazi. They'll take a joke I've made, take it out of context, strip it of any sort of context, and then make it an affirmative statement, like it was some sort of Ph.D. dissertation.

It's also that they're unbelievably lazy. The journalism job is not the *Watergate* job it used to be, with the press and your fedora, and the notepad and the...running from the courtroom until all the tollbooths fall over with all the exciting news about the judge's verdict. Those days are *gone.* These people don't leave their desk. And this is true of the right *and* the left.

They'll sit there and they'll Google and talk about a "backlash", and you'll go check the evidence of this backlash, and realize it's just *tweets*, and I have these tweets come from 16-year-olds with three followers. So this sort of cultural litmus test is based on you coming up with a hypothesis first and then finding tweets to fill it in. They just Google. In fact, I've seen a local news once — they go, a common thing they'll say: "If you Google 'planking,' over seven thousand results come up," and then they'll show on the news the scrolling of the Google results and you go, "I actually have access to Google. I can do that on my own." And one fun way to figure this out, too, is: I think everyone has read an article about something they know a hell of a lot about. Whether it's your home town of Kanata, Ontario, and they go, "Kanata, Ontario was founded as a hockey town in the 1960s. And, since then, it's been mostly Amish." And you're reading and going, "That's not true...that's not true. No, that was in the '80s. No, he's not from there, he's from Napean." And you go through, and you go, "There's 37 errors in this!" and that's when you realize: Wait a minute. That must be true of all the articles I read about other stuff where I'm *not* an expert...any time it's about your family, your hometown, your thing, your sports team — actually, I shouldn't comment on sports...I'm not that well-versed on it, but — the area that you know intimately well, and the reporter comes by — you'll say: "Wow, these people have reached peak incompetence, so they have a leftist agenda, where they inject swastikas into *everything*, and they're incompetent. And that includes lazy and stupid. So you have someone who's lazy, stupid, useless and obsessed with Nazis, and we wonder why the media has become such a joke.

Do you think that since they're using tactics like speculation — they're using things like taking things out of context, humor — that the backlash against them from alternative news sources... do you think it's justified for alternative news sources to then do that to them? Or do you not view it that way?

That's a tough question, is: should we retaliate? Like when Kathy Griffin — is that her name — "Kathy Griffith?" I always get confused with Family Guy. When she was holding Trump's head up — we're about free speech. I don't want to live in an America where you can't have a mock head of the president up. That's Stalinism. I don't want that. So I don't want her to be fired.

However, that's not high on my priority list or say, when-, when Laura Loomer and Jovi Val went and disrupted that Shakespeare thing, *Shakespeare in the Park*...that was an SJW thing to do and it would be-, it would be hypocritical of me to say, "Well, we should shut down plays and we should shut down art when it criticizes the president I like." So I just avoid that altogether. I didn't comment on Kathy. I didn't comment on *Shakespeare [in the Park]*. Someone asks me, I'll say: "all art should be permitted and you shouldn't shut down plays." But I think it's-, I totally respect those people playing dirty pool. I respect-, I respect people calling for a boycott of liberal shows. It's not my cup of tea, but I'm not going to stand in the way of it, because these people play dirty pool, and I've been playing dirty pool in my own way...like these journalists who say these things — I find pictures of them. I expose them, because they like to sort of hide in the bushes with their BB gun and shoot me in the back of the neck when you're walking, so I like to go to the bushes, pick them up by the back of the neck and go, "*This* is who wrote that. First of all, he's British and he's talking about about NASCAR and gun culture. This guy doesn't know what he's talking about." I think that's a way to stay sort of philosophically consistent and also play dirty pool.

But as far as dirty tricks go...I'm just standing out of the way, because if someone wants to, you know, "fight fire with fire," then it's not my first priority to call them out on it.

Do you think there's a problem in the country with, like, the filter bubbles, and that whole discussion of how nobody is following each other with different points of view? Do you see that as a problem?

That is thc problem right now with America: the bubble. You know, it's highly possible this could be a whole other documentary-, that it's "Facebook's fault." They've [taken] this innate human tendency where you don't want to see bad news. So you click away and you unfollow. Same with Twitter. You separate yourself from people with contradicting views and then you end up with this sort of snowball of your own narrative.

And there was a study awhile ago that said, "When people are confronted with data that contradicts their belief, they become more steadfast in those beliefs." Like, if some-, if some cult leader said, "The world's going to end on November 1st," on November 2nd, that guy has more followers than he did before. Which is-, I think that's a relatively new trait, or at least it's gotten worse [with] this bubble. And that's what Charles Murray talked about in *Coming Apart*. And I think we have to discipline ourselves, too. If you're a rich liberal, Upper West Side, or with no kids, go see a Transformers movie, drink Budweiser, join the Knights of Columbus, hang out with union guys, hear their dirty jokes, sit with the police and do a ride-along. You can do that anywhere in America. You don't need to be a citizen of that state. Go there, then book it. They call you up a few-, a couple of weeks later, you go ride with the cops.

You know, being a right-winger in New York City, I'm drowned in the air [of] the opposition. And you learn to enjoy conflict. You learn to enjoy arguing and I think it makes you-, it definitely makes your arguments more thorough, but it makes you a more *complete* person. You know, the whole reason we have "trigger warnings" and "safe spaces" is because we've become mentally obese. We're out of shape philosophically; we're out of shape when it comes to our own political beliefs and that makes us weak people. So now we're weak and ugly on the outside *and* on the inside. And it's a pretty easy thing to avoid. Just, I don't know, follow some conservatives on Twitter, allow conservatives back in your life on Facebook, debate the right if you're left — debate the left if you're right. I mean, talk to Tucker Carlson about trying to get liberals on his show. It's a near impossibility. And, I find on my show-, I feel like I'm feeding a squirrel in the park. I have to go, "Come on...okay, okay. You can just hang up the video Skype. You won't be at my house. And if you feel that it is going bad, turn it off...turn it off, [then] radio silence... they're out." So, yes, the problem isn't just that we're polarized.

The problem is that we're willfully polarized and we want to blame Trump, we want to blame Russia. We want to blame the media, but it's our own fault. And I'm sorry, but the left is way worse at it than we are. You know, the right wants to have you over for dinner. Dennis Prager says — and I think he's stealing from Charles Krauthammer — he says: "They think we're *evil.* We just think they're *wrong.*"

— Well, that would be a great ending.

What do you think this current era of journalism-, what is the "ideal journalist" to you? How should they fact-check, approach sources...what's your ideal?

I think the future of journalism is-,and if you ever had a kid, but when they take off the umbilical cord, they sort of clip it and they leave it there and eventually it just dies, and it gets sort of brown and rotten and it just falls off. It's like the opposite of a circumcision, where you really got to get in there to get off. And that's what's happening to this dinosaur media.

You look at Anderson Cooper's ratings and they're pathetic. They're one hundred thousand, two hundred thousand. Alex Jones, if he got under five million, he'd slit his wrists. He'd say, "What's happening to me?!" Even with right-wing journalism — like, a right-wing media — like, Hannity is probably the king, and he gets three-, five million sometimes. That's pretty standard for *Infowars*, and for some of these — Paul Joseph Watson, for Lauren Southern, for Shapiro, for Crowder...I mean, I would be-, when I see I get a million hits on something, I go, "Not bad. That's pretty reasonable." Where, with MSNBC, that would be-, I mean, they'd have a party that night. They'd be screaming, drinking champagne. In other words, that media is dead now, and the new media is amateur journalism and these people have become the sources of most of the major scoops of this past year.

The guy-, there's no more Watergate from the beat reporter talking to people on the street, because he just uses Google. These kids go out there and they know what's going on. And when it-, when they do use Google, they're accruing millions of other peoples' info. They look at how we found that bike lock guy — some guy smashed a pro-Trump guy in the head, split his head open — the autists on Reddit found the lock, found the face, people did all these codes thing. I think Jeremy Piven has a show — a fictional last cop show — based on him. But we tracked him down using all those people working. And we now have a system where, for the past three or four generations, both five percent three percent of the fifteen-to-twenty would call themselves "conservative." Now it's above seventeen percent of these young people calling themselves "conservatives," and that's because the left blew it by being lazy and making themselves antiquated. And the irony is these kids now are turning to themselves for information...they're their own journalists, and that's what's so exciting about this time, is someone like James O'Keefe can come along with an undercover camera and totally blow up *The New York Times* — totally blow up YouTube, and their fake algorithms, and all their bias in getting videos up. He exposes Hillary, fake voting. All of this stuff by going out there and just doing it themselves-, themselves-, himself. So the the answer to this question is the question of who are the great new journalists? I would say it's you. It's the guy in the mirror, because the dinosaur media has ruined itself. They've destroyed their brand. And no one takes them seriously anymore. Look at the numbers.

When you get lied about, do you get upset at this point? Or do you think it's just "par for the course?"

That's a good question. When I read these lies, I mean, it depends on the time of day. If it's just *me*, I love it. I don't mind getting yelled at. I would say eighty percent of the time I get stopped in the street — way too many times — I don't-, if you don't want to be noticed, don't do five YouTube videos a week, for several years, because your fame lives on and it's just, "Hey, Gavin, can I get a selfie?" So many selfies 'cause they're so boring. The camera is never ready and, "Hold on...hold on. I'm going to go somewhere, dude." But four-out-of-five times, it's, "Hey! Love you! Proud of my boy!" and then, one-out-of-five times, it's, "You're a Nazi!" Or one I got: I was playing baseball with my son, throwing my ball back-and-forth, and this guy rides behind on his bike and goes, "How's the hate and ignorance industry working for you?"

It's problematic being a dad because, you know, your wife reads these. Your-, your-, your in-laws read it...your aunts and uncles believe it, and people are incurious, generally. You know, I was traumatized at my bar the other day where a guy-, the wine salesman pulled out a bottle from South Africa — I'm sorry to keep telling this story, but I think it's very indicative of the way the general populace thinks — and goes, "Oh, I don't want any bottles from South Africa."

The SPLC had a good reputation for a long time. Now they're a joke. The ADL — the Anti-Defamation League — all of these things were read. Those are four very reputable sources. They're yelling, "Nazi! Nazi! Nazi!" today, at me. And people take it seriously because they only remember those brands, those news sources, those-, those projects from ten years ago, twenty years ago, thirty years ago. So it's frustrating when these lies are said about me. But, you know, let the dogs yap. I get a lawyer. I send them a letter and make them do a retraction. And if someone's going to not, you know, invite my daughter to a party or-, or, you know, be awkward around me, good riddance.

But doesn't the fact that people are incurious — that they're repeating talking points about South Africa from the '80s — speak to the fact that the mainstream media still has enormous power and influence?

No, it's a lingering power. The mainstream media has a lingering power. If the sun blew up right now and blacked out, I believe it would take us eight minutes to notice. And that's what we're having with media now. They're dead, but we're still seeing their star shine up above. And it's only a matter of time before we realize they're dead and you know what's going to happen is: the left is-, they've created this monster and they're going to start cannibalizing each other, and that's when they're going to realize that these people are evil.

So there's two things at play here...one is: it takes a while for society to realize that the mainstream media is a joke, and two: as they keep eating themselves, people are going to realize that they're not just dumb and crazy, they're sinister.

What role does comedy have in terms of influencing culture, commenting on news, allowing tensions to be defused...?

Comedy is a funny-, in a funny place right now. Get it? And I think comedy is like sex-, sexuality: you can't stifle it. So if there's no kissing at school, and all the girls have to wear long dresses, they're going to find a broom closet to make out in. Now, what the liberal fascists have successfully done is killed comedy in Hollywood. You know, Adam Sandler had that movie with

Indians in it. The liberals got in their ears like little Rasputins and said, "This movie is racist! Quit!" So that movie was canned. You know, it was probably super-funny and I believe the Indian in that movie is a superhero because he's so awesome. But, no, that's not good enough.

So they ruined movies and they've ruined stand-up. Go to a stand-up show. And it's only three jokes are, "Trump is Hitler!" "Trump is Satan!" and "2016 sucked!" Again and again and again, on a loop. And it's so *unfunny*. But you can't kill a comedy...and now you see comedy in memes, you see it in parodies, you see it all over the Internet, anonymously, where people won't get fired if they dare to make fun of this liberal.

What's the future of journalism?

The future of journalism is "amateur journalism." The future of journalism is James O'Keefe. The future of journalism is someone building it from the ground-up themselves and not really caring where it's reported. I mean, someone like Lauren Southern, she was at *Rebel [Media]*, she was with someone else...I don't know where. I don't even know where she is now. I don't care. I want to watch her videos. I don't care if she's hosting it on YouTube or if, you know, [*The] Daily Caller* hired her. That doesn't really matter to me. So the idea of brands, I think, is dying — where you're located doesn't really matter. The gatekeepers have had-, the gatekeepers have died. You read the article, you double-check every fact that's important to you, and you go, "Oh, that's fascinating...I never heard that." You know, when I read young men, you know, arguing on the Internet these days, they'll say things like, "Big if true." They never say [just] "Big" anymore. So now young people will double-/triple-verify everything that shocks them. And that's a very healthy way to be and that is the death-, that's the end of Anderson Cooper. And the beginning of "You-derson Cooper." *You're* the new TV host.

— That's not such a great ending.

RYAN HOLIDAY INTERVIEW

Who are you and what do you do?

I'm Ryan Holiday. I'm an author. A media strategist. Media columnist for *The New York Observer*. I wrote a book called, *Trust Me, I'm Lying*, where I tried to expose or rip back the curtain on how the media really works, both from a marketing standpoint and a journalistic standpoint.

One of the main subjects in your book is about "trading up the chain." How the blogs run the media, to a large extent. Could you talk about that?

One of the things I noticed as a marketer is how often a seemingly inconsequential tweet or blog post on a small site could go from basically nothing to national news. So it might be, you know, some reporter at *The Huffington Post,* or some local blogger in some small city writes a 250-word article and then, three days later, you're forced to respond to this on CNN.

So I was interested in how that happened. How does this disreputable source of news find itself being — if not reported on widely by the mainstream or the international press — how, at least, are you not finding yourself responding in those mediums? So it will be like: "Rumors online are saying this. Is this true?" So even if the media isn't outright reporting on the rumors or reporting the rumors, they're reporting on the rumor.

So it's this kind of process where, if you think about what it would be like to be a news producer or a journalist at a top paper today, you're not sort of pounding the pavement looking for stories. You're logging onto the Internet and seeing what people are talking about on Facebook or on Twitter or on the various blogs that you find. So it's this sort of process where you have a really small source. It could be a subreddit. It could be a Wikipedia page. It could be just some random person's social media account that leads directly to news reports on a major outlet. I mean, the slogan for *Gawker* was always that, "Today's gossip is tomorrow's news". I think that sort of encapsulates how the media system really works now.

You mentioned a statistic that eighty-nine percent of journalists get their news from online sources. Could you mention that?

If you ask journalists, "Where are you getting your information? What are your best sources?" It's not, "Oh, I have, you know, some mole in the State Department." It's their network of people that they follow. And those people are going to be right a lot. And those people are going to be wrong a lot. And so, when-, when you look at-, one of the reports now is the amount of fake Russian tweets that were picked up by something like eleven thousand different media outlets. This single Russian troll was quoted like eleven thousand different times. And part of the reason that happens is that journalists have figured out — these are journalists who are often-, their success is measured by how much traffic their articles do, and so, that means that they do a lot of articles — and so, one of the easy ways to get an article out very quickly is to say, "Here's what people on Twitter are saying about something." Right? So people are mad that Trump said this and then they'll have twenty or thirty sort of high-ranking tweets or viral tweets about it. "Here's what people are saying on Facebook...here's what people are saying on other blogs...," so these sort of roundups of content. And that happens because these journalists spend all their time on social media as well. So...I think people have started to realize that this is where the sausage is getting made, and what comes out the other side is seemingly reputable, well-sourced accurate news. But it's really kind of coming from just this noisy sphere of content and there's not a ton of vetting done of that content.

Let's talk about how you have manipulated that system — especially sources. "Oh, I got a tip from this reputable person," when it's really coming from someone like you, who is trying to game the system?

Media outlets have gotten very addicted to breaking news leaks, right? And so, they put up tip lines on their website. And I think it's silly to think that people who want to be in the news aren't realizing, "Okay, if I go through a publicist, if I-, if I pick something through these traditional channels, there's all sorts of competition." There's sort of a reluctance to do what somebody wants you to do from a journalistic standpoint. But if that same pitch — if presented as a "leak" — somehow comes off as being "exclusive" and attractive and interesting...I remember when I was the Director of Marketing at American Apparel, we-, we were sued by Woody Allen over some copyright dispute or something and were getting savaged in the press about it. And every time we would try to talk to a reporter about what our side of the case was, we weren't getting it done. No one was really interested in telling that side of the story.

So what I did was: I wrote a memo where I outlined our entire case — why we did what we did. I presented it as though the memo was being written from the creative director to her employees. Then I printed the memo out. I had the creative director sign it. And then I scanned it. And I leaked it to a number of websites as an employee of the company who'd just gotten this memo from my boss. And so, now the *same* set of facts and quotes that the media hadn't been interested in reporting before, they're now presenting as a response to this leak of information.

You see this all the time, too — even on media outlets, right? If you're the CEO of *BuzzFeed,* or you're the publisher of *Gawker,* or you're the editor of some website that's embroiled in controversy, or that you're trying to send a message to investors...right? You don't set up a pitch for *The New York Times* reporter and hope they come up and profile you, and that this information is buried somewhere in the story. You write a memo to your employees, but it's not really to your employees. The memo is designed for publication. So it's-, in some ways, these leaks are more press releases than they are anything else.

How does anger and controversy sell? How have you used that to your advantage?

Well, look, you don't tend to share things that you don't have a strong reaction to. And, so, I think social media thrives on anger. Some of the research shows this, too. That virality is a very strong predictor of social sharing. They did a study of [*The] New York Times'* pieces. And anger was the number one predictor of that virality. So it shouldn't surprise us, then, that we see lots of things that make us angry. Right?

It's important to note that — although there might be higher ideals behind a certain media outlet, or even reporters' sort of internal ethics — that they are still making a *product*. And none of them get paid. And they can't keep the lights on if that product isn't sold. And so, if anger is driving the social sharing — which is where traffic comes from — it shouldn't surprise us that we would see lots of things that make us angry. On both sides, right? So the right is in a perpetual state of indignation and the left is in a perpetual state of outrage. And then those positions flip all the time, right? "They're doing this terrible thing. Can you believe it? They're doing [that] terrible thing. Can you believe it?"

I saw a report that was really interesting: They were showing that a number of the fake news sites like-, there's different types of fake news, obviously, but in a number of the fake news sites, [they] are owned by the same companies. And they'll take the same story and present: "Here's why you should be outraged by what Kellyanne Conway said...and here's why you should be outraged about what they're saying about Kellyanne Conway," right? Or, whatever: "Here's why you should do this." "Here's why you absolutely should not do that exact same thing." And so, what they realize is that — if the truth is somewhere in the middle, and the truth is kind of boring it would be much better to take two diametrically opposed, but outrageously inciting anger-inducing articles for each poll, because those are the people that are going to drive the traffic.

In your book, you used an image of a funnel to describe our perception of reality. Could you illustrate that for us?

It's based on a sociologist's work that I'm forgetting. But if you think about what the news is — what you see in a newspaper, on TV — it's a small fraction of reality. There's all the things that have happened. There's all the things that they know about. There's all the things that they decided to write about. There's the things that they decided to write about that you saw. And it goes down...and down...until you're at that individual article. And so, you think that when you're reading the news, that you're being informed, that you're educating yourself, that you're seeing how the world is...but you're seeing such a tiny fraction of the world.

And what I would add to that thing now is, like, one of those things: Did social media decide to put [that] in front of you? — so, if Facebook's algorithm is selecting for engagement, for it's truth or falsity, whether it's looking to filter out fake news. If what you're seeing is what your friends happen to like. If what you're seeing is based on what Facebook thinks you're going to like, based on your interests and your location and all these things. You think that you're being informed, but you're really just seeing a tiny piece of landscape in front of you. And so, you could argue that, in a way, that the media is designed not to inform you, but to keep you uninformed. And that's really scary. That the bubble that we all live in — that has no real higher obligation anymore to this sort of philosophical idea of truth — is a scary thing.

How can we get better-informed?

It sounds weird, but perhaps the best way to be informed is to consume as little news as possible. One of the things I talked about in the book is — and this is from a memo that Nick Denton had written, who is the founder of *Gawker*, six plus years ago, he was saying-, he was talking about fake news, and — fake news isn't just deliberately manipulated/deceptive information. Fake news is also the stories that you read that turned out to be nothing. The speculation. The guessing. "Is this going to happen?" "Is that going to happen?" The analysis. The opinion on top of the analysis. All of this information...you know, you could be reading a story on Monday about a thing that may or may not happen on Friday, when you'd be better off waiting until Saturday to read about what *actually* happened. Like, how much of the news do we consume that we actually make decisions based on? The equivalent I've started to use is like: watch football on Sunday. Football is great. But you don't need to watch *SportsCenter* on Thursday speculating about who may or may not win. What players may or may not play. You know, who may or may not stand for the national anthem. These are-, these stories *feel* real, but they are fake. They are designed. They are people constructing additional information for us to consume that is in no way important or imperative in our lives.

And so, I would think the first thing you could do, if you want to escape the cycle, is to step back and ask yourself, "What do I use this information for? What is the purpose of this? Am I actually being informed or am I just making myself feel like I'm doing something?" You know, I think it's interesting that in the State and the Defense Departments, they've been reading through Thucydides — the history of the Peloponnesian War — to understand what to do about the rising threat of China. So this idea that the most-informed people on the planet — if you think about the people that had-, our intelligence and armed forces have — they had the greatest access to information, and information that you and I can't possibly get. And what they're reading is a twenty-five-hundred-year-old book about a conflict long, long ago. And I think the reason they're doing that is there's some sort of timeless truth in that; whereas, so much of the information in the media and even in intelligence reports is noise. And they're looking for the signal inside the noise.

And so, I would think that people need to consume far less news. And they need to stop equating: following the news and responding to the news and talking about the news, with civic engagement. Because they're not remotely the same thing. Reading about something and talking about it feels like you're participating. So, you know, we're talking-, in Austin, I remember a year and a half ago, we banned the city. Banned Uber and Lyft, right? They passed this law, then Uber and Lyft threatened to leave. And there's a special election — basically a referendum — on whether they're going to stay or not. And voter turnout for the thing was abysmal. And then I remember, the next day, the Internet's obviously outraged that this happened. And I got invited to join in. It was a Facebook group that was supposed to be an online petition and then there would be a march about this, like a protest of what just happened. It was like the way to protest this thing that just happened would have been to vote in the election yesterday. And so, we-, we-, we've come to associate sort of talking and chattering and thinking and sharing with civic engagement, and we neglect the actual one piece of civic engagement that we have, which will be *voting*. I don't know. Psychologists have talked about this idea of the narcotizing dysfunction, which is basically the more you consume-, if we have a finite amount of energy, the more you consume and the more you talk about it and the more you think about, the less room you have for these other things. And the worst part is your brain excuses your lack of energy for these other things with the fact that it already spent all this other energy. And that must count for something. And the truth is that it really doesn't. You know, the article that you're reading that has room for comments at the bottom. That comment form is not there because they care about your opinion. That comment form is there because the longer you spend on that site, the more they can monetize your engagement. The "Tweet" and the "Share in an Email" buttons at the top of the article are not there because they want your friends to be *informed*. It's that they want you to give them your friends, so they can sell advertising to your friends. And it's to understand that the product that the news is selling is not truth. It's *audience*.

What do you think about people like Mike Cernovich?

Yeah, I think it was Frederick the Great — might have been Voltaire — he was saying that the first thing that Machiavelli would tell a prince to do would be to write a book denouncing the Prince. And so, I think it's interesting, you know, to have someone like Mike doing a documentary about fake news because it's owning a term that has been directed at him and people like him. I think one of the reasons that someone like Mike aggravates journalists so much is that he's sort of like a carnival mirror. Like he's projecting back at them what they do. And almost all their-, but to an absurd and almost offensive level. You know he calls himself a "journalist." He breaks scoops. He's partisan on Twitter. You know, he is sort of doing-, it's the exact same playbook that these other journalists are doing. And so, I think that sort of mimicry is-, is very upsetting. I don't know. I mean, I think what we're seeing is this sort of a devaluing of a lot of these terms. So when Mike calls himself a "journalist," is he? Who determines what a "journalist" is? Who determines what a "scoop" is? Who determines what a "source" is? Who determines what all these things mean? And, then, what that's extended to is like: "Who knows what's true or not?" We can't even agree on *reality* anymore.

Do you think there's a value in holding up that mirror to the media?

Yeah, I mean, look: I'd say there's more than enough blame to go around. Part of the reason [that] we've seen the rise of a lot of these figures is because the media has not done their job. The media has not held themselves to a high-enough standard. They sort of violated a lot of their own norms. I mean, I wrote a piece a couple of months ago and it's like, you can't decry Trump for not following the norms of democratic society. Meanwhile, the media is violating all its sort of stated and unstated norms: about bias...and about partisanship...and about calm sobriety...about unpleasant truths. *All* of these things. So I think the system is definitely broken. I guess I don't know if the solution is-, is to introduce more speculation and conflict and hyperpartisanship into the mix. So it's interesting, you know...okay: A guy kills fifty people in Las Vegas, and the right says, "This is not the time for politics. Let's not exploit a tragedy to make a political point. Let's...," you know, "...thoughts and prayers," whatever. And then a guy in New York kills one person with a car and it matters that he comes from Uzbekistan. And we should use this as a chance to politicize this and, "extreme vetting," and blah...blah...blah. The truth is somewhere in the middle. That-, like-, you shouldn't exploit tragedies. And yet, you should also be able to have unpleasant conversations that need to be had that the tragedy brings up. And so, the problem is if the media is hypocritical, the response is not to respond to hypocrisy with *more* hypocrisy. So, I think we're seeing this sort of-, almost a death spiral into just chaos and deception and untruth and propaganda. And I don't exactly know what the solution is, but clearly whatever we're doing isn't working, either.

Do you think that stepping back — unplugging — is the answer? Because one could say, "If I step back, we lose."

I love this idea that Nate Boyer was talking about. This sort of "radical middle." I think the problem is that the-, there's this "horseshoe theory." The horseshoe theory says that, "At the extreme ends of the political spectrum, they're basically the same." And I think the debate has been sort of hijacked by the people on the extreme end of the spectrum. And so, instead of choosing which extreme end of the spectrum you're going to work with, I think the individual needs to step back and go towards a deeper, more sober understanding of what's happening. You need to find truth through your own research. Your own-, I guess it's very hard to find out what's really happening in the chaos and dysfunction and the noisiness of the media system. Whereas, if you step back, a lot of these things are pretty intuitive and obvious.

And so, I think what we're really lacking is *perspective*. So it's like, on the one hand, right now looks like the worst time to be alive and in truth, with some perspective, it's not as bad as you would think. And when you step back, you also realize what is *urgent* and what is desperately broken and what does need to be fixed. So instead of being seesawed around by, you know, this offensive comment or this ridiculous protest or this breaking news piece, it's better to let that stuff sort of sort itself out. If you're stepping back and you're letting the process do a little bit of that, and then, when you're-, when you are consuming this information, it's not in the same environment of chaos and immediacy. I think the idea that we need to be consuming this news in real time is probably the main problem right now. Because we're forming our opinions before the facts have really come in.

And the reason the media wants us to consume the news in real time is that-, because of-, the story is always changing, we have to stay tuned into the story. So instead of them doing their job, and then you come in it after they've done their job, and they've said, "Look, here's everything that we know. Here's what experts have said about it. Here's what's been fact-checked and verified. And overall, here's our comprehensive take on this event." We're reading: "Okay, there was a shooting. Okay. ISIS took credit for it. Okay. ISIS actually probably wasn't involved. Actually, okay, this guy's a lone weirdo. Okay. Actually, the FBI could have stopped it here. Okay. Actually...

So, instead of consuming one story or two stories, it can consume in fourteen stories over two days. You're upset and anxious and frustrated the whole time. You're mad at other people the whole time. You're forming your opinions as this is happening, and you think that you have the ability to change and update your opinions as the new information is coming in. But, almost no research supports that. In fact, the research shows that once you form an opinion, even if that opinion was based on totally bogus information — and then you're almost immediately given the correct information — it doesn't make you change your mind. It actually makes you believe the fake information even more, because now you've processed it more than one time. And so, this real time imperative is really great for media companies and it's really terrible for everyone else.

You updated your book for the Fake News Era. Why?

Donald Trump has been talking about running for president since I was born. So he started in 1987 — that's when I was born. And, in every election cycle, he toyed with being president. He sort of put his foot in there [to gauge] the reaction. And, in every election, it was obvious that it wasn't going to work. And, clearly, he wasn't too serious about being president, or he would have learned even a tiny bit about policy. Even if you disagree with that, he probably wouldn't have said so many dumb things in interviews and when there were microphones around. And so, what is the difference even between 2012 and 2016? I think it's that if Donald Trump is here — and he's the same crazy person the whole time — and the media system is going like this, in terms of its sort of ability to separate fact from fiction-, its ability to make good long-term decisions, its relationship and trust with its readers, etc., it's that they intersect. And, suddenly, the same Twitter tactics that didn't work before suddenly propel the least-qualified person in probably the history of the modern world to the Presidency. And so, I always knew these forces were there and I always knew that they could be exploited. And I knew they could be exploited, because I've done it myself. But I think people need to realize just what's at stake. Like, what can happen when you have a media system that not only has so many enormous vulnerabilities, but refuses to do anything about those vulnerabilities. And when, sort of, public media and information literacy is the way that it is, people are basically defenseless. So, the updating of the book for me was, you know: "Here's why we are where we are."

What are the consequences for being able to game the system so easily?

Just think about a world in which nuclear policy is being debated in a 140-character Twitter War between world leaders. That's terrifying. But I think, generally, you can have a media system however you like. What's happening in the media is not real. People are reporting and saying things. They can say, "The sky is blue." That doesn't change what color the sky is. But when they say, "This is happening," or, "This is what people believe," or, "This is what people are worried about." That exists in the netherworld of information.

But the problem is, we then make decisions based on this information. And so, the unreal becomes real, or what Daniel Boorstin will call "unreality" or "pseudo-reality" ensues. Where we're given-, look how many people have opinions about Hillary Clinton that are not at all based on any actual facts about Hillary Clinton. [I'm] not saying, "Hillary Clinton is great." I'm not saying people should have a positive opinion about her. But many people think very clearly and strongly [have] opinions about her that have no basis in reality. And the same would be true with Donald Trump, obviously, as well. People then make real decisions based on this information. They form real opinions. If we could see this in the financial space-, if you're able to create the impression that the iPhone is going to be delayed because a tweet led to a blog post, which led to another blog post, which led to a Fox News report about how people on the Internet were reporting on this — and it takes Apple stock price down ten percent — you know, that's tens of billions of dollars of real economic impact that affects people's pension funds. That affects retirement savings. That affects hedge funds. That affects tax revenues. It ripples through the real world very quickly.

And so, this idea of fake news is sort of a misnomer. Because fake news creates real opinions, which creates real actions. And then we live with the real consequences of that. No amount of reporting makes Pizzagate real. But the bullet that goes through that pizza shop is very real. And very dangerous. And could have killed someone. And so, when you see these people, they get radicalized by fake information or by speculation or by disingenuous online posturing. It might feel harmless. This might feel no different than creating "LOLcat" memes. But these memes have real consequences in the real world — for real people.

Do you think it can happen in the mainstream as well? You have an example from your book about Dick Cheney and the Iraq war.

People forget: So Dick Cheney leaks information to *The New York Times* about weapons of mass destruction. He's an anonymous source for the article. And then he goes on *Meet the Press* a few days later, and he goes, "Look, this isn't just coming from me. *The New York Times* reported this earlier this week... *The New York Times*!" So what he's doing is basically doubling himself. So instead of just saying, "This is what I think." He's going, "Look, *The New York Times* agreed with me." Even though they're the same thing. The good news is that that kind of outright deception with the mainstream media is relatively rare. It's difficult to hoodwink the paper of record in the United States, which has fact-checkers and editors and reporters, who really care about their reputation. Even if you just look at the reporter that-, that happened to, her reputation is not doing very well. But that does happen. The problem is what happens in an online media world when there are none of those protections. There's not even the reservation. Like, it's all-, you take someone like Mike Cernovich. If he gets it right, it's great for him — gets lots of attention. He looks-, he can throw it in other people's faces, etc. But, if he gets it wrong, what are the consequences? You can't get *fired*. His fans all sort of stick with him, regardless.

And so, what that creates is a lot of guessing. But the problem is there are real consequences for the guessing for everyone, [except] the person doing the guessing. And so, that's the dangerous thing. So we have this system now, where people are masquerading as journalists or masquerading as media outlets when it suits them. And then when they get it wrong they go, "Oh, I was just speculating," or, "Oh, I was just guessing," or whatever. Alex Jones gets to talk about whatever he wants, and I'm not saying he shouldn't legally be allowed to do this, but Alex Jones speculates and speculates this crazy thing after crazy thing after crazy thing. And he doesn't lose any reputation for that. I think that's the problem.

I'm surprised that you think the mainstream media can't be gamed in the same way. In the same way that you can manipulate the system to sell American Apparel, can't corporate interests and government operatives do the same thing?

No, no...I absolutely think that they do. I think it happens. What I'm saying is that it's-, part of the reason you're saying that government officials and corporate interests do it is because they have the resources to try to do it — given how difficult it is — so it's not impossible. And the Dick Cheney example is obviously one of them. But it is-, the fact that even their critics can only seize on a handful of examples — many of-, many of which are not exactly new — is sort of an indication, the fact that it is not as commonplace as, say, a blog getting it wrong. But look, the whole system is rotten and toxic. So I wouldn't disagree with you that there aren't leaked reports from one administration or another administration that is very much intended to paint the picture that the person wanted to paint. *The New York Times* loves leaks as much as *Gawker* loved leaks. It's a little bit harder. It requires more effort. It requires more legitimacy. But sure, it can be done.

Could you talk about *Help A Reporter Out* and how stories are reverse-engineered, to some extent?

There was an interesting thing that happened after the Super Bowl...not the most recent Super Bowl, the Super Bowl before. This is the one where Beyonce performed. And there was a producer for the BBC that tweeted after the thing that Beyonce had done — some sort of political protest during her performance — and he said, "I'm looking for someone to comment on Beyonce's performance." And someone replied on Twitter, and they said, "Oh, you should talk to some superfan." And the guy was like, "I don't really care if the person-, person's a fan or not. I just want them to say they were outraged by what happened."

And so, this is basically how the sausage gets made in so much of our news. Whether it's in blog form or in a reputable media outlet like the BBC, which is that: a producer or an editor or writer or an anchor knows where they want the story to go and they look for confirmation of that viewpoint. So instead of assembling all the facts and information, and then publishing where the information takes them, they go, "I want to talk about how people are angry about this thing. Who wants to say that they're angry?" And this is a systemic media problem from top to bottom. There's even a service called, "*Help a Reporter Out*," that basically says, "Journalists don't have time to find expert sources." It's almost like Craigslist for journalists. They go, "I'm looking for someone to be an expert about 'X.' I'll promote you in this story if you give me a quote." And it's basically an exchange for information.

So when I was writing *Trust Me, I'm Lying* I wanted it-, to me that encapsulates everything that's wrong with the media system. And so, one of the things that I did was I signed up to be a source, as myself, even though I wrote a book about media manipulation which had been announced. And I answered every single query that I possibly could. You know, I was an expert about being a germaphobe, being afraid of the market, that I sold all my stocks. I was an expert about boat winterization. I was an expert about being an insomniac. I was an expert in *The New York Times* about vinyl records. I learned what "LPs" stood for in the article in *The New York Times* that I was quoted in. Like, that's how little I knew about the topic that I was quoted as an "expert" at. And, eventually, this was revealed and it was a big controversy. And I remember *The New York Times* reporter said something like, "How else was I-," he said-, he said, "He seemed somewhat credible. So how else was I supposed to know that?" Well, I would hope that the standard for *The New York Times* would be more than, "...seemed somewhat credible." But two: Why didn't he call a vinyl record store? Or go to a vinyl record store? Or call a record label? There's so many ways to have gotten legitimate sources for this thing. But that would have required more effort and it would have required something less instantaneous. That system-, so you would think-, you would think that something like that would have eliminated-, like the controversy surrounding this would have-, would have destroyed *Help A Reporter Out*'s credibility.

You mention regulations in your book. Would you regulate the media?

I don't know necessarily about regulation. What I was talking about is that in past generations, media outlets have been forced-, media outlets over a certain size have been forced to post libel bonds or defamation bonds. Which I think is-, you look at something like the Hulk Hogan *Gawker* lawsuit where there-, they would do something that a jury would find that they were not allowed to do. And it took a billionaire writing a blank check, essentially, to hold them legally accountable for that. And so, I think on all sides of the spectrum, whether you're talking about *Breitbart* or you're talking about *Gawker*, we have a system where media outlets basically believe they never have to be held accountable for the things that they say and do. And the lack of that escalates the risk they're willing to take. The things they are willing to say about people. It prevents them from needing to stop and think. So they've been talking about how there's this *Gawker* effect since the verdict of that lawsuit. Where there was a 140 million dollar judgment against *Gawker*. And so, when they talk about stories now, outlets are really having to think before they hit the "publish" button about these-, they write about an important person or some scandalous allegation or some leaked piece of material [and] they're having to think about it before they hit "publish." As if that's some sort of bad thing. That's what they *should* have been doing from Day One! If, on advice of legal counsel, they've got what they need to proceed, then they absolutely *should* proceed. But I think in some ways that sort of chilling effect is not the terrible calamity that other people are trying to make it out to be.

You talk a lot in your book on the incentive problems. Could you talk about that?

So I subscribe to the digital version *The New York Times*. So, if I didn't subscribe, I could read ten articles a month from *The New York Times* for free. So, first off, I subscribe. If I were to read some disgusting, terrible, awful article, I would have recourse. I could stop paying them if I found that it just wasn't delivering enough value to me. Like, for instance, I was paying for the physical newspaper, but I found that I never read it. So I scaled back my subscription. If I found, "Hey, on a given month, I'm only reading like eight good *New York Times* articles and the rest are garbage," well, then, I would unsubscribe. And so, in that case, they now have an incentive to create eleven good articles and then, obviously, lots of-, they have to make lots of good stuff or people stop paying. And so, I think that's an example of a good incentive. If you're reading an outlet that you're not paying for, an outlet for which most of the advertising is sold on advertising exchanges, etc., that outlet doesn't care about you. They just want you to click and stay on the site as long as humanly possible. So, like, think about YouTube: You're watching the YouTube video, and it's automatically queuing up the next one and the next... they're designed to suck you in, to consume as much of your time as possible. That's a bad incentive.

And so, I think really looking at the incentives that our media system operates under and asking yourself: "Does this media outlet align with me or is this media outlet hoping to exploit me?" And deciding what to consume based on that is, I think, important. And then [for] the media outlet to ask themselves, "What do we want in our DNA? Do we want to be motivated to exploit people? Or do we want our people to be motivated to create really good stuff that's worth paying for?"

How are we fake news?

None of this would work if we didn't share it. So I think what fake news tends to exploit is the fact that it vibes with what we *want* to be true. And so, if you could take an absurd *Onion* article and put it in front of two groups: And if the fake claim in that *Onion* article aligns with what you wish to be true, I would imagine you're going to be more likely to forget the fact that it's an *Onion* article. Whereas the other person whose identity is not at stake can see it for what it is. So the reason that — for instance, there's so much fake news about Hillary Clinton — is that people really don't like Hillary Clinton. And [they] really wanted a lot of these things to be true to justify this deep emotional reaction that they had to this person. I'm not saying that's right. I don't think it is. But that is the truth. There's lots of fake news about Donald Trump, too. There are literally-, let's say half the population, if not more, is disgusted and incensed by this person. So any news that confirms that emotional reaction, they want to be true. And so, because the public doesn't take the time to think through things — to ask themselves, "What evidence is this based on? Where is this coming from? Why would this be shared? Could this possibly be true?" — we end up propagating this thing that we then denounce Facebook and trolls and Russia and all these other people for creating, but it wouldn't be possible without us.

You mention James O'Keefe in your book. Do you want to talk about him? Do you think it's all selectively edited or not true?

I think it plays into what we were just talking about, which is that people don't like certain groups. Or they don't like certain causes. Or they don't like liberals or conservatives. And so, what that creates is an opportunity for investigative journalists to create exposés or breaking news that again confirm the worst of what people want to suspect about those things. And then these things are super viral, because nobody wants to take the time and go, "Could this tape about these people that I don't like — about this cause that I fundamentally disagree with — could someone be being unfair to them?" It's very hard for us to to insist on fair treatment for groups and ideas that we despise.

And I think someone like James, and I think someone like *Breitbart...Gawker* are certainly guilty of it, and so is *AlterNet* and all these other partisan sites. They exploit that weakness in the human psyche. They are unfair to people who we disagree with. Or uncharitable or disingenuous when they make their points and then nobody has the intellectual courage to go, "Look, I think ACORN is a group that I disagree with, or that I think Planned Parenthood, you know, is a bad force in this world, or whatever you believe happens to be, but my ultimate allegiance is to truth and accuracy. And what you've presented here is not true." And so, therefore-, like, I'll give you a great example: Ben Carson made these comments right after he was appointed to the Housing Department, where he said — he was he was talking about immigrants who came to America and then he said — "...and then another kind of immigrant came here in slave ships and they had the hope of a better life." And he sort of goes on like that. And the headline in *The New York Times* and CNN and a bunch of other outlets is that: "Ben Carson says that slaves are immigrants." Right? Now I don't like Ben Carson and I think he's utterly unqualified to hold basically any office in this country — I think he's a fool — but he did not say that slaves were immigrants. He was making a pretty accurate rhetorical point, which is that slaves came here and want the same things now. You know, their descendants want the same things that the descendants of other kinds of immigrants wanted.

And so, it's completely unfair to manipulate the comments of another person to make them sound like they are much worse than they actually are. So it's like, "Look. I don't like Ben Carson because I don't like Ben Carson." So if I'm going to disagree with him, I'm going to disagree with him on the facts. What I'm not going to do is paint him in an unfair light and I'm not going to engage or propagate other people doing the same thing because that's just as much fake news as any of the other things that we're seeing. So I think people need to have the intellectual courage and strength to say, "I disagree with this person, but not for made-up, manipulative, or deceitful reasons. I disagree with this person because of "X, Y, and Z".

What is truth?

Truth is everything. Look, there's philosophical truth. You might call that, "Truth with a capital 'T.'" And then there's literal truth. What the temperature is today. How old you are, etc. There's probably some middle ground between those two truths. But I think as a human being, your job is to find truth in your life. It is to hold truth up as the ideal that we're all striving for. And to not accept sort of shortcuts to that truth. And to not tolerate the propagation of untruth in order to achieve what you think is truth. Which I think is the main political problem that we have right now.

You mention the history of the partisan press in your book. Could you outline that for us?

If you want to look at an analogue in our media system, this world where we don't pay for news or we have hundreds and hundreds, if not thousands, of sources and where all those sources are competing against each other: It really goes back to the early 1900s/the late 1800s with the invention of the penny press — which was the cheapest form of a newspaper at that time — New York City would have had dozens of daily newspapers, and as you got off your train into Grand Central, would have had competing newsboys shouting for your attention on your average street corner. There's some argument that the Spanish-American War was driven by the newspaper war between Pulitzer and Hurst: Two competing newspapers escalating the story until it got worse and worse. And I think that's sort of what we have now. You know, early on in American history, newspapers were owned by the political parties. But you were a subscriber to that press. So it was somewhat subsidized. It had a readership that was defined. But I think an environment in which the news is not openly partisan, but driven by one [from] purchases or one [from] viewing. I read a *Huffington Post* article. I read a *Real Clear [Politics]* article. I read a *Breitbart* article. I read a *Fox News* article. All of this is really just creating competition for more and more noise. And, thus, more and more fake news.

Any thoughts for our audience?

Yeah I would say...I'd make sure that what you consume and what you read and what you share doesn't conveniently or constantly overlap with what you already believe. If we think of the news as truth, a lot of times the truth is not going to line up with what you want to be true. What you thought would be true. What you hoped would be true. Just as this is the case in life. And so, conveniently over and over again, your assumptions are being confirmed if things are feeling like they're getting worse and worse. Exactly along the lines that you knew or thought or predicted or that people that you follow said would be. You're probably trapped in a bubble of some kind. And you're not pushing yourself to be challenged. And you're probably being misled.

JAMES O'KEEFE INTERVIEW

What is your name and what do you do?

My name is James O'Keefe. I'm an undercover journalist and President of *Project Veritas*.

So tell me about *Project Veritas*. How did it start?

Project Veritas started with the mission of investigating: exposing waste, fraud, abuse, corruption, dishonesty, self-dealing in order to make a more ethical and transparent society. We believe that our country is in a state where a lot of the solutions are not going to come from government or from legislation; it's going to come from information and education. But not just any type of education. Sort of shocking people with the truth of what's happening. And that's our job. In order to do that, we have to go undercover. Because a lot of these people are not going to tell us on the record what's happening. So we've brought back a lot of these old-school, shoe-leather journalism techniques from *60 Minutes'* Mike Wallace. Some of the newspapers in the early part of the 20th century used to go undercover. That's what we do. And we brought it to a new Information Age. A Digital Age. And our work is enormously effective. We would argue that we've gotten more results and more accomplishments than pretty much any other journalist in the 21st century.

What are the ethical concerns involved with going undercover?

It's a sort of utilitarian calculus. Which is: "Does the information you're exposing exceed the damage done by using deception as a technique?" And traditionally throughout the 20th century the answer was, "No." A lot of the old Emmy Award-winning and Pulitzer Prize-winning journalists went and used this technique to discover things that were far less important than the things that we've discovered. *Chicago Sun-Times* did many undercover exposés in the 1970s. And they would expose maybe a local police officer taking a twenty-dollar bribe. Or one of the-, one of the individuals in the *Chicago Sun-Times* actually went undercover and strapped a camera to their ankle and went into a poll booth and exposed chicanery at the polling booth. That won a Pulitzer Prize. So you look at the work that we've done — we've exposed high level officials in the Hillary Clinton campaign talking about how they're busing people in for decades and using fake IDs, and the idea of using fake IDs to get illegal votes. That's a far more systemic and far more elaborate example of a discussion about fraud. So if it's a virtue for them to have done it, it's certainly a virtue for us to do it.

The real reason that people stop doing it is not because it's immoral or wrong to use undercover work. I think that "when push comes to shove" everyone can agree that it's necessary in a democracy. The real reason people stop doing it is because they're afraid. Because of the repercussions. Because of the retaliation from these powerful organizations. And that's the real-, the heart of the matter is journalism is about exposing things for what they really are. And there's a lot of powerful interests that do not want things exposed for how they actually are. That's really what it's about. The undercover camera is merely a vehicle to make things so incredibly real. And a lot of times people don't want them to be real.

Why aren't you afraid of the consequences?

The answer is: I am afraid, but I think the definition of "courage" is facing it or overcoming it or doing things despite your fears. Also I think we are in many ways the ones that got away. Right? To put it-, to put it in those terms, I mean, I've been-, there was a time in my life when I was arrested and falsely accused. You would-, you would think that people on the left wouldn't even understand the nature of what it means to be falsely accused. But that does happen sometimes. But I think that there is a time when you're so passionate and committed and so focused on the idea of justice — justice is just a derivative of exposing truth — I think when you're so passionate about those things, those other concerns about your reputation — if *The Huffington Post* calls you names — those tend to be less important. When you really are concerned about society, and making society better through exposing, I think you're focused on what matters. And those other concerns go away.

But we're definitely the ones that got away. The barriers to entry are so great to do this. We've been able to build here at *Veritas*. It's certainly not just me; it's a whole team of people now. We've been able to build an institution and build up an audience and build up a support network of thousands of small donors, that when they-, you know — just last week I got served with a federal lawsuit — but when we get served with lawsuits, our people rally behind us. And I don't know what the future holds, but I'm going to-, I'm going to keep doing it until they stop me from doing it.

One of the main differences between *Project Veritas* and mainstream outlets is that you're donation-based. How does money influence coverage of news?

Yeah, that's a great question. We are a nonprofit organization. So one of the things I learned during the election was-, one of our stories was spiked by, for example, a large media conglomerate. And one of them was Fox. There was another one. And these corporations, it's really all about-, their decisions are done by economic necessity. And decades ago, it used to be the case that news divisions did their investigative reporting operating at a loss. They did so in the public interest. That's gone by the wayside. These days, news organizations do specifically what behooves their bottom line. In our recent undercover exposé of *The New York Times*, the *Times* said as much. They said that they give the readers what they want to read — what they want to hear. They don't give them the truth. They give them what they want to hear. And that's true, left or right.

Now we don't have that concern. We don't have advertisers; therefore, people can't boycott us. We truly try to go places and expose things that are not supposed to be exposed. But when you expose the Hillary Clinton Administration, and you go to a media conglomerate, and say, "Please air our tapes," their concern is going to be, "Well, what happens if Hillary gets elected? Is she going to revoke our FCC license?" and so forth. That's what happened during the election. They were concerned about the journalism, not because it was bad journalism, but because it was so incredibly devastating. So those are the types of concerns you have when you do this. At *Veritas*, no one really has a fiduciary control over our editorial MO. No one-, no one says, "Don't do that or I'll take away funding." That just doesn't happen here. And I have the scars to prove it. I mean, the ACORN story: *The Washington Post* dug deep to try to find, you know, who are the billionaires behind them. There were no billionaires; it was me and a credit card and a pimp coat and an iMac. You know, two thousand bucks. It defied conventional understanding in the news business. It was beyond-, they couldn't accept that as a truth. It had to be that there was a Koch brother. It had to be. It wasn't — it wasn't.

So these days, the barriers to entry are so low and it allows us to do things that have never been done before, and "boldly go where no one has gone before." Going after *The New York Times*? Who would ever want to do *that*? You want to get your book reviewed by *The New York Times*, right? So we're doing things-, we're going after the sacred cows that no one would go after.

You touched on access as one of the considerations journalists have when they are reporting. Could you talk about that relationship and the considerations involved?

That's a huge consideration. So there is-, there-, I would say there's a couple of different considerations. Number one: There's just fear, right? People are afraid. Number two is: Shared politics. Number three: It's the economic considerations we just touched upon. Chomsky wrote a whole book called *Manufacturing Consent*. Chomsky was a leftist but Chomsky was talking about market dynamics. And there's nothing wrong with having market dynamics as long as you understand how those dynamics impact your business. And that's where-, that's where it's hard for me to reconcile. Again, it's hard for me to reconcile. How can you operate in the public interest and yet be beholden to advertisers? It's very...I don't know if anyone's figured out the answer to that question. But what you talk about is another factor. Access. Access. And how does access impact-?

So most journalists are afraid. Like, for example, *The Wall Street Journal* would be afraid to talk about the impending economic crisis with the credit default swaps and derivatives because all of their sources are inside the financial institutions. That was that movie the-, *The Big Short* highlighted that beautifully. Going after Hillary Clinton. Why would you go after Hillary Clinton if *The New York Times* predicts a ninety-six percent chance that she will win the presidency? You will be cut off. That's what the Clintons did. So journalists cannot succeed in the status quo without access. Now we come along, and we don't need the traditional access because we do undercover work. We burn every single person we talk to. I mean, at least in the abstract, we do when we release the story.

So access is a huge problem and adversarial journalism is gone by the wayside because journalists don't want to ruffle feathers. They want to make friends. They want to be cozy with the Establishment. And you see that with the White House Correspondents' Dinner; although up until this past year, you've seen that in the past. They're sipping champagne and swirling Chardonnay amongst the people they're supposed to be aggressive with. And I just...I couldn't-, I couldn't live with myself in that environment. It just doesn't make sense. You have to be a watchdog. So access has been a huge reason why journalism has gone by the wayside over the last twenty, thirty years.

Critics of *Project Veritas* claim that you use selective editing. Could you talk about that?

One of the things they throw to us is the "selective editing" thing. This is silly. And, in fact, it's just a bunch of hyperbole. The notion of selective editing — if you want to see *real* selective editing, you look at Katie Couric and her gun documentary where she got sued for defamation, because she ripped out someone's comment out of context. Or you look at *Rolling Stone* magazine going after that rape case at the University of Virginia. It didn't even happen. When you Wikipedia, "Rolling Stone," do you see, "*Rolling Stone*, who's been sued for defamation?" You never see that. You'll never see that. Katie Couric isn't known to be accused of selective editing. You look at my entire career. Look at the hundreds of videos I've produced and actually name for me *the* edit. The best they can come up with — truth — is that I didn't wear the pimp fur into the ACORN office. Well, since when does pimp protocol require the wearing of a pimp fur to be a "pimp?"

So this whole thing is just sort of a conjured-up thing that people say. Why do they do it? Well, the motivation is clear. They do it because there is nothing else for them to say. So the only thing they can do is attack our work product. But I would simply ask them to name the *one* edit in the entire career of what I've done. *Name* one. *Name the edit.* And they can't do it. So it's really just a bunch of hyperbole. And by the way, newspapers, when you want to talk about selective editing, take a look at *The New York Times*, *The Washington Post*, *The Associated Press*. The words are placed selectively together in sentences. *Veritas* uses video. We use time slices of reality. So it's-, there's no actual meat on the bone. It's just another thing they're going to throw at me. Like they've thrown "racist" and anything else. But in the end, in the final analysis, the people resign. People resign. They admit they said what they said. *The New York Times* Executive Editor said, "Yep. He did say what he said. That young guy behaved unethically." CNN said, "We support diversity of opinion." Scott Fogel was fired from the Hillary Clinton consultant firm. Bob Cramer was fired. People keep getting fired and they admit they say what they said. So where's the edit? Show me the [selective] edit. They can't do it, because there is no selective editing.

Let's talk about *American Pravda*. How did that exposé originate?

American Pravda is a series we're doing on the mainstream media. And we've, so far, released two major series: Number-, Number one on CNN and number two on *The New York Times*. And the whole idea was to expose the real motivations behind the people in the media. The media has more power than the legislature in this country. Everything flows from media. Everything flows from what people read and hear and see. It's simply not possible to say anything else. So we want to expose what their agenda was. What they're leaving out.

And you see it in the CNN story. Probably one of the most overlooked parts of our first story was how we took the raw audio from an interview and juxtaposed it to the five-minute version, and they literally "edited out," to borrow their coined phrase, they edited out all the things they didn't want the readers to see. It was devastating. How the CNN producer in Atlanta says, "Well this is all B.S. This is all bullshit. We don't think there's any proof there." He says-, "The CEO of CNN set an internal meeting to stop focusing on all this other stuff and focus on Russia because of ratings." That's what this producer said in Atlanta. And-, and then CNN responds with, "Oh, he's just an Atlanta producer."

Really? I don't care if he's the cleaning lady. The fact that he's saying the CEO of CNN told him that, that's *truth.*

So there's many videos [in] the series. We did another video of Van Jones saying, "The Russian stuff is a nothingburger." I mean, this is not a low-level guy. This is *Van Jones*. And when we release these stories, we have to do so in a way that prevents people from belittling them. They'll say first that the guy is a "low-level" guy. Then we will release the high-level guy. *The New York Times*? We released the low-level guy — [he] wasn't really low-level, though. He was an Audience Editor of *The New York Times*. And then we release the Senior Editor. And that's how we work. They keep on lying. So we have to keep releasing the videos in such a way to catch them in their lies. They keep on lying. So we have to catch them in such a way as to reveal their lying in how we release the videos.

How would you respond to those who say, "It's just a few bad apples?"

My response is it's prima facie in what the CNN Atlanta producer said. He said-, the CEO said in our internal-, Jeff Zucker, that's the top guy at the top of the organization, so how can you say that it's not a systemic cultural thing when he says the CEO said in internal meetings — I'm quoting him now — the CEO said in internal meetings to, "Stop doing that and focus on Russia." That-, that can only be a systemic thing. And CNN didn't say it was edited. They said they support-, the guy has a right to say what he said. Now that-, that's kind of a cop-out because he's quoting Jeff Zucker. So I mean, it's just people are-, they're never going to do the right thing unless they're compelled to. They're never going to be honest or be transparent or be virtuous. Harvey Weinstein: same thing. They're only upset they got caught. They're just upset they got caught. We caught up with Jeff Zucker recently, in another meeting a few weeks ago, and we secretly recorded him. He was most upset that he got caught. He's like, "Be careful what you say," is what he said. So it's never about reforming the behavior. It's about making sure that we behave in such a way as to not be exposed by James O'Keefe.

Why is it wrong for Jeff Zucker to want his reporters to focus on the Russia scandal if it both drives ratings and is of national interest?

Well, it's wrong if they're doing it purely for financial interests. Just for clicks and just for dollars. If it's all just because of ratings. If it's all just for money. If-, if his own staff — more than one person — thinks that it's B.S. If there's no proof, according to them, and they're doing it in order to make money only, that's something the American people need to see. I'm not making a value judgment about it. But that's information that people need to see. Because, and again, same thing with *[The] New York Times*. Their Ethical Code of Conduct says you must do nothing to compromise your objectivity and neutrality. It may not be a shock to you, or the people watching this film, that *The New York Times* is *biased*. But it's a shock to *The New York Times*. Their credo says, "You cannot say or do political things that compromise your neutrality as a journalist."

So my point is: Just be honest about who you are. Just-, just tell the truth. There was a *New Yorker* reporter who was supposed to be here physically today as we talk to each other. And he's pretending as though he's this-, is this neutral, objective guy. And I said, "Just tell me. Just say you're a leftist. Just say it. It's okay." I am no more right-wing than they are leftists. I don't even express political opinions and they consider me right-wing. So it's like that-, in an argument by analogy, if I'm a conservative activist, then, "Rachel Maddow is a left-wing, left-wing activist," is an understatement. The person-, that person doesn't even do journalism; she just spouts opinion and conjecture reading off a teleprompter. So if our going into the field and exposing facts is considered the right-wing activism, then Rachel Maddow is a far-left political thespian. I don't know what you'd call it, but it's certainly not "journalism," right? So I'm just asking people to level the playing field and to be open and honest about who they are and what their motivations [are], and if they're not going to be either-, going to lie about them, we're going to go expose them.

Does *Project Veritas* have an Ethical Code of Conduct? Do you think the new media should abide by one?

I do. I do think it's important. First of all, one of the things you said in your question was: I think it's important to establish, "What is journalism and who is a journalist?" Right? Just like the Code of Conduct. And my argument, and I've been making this argument for years, is that basically everyone is a journalist. Journalism is not just an identity, it's an activity. It is what you do and you judge people based on what they produce.

So the biggest rub on me is that I'm "not a journalist." That's what they will say. Constantly. Every time. That's what Dean Baquet at *The New York Times* said. He said-, the first thing he said [was], "James O'Keefe is not a journalist." Okay? Now they can call me, "SpongeBob Squarepants," "Captain Kangaroo," one-eyed salamander. Whatever they want to call us. It doesn't matter. What matters is the thing that you are producing. The action. Okay, so, if you're out on the street, out there and with your iPhone, you capture a mugging on tape. Congratulations!

You just did an act of reporting. Okay. And, therefore, you have the protection of the First Amendment. The First Amendment doesn't protect someone more than the other. In fact, if you actually open up the whole Pandora's Box and take a look at the activities of the establishment journalists, you realize that you can pick someone at random off the street and they're more of a journalist than the people on TV.

So the most important thing to establish when we're talking about this is: Everyone is entitled the protections of the First Amendment. They would disagree. They would disagree. They would say that I don't have the protections. That's why when I cross the border, I get detained. And government agents ask me who I'm voting for. If that ever happened to a CBS News reporter or a *New York Times* reporter, there would be riots in the Establishment over it. And that person would want all types of prizes. But they're able to change the rights of people based on the identities that they ascribe to them. Which is why it's so important that we rip apart that artifice and show people what really is going on. But I think the definition of "journalist" is key in answering that question.

If journalism is just an activity, what about the times when people perform that activity, but not in a professional manner? So, for example, a man takes a picture of buses in Austin, Texas, and tweets out that Hillary Clinton is busing in voters. That went viral and it was false. When asked about it, he replied that he wasn't a journalist. He was just a guy and shouldn't be held to the same standards. Was he a journalist?

Well, first of all, I think he did so from his computer screen in his apartment, right? So I would say that real journalism is about getting out into the street. And actually interviewing people.

And checking your sources. And actually reporting real factual information. We don't just talk and opine about, "buses." We actually interview people and record people in their own words. And show that. That's not even at a level that newspapers do. When *The Associated Press* does an article, do you get to read their source material? Did you get to open up the notebooks and see what they said? *No*. You have to take their word for it. Why? Why should you take *The Washington Post* reporter's word for it that the source said that and he didn't cut up the sentence? Why? *Why*?

I could give you example after example. *The Washington Post* basically defamed me and said that I omitted something, when I didn't, in my interview. He just *lied*. He lied so bad that he got disciplined by *The Washington Post* editors. So why should we trust the mainstream media when every single time we open up the notebooks and open up the raw recordings and open up the facts, we see that they're twisting things. Okay...why? Why are we supposed to trust them when they use "anonymous" sources?

Think of it like a bank account — this is something I think Jay Rosen said: It's like a bank account, and every time you use, "anonymous source," you make a $100 withdrawal from an account with $50,000 in it. If you keep on using anonymous sources without actually doing something to show me that you're credible — by, actually, I don't know, giving me a smoking gun — you're relying only upon the credibility of your masthead. You're relying only upon the credibility that you built through-, through years of results. Name the last time a mainstream journalist has actually shown me with-, so I can hear it and see it, something of importance when it comes to "Russia." I don't see anything. I see an indictment. Okay, today I see an indictment. But I don't see any actual proof. "Don't take *my* word for it." That's what the CNN guy said when we talked to him.

Veritas shows you proof. We show you people in their own words. Then they go, "But show me the two hours of raw tape." I say, "No. I want to see your two hours of raw tape." So it's, you know-, I am so-, things are so lopsided. Things-, things are so out-of-whack that I'm not going to even begin to talk about some guy on Twitter in his basement when I got the whole mainstream Democratic Media Complex having all of the vices that they accuse us of. But having none of the virtues. "Hypocrisy" is an understatement. And the only thing that matters is exposing them all. Exposing them all, so that *all* Americans can see just how wrong it is. A lot of American people don't trust random people on Twitter. Okay? But the difference between-, this is why we're calling it *Pravda*. The difference between the Soviet Union Pravda — which is the Russian propaganda organism — and, say, *The New York Times*, is that people in the Soviet Union-, they knew they were being lied to. And they know when they go on Twitter: Should I really trust that? But there is a lot of people in this country who one hundred percent believe, and they're gullible enough to believe, what they read in the papers and what they see on TV. And that's what we're trying to change.

What are the different ways the mainstream media can manipulate information to mislead?

This is an example of projection, but when they say that I "selectively edit." That's because *they* selectively edit. So that's the first way — is just through doctoring tape. And if you read a newspaper article, and you see the way their headlines are written, and you see the way they paint a portrait using words, they're just painting a portrait is all. They're just painting with a paintbrush.

I want to see the raw notes. Show me the source. Show me your sources. "Well, we can't do that. That's our protected information." Well, why should I believe you if you don't show me your sources? Why should I believe anything you have to say?

Recently, they were saying Trump said something in the Oval Office to somebody. I think it was a "he said/she said." It's all he said/she said. It's all he said/she said. Ferguson: "Hands up — don't shoot!": he said/she said. It would be all black-and-white if it was caught on *video*. But they have an ability to paint a portrait using words. I saw a Phelim McAleer production where he just took the-, literally took the depositions from the people who were in Ferguson and just-, people were just *reading* the deposition. The media omitted all of those depositions. They didn't show you what local African-American citizens saw that day. They saw him not putting his hands in the air. I never read that. So by virtue of the fact that-, do you not want to make that your *headline*?

What do you want to focus on? What are the things that you focus on in how you report things? And how do you choose what the priorities are? The media just chooses one specific priority. And it omits and ignores the other ones for a virtue of making the world a more "just" place. So they have a sort of "social justice warrior." They have a specific ideological agenda. Which is fine. Saying you have an "ideological agenda." For example, say you want to tackle racial injustice. But if this case doesn't fit in with that narrative, your responsibility as a journalist is to report the facts. And, ultimately, it's a conflict of visions that these people have with someone like me. I believe-, I have an infinite faith in the power of free people to make the correct policy decisions if they're given the facts. The mainstream media adheres to a sort of propaganda premise, which is that people are stupid. And you have to guide them like you would a herd of sheep. You have to guide them because they're ignorant and stupid and if left to their own devices, can make wrong decisions. It's a conflict of visions. So it's how they paint the portrait using the words on the canvas in order to direct them to a certain policy outcome.

If you were made the CEO of *The New York Times*, what would you do differently? How would you make them succeed?

How would I make them succeed? I think that as a thirty-three-year-old young man who's been in this for a while but not a lifetime — I'm probably not ready to run a division of a thousand-to-a-few-thousand people just quite yet. But start with the basics. I mean report facts. Admit that you have an agenda, if you do. Don't pretend like you don't. If you have hundreds of employees who have a left-wing editorial agenda, then what I'd probably do is hire some people who don't have that agenda. I think-, was it Gerard Baker at *The Wall Street Journal*? — the Editor of *The Wall Street Journal?* — Can't remember his name... but he brought in all of these journalists, and said, "Guys, you've got to stop leaking your opinions into your work." I think that would be the first thing I would do is stop leaking your opinion into what you write. And then, if they can't do that, then I would fire them and hire new people.

If I were the CEO of *The New York Times*...I'm sure there's a lot I have left to learn in this business before I become the CEO of *The New York Times*. I think one day, by the way, *Project Veritas* is going to become more powerful than *[The] New York Times*. I also want to say that I think the mainstream media is very reactive to what citizens do. So, in many ways, *Project Veritas* has an even greater responsibility than *The New York Times*.

Here's what I would say: If I was the CEO of *The New York Times*, I would say-, I would bring all my reporters in a room and say, "Here's the deal: If you have an opinion, and it gets injected into your article, then state that to the public. Make a little asterisk saying, 'By the way, I'm an activist for Hillary Clinton all the way. With all of my heart I want her to win. And that's the truth.' Just say that." If I was the CEO, I'd probably at least hire as many people to the right of me as to the left of me in the sense that there would be some balance, and in the sense that I make sure that-, that the people that were professional enough to not let their opinion get into their work. Here at *Project Veritas,* we're very careful not to insert an opinion — even an ad hominem attack — anything into what we do here. We don't inject our opinions into things. It doesn't add any value. It's just opinion. So I would be very, very disciplined about making sure that that doesn't happen.

What do you like and what don't you like about the New Media?

Michael Hastings said right before he died — he was at *Rolling Stone* and *Newsweek* — he said he really had to leave the corporate culture in order to pursue the stories that were of interest to him. The greatest thing about the independent media is that they're able to go places that nobody else can go. They're able to go after people. And the irony is that when you go off to, like, Silicon Valley targets, like, we just did a story on YouTube — like, that's owned by Google. And the first thing that-, that occurs to any rational person is, "Oh, my God! They're going to, like, leak my G-mail or something!" Independent people don't-, don't care about that. They're fearless. They're brazen. They have nerve. That's the greatest virtue is the lack of fear.

> The biggest issue is accuracy-, is making sure that you're factually-, and I don't want to say any names, because I don't want to throw anyone under the bus on the record. But there are people, independent people, on social media — they have like a sixty percent accuracy rate. And I say, "That's not good enough." Andrew Breitbart told me early on that you have to be better than them. I have no problem sitting here right now and telling you-, you take anything we've done and match it up to any Pulitzer Prize winner and we have a higher ratio of success. Don't take my word for it. Carol Leonnig, of *The Washington Post,* has had a print two front-page retractions about me and she is a Pulitzer Prize winner. I've never had-, I never had to retract a video. She has had to retract.
>
> So the key thing is *accuracy*. Is making sure that your story-, and people say, "Well I'm not a journalist." Well, don't do journalism. If you're going to say that, "I'm not a journalist," then shut up and go away. Because you've got to make sure you rise to a standard. It's your responsibility as a citizen in this democratic republic. If you're going to inform your fellow people, you better make sure that your facts are correct. That's your responsibility. Or don't do it. But what I would say is that's the top issue I have with the independent media.

What's the worst example of fake news, historically speaking?

> Fake news is a big, broad, vague issue. So let me just focus on what I think needs to be focused on: is that the news companies will produce bubblegum journalism — Pop Culture segments that are just void of any informational value — in order to get clicks. Like, there's a scene that I always point to, and, you know, at the end of, like, The Five with Greg Gutfeld, and there is an image of, like, a gerbil or, like, a cat, like, playing patty cake with

one another, that-, that was aired the same day that our stories on Democracy Partners were spiked. Right? Because they were about the Clinton Administration. And it's a lot easier to show squirrels on a skateboard or Good Morning America. It's just crap that makes people feel good about themselves than it is to show them the truth.

That's probably the greatest problem in our society: People don't-, people don't really want to see and know what's true. They don't. They want to live in a fantasy world. I think that transcends the issue we're talking about here. It has more to do with the American consciousness. But that's a factor. People don't-, people want to be ignorant. They don't want to know what's really going on. A lot of them don't. So the news companies sort of play into that. They give the people what they want to hear and see. At *Veritas,* we give them the truth. We give them the facts. And, oftentimes, we don't air it unless it rises to a level that shocks them so much. So I don't know if that's technically "fake news," but I consider it all part of the same umbrella.

How do you make decisions of who you go after?

Well, let's first talk about how we *don't* make the decision. We don't make the decision because a donor tells us who to go after. We don't make a decision based on who an advertiser tells us to go after. We don't get paid like a quid pro quo, where I could point you-, I can tell you a lot of companies who do that. We don't do that. We genuinely pursue stories that are in the matter of public interest. And we have an internal editorial process just like any other news company. We sit down, we talk about it...we get tips. We send people out to the field for weeks at a time to do reporting to corroborate whether it's a story.

What I found is that there is always a story. It may not be the story you think it is — but, whether it's Antifa or fake news or government corruption or judges being bribed — there's *always* a story. The question is: How many-, how much time and money and manpower do you want to go in finding that story? There's always a story. We have a hashtag here — it's: The Whole World Is A Fraud. Man is Fallen. And people will always do what's in their own self-interest. So it's just a question of how much time you want to spend. But we have a process where we consider what needs to be exposed versus what is being exposed. And we sort of triage on where to direct our resources.

What is truth? Are we living in a Postmodern Age?

Well that's one of my favorite-, he is quickly becoming one of my heroes: is Jordan Peterson. I don't know if you're interviewing him for this documentary, but have you already [spoken] to him? No, he's-, I mean, he could-, he can take me for a ride with my answer, because my answer will be nothing compared his answer, but I would just sort of talk to Jordan Peterson. But, no, he is-, what are the three transcendentals? "The good, the true, and the beautiful." And I think, as a society, we're getting far away from those virtues. And the other-, the other thing I would point to is-, is Solzhenitsyn's Harvard Address he made to Harvard University in 1978. Where he sort of said, "Western society, you forget about-, you forget about truth." And when he said that, like, the audience was clapping and then they sort of stopped clapping. But he said-, Harvard University where the motto was *Veritas*. Right? *Veritas* is the model of Harvard. But people don't want to know about that. People don't want to hear about what's true. So I think that the Postmodernists, I mean, their whole thing is about, you know, relative-, what is relative? What is your truth? And that's something that we're up against.

You also have this sort of, "What's happening now in society?" is virtue signaling, right? Virtue signaling and where it's happening, where people just are identity politics. Race. Sex. Class. And things that have anything to do with what's objectively true or not. So that's-, those are issues that we're constantly running up against at *Project Veritas*. We actually tend to use them to our advantage undercover. If we're trying to expose something that's wrong, we actually use these techniques of identifying with someone's race — someone's propensity towards feminism. We use that language. Try to ingratiate ourselves with them in order to get them to open up to us. So, in many cases, what's funny about *Veritas* is that in order to expose the adversary, you have to sort of adopt their language and their customs.

But, you know, I think in many ways, truth runs contrary to what's happening in the culture right now with the Post-modernists, and they don't even believe in facts. Like facts are bad. Because facts run contrary to the thing that they want to advance. Another one is F.A. Hayek, right? He wrote this book called, *[The] Road to Serfdom,* and he said in one of the chapters that the Postmodernists, the Marxists, actually don't even believe that certain facts should be-, if it doesn't advance a specific social agenda, they should not be allowed to exist. We only allow discussion that advances a particular social agenda. That's what it comes down to. If it doesn't advance the agenda, it shouldn't be allowed. It shouldn't-, "Pay no attention to that man behind the curtain. Pay no attention to that James O'Keefe guy in Westchester, New York. He doesn't exist. He's a nobody. A no one." Because they don't want facts that aren't directed toward their specific destination. So what do we do? We bring in facts that are so emotionally damning and so manifestly damning that sort of shock and shake people. And that's how we sort of deal with the Postmodernists. I don't think anyone else is doing it. At least not in that visceral way. You can't convince them through argument, right? So you have to do it this way.

What is your dream for *Project Veritas* moving forward?

To do more of what I'm already doing. So, to do what I'm doing to a factor of one hundred. Just do more of it. It's that simple. If we-, imagine if we had one hundred employees at *The New York Times* on tape and we just release them every day. I mean, you might-, "you might think I'm a dreamer, but I'm not the only one." I mean, we have hundreds and hundreds of undercover people that we're trying to hire. We already have hired a bunch. So it's just a question of building a business. I hate to put it-, it's not only a business, but building a movement of people. I have to pay them, too. So it's sort of-, I have to raise the money to pay them. It's all these ingredients. But it's just doing more of what we've already done. So teachers' unions is an example: We've done some stories on education reform. I believe that's a civil rights issue of our time. You know, the sexual abuse within the teachers' union makes the Catholic Church spotlight investigations like a walk in the park. There's no accountability whatsoever inside the teacher's union.

So again, I just need to expose hundreds and hundreds of people on tape covering up the abuse of children saying that, "It's not about the children; it's about their own money and power." And that's the truth. It's not my words. It's what's happening. What are they going to do? Say that I'm "against children?" No, but they're the ones who are against children. So the truth — the key

— is just doing it on a massive scale and somehow not getting shot. Which is true, if truly a threat. I'm not trying to sound like a martyr, but I am. I know there are wacky people out there... and not being shut down with lawsuits...if I can get past those things, I should be fine.

My vision for the future is to scale what we do and to do more of what we're already doing. My vision is to-, is to just simply, instead of catching a few people on tape, catch hundreds of people on tape in any given institution. Whether it's in the media or education reform. We caught a couple of teachers' union people on tape saying they want to cover up the abuse of children to protect their own money and power. What if we had *hundreds*? It's to show that everything is systemic. And make it undeniable. And when we've done this to great effect, it's prompted legislation. It's prompted public policy changes, so it's simply to do more of what we've already done.

Do you have any upcoming targets?

None that I can talk about. But we have another one coming out on the mainstream media. To continue the *American Pravda* series. And beyond that, you'll just have to wait and see.

Do your undercover reporters feel bad about what they're doing after the fact?

You know, to the best of my knowledge, no undercover reporter that's worked for me has ever really felt guilty or bad about what they've exposed, because of the nature of what's being exposed is so-, sometimes so awful. That the undercover technique-, the deception to go on under there using a false name is justified. But what I do know about it is it's really hard. I mean, it's really painstakingly difficult/challenging work to pretend to be something you're not. Sometimes pretending to be multiple people on any given week during different assignments. You're away from your family. You're working long hours. You're in airports every day. It's tough work. It's really hard. It takes enormous sacrifice and the biggest challenge is when you're burned. And when you're compromised, and when you're humiliated, and when *The Huffington Post* does a hit piece about you. And that's the real tough thing that we struggle with here. And it separates the men from the boys sometimes when it comes to doing the work.

You have a picture of Saul Alinsky behind you. How have you been influenced by Saul Alinsky?

So let me talk about Saul Alinsky for a second: I mean, Saul Alinsky is an inspiration to me. We have borrowed a lot from-, I wouldn't say he's my only source of inspiration, but what I-, what I learned from Saul Alinsky was *tactics*. He was a tactician. He was about organizing people and showing what's in people's self-interest. The problem with people on the right that I found is that a lot of them are afraid to be effective. They are afraid of the byproduct of what happens when you do the effective action.

Because to be effective is to be hated. I think Saul Alinsky once said to his team when they were praised, "Don't worry, boys — we'll weather this storm of approval and come out as hated as ever." And Rush Limbaugh once said on the air, "You know, I'm so hated. How do you deal with it? It really comes down to dealing with being hated for doing what's right." And most people don't have the stomach...the wherewithal.

So what do most people do? I think they choose to do the thing that's going to be not as effective as the thing they could have done, because they don't want to deal with the consequences and the aftermath of taking the effective course of action. Saul Alinsky was teaching people about how to organize in order to achieve the greatest possible victory. And through his book, *Rules for Radicals,* we picked up on a bunch of things. But number one was making them live up to their own principles. So we talked about these Postmodernists who are the enemy of truth. We simply make them look to their own book of rules. When we ban Lucky Charms, we said, "I'm Irish. I don't-, I think that this cereal represents a racial ethnic stereotype." It was out of *Rules For Radicals* and it worked beautifully. Because it forced them to confront their own-, their own duplicitousness. That's straight out of *Rules For Radicals.*

People say, "Well, Saul Alinsky was a Marxist/Communist [leftist]. No, no...he wasn't. He wasn't really a guy with any dogma. He just believed in organizing people for power. So the problem with people on the right is they can fuse tactics with ideology. They think that tactics *are* ideology. That's not true. And many times — and I hate to put this in ideological terms, but that's just the way it is — if you-, if you have a specific mission — our mission is truth, some people's mission is pro-life, whatever — you owe it to your mission to apply the most effective tactics necessary to accomplish that thing.

So I have a huge problem with people on the right because they don't really get this. They-, they don't really understand. And in the final analysis, they don't want to be effective, because to be effective is to be *hated.* And they don't want to be hated. So the Republicans don't actually do the effective thing. They don't actually vote on the legislation because they'll be hated by the media. They'll be humiliated by the mainstream media. They don't want to deal with that. So that's where we draw some of our inspiration from Saul Alinsky. But there are others who inspire us too.

Do you have anything you want to add about fake news, media bias, media manipulation?

One of the things that distinguishes us from the mainstream media is these infotainment shows typically go after pedestrians and innocent people with hidden cameras. The analogy we use is, "They use a bazooka to kill a fly." Like, they'll dress someone in a MAGA hat and they'll go around screaming, "White Power!" And then secretly record people walking by, and if the people walking by don't disavow the guy with the red hat, then they're "racist." Like, this is not exposing corrupt people. This is just going after innocent pedestrians.

But why do they do it? Because it's easiest to go after innocent pedestrians. It's harder when they go after big corporations and governments. You ever notice how the more money and power a media corporation has, the less likely it is to go after people with money and power? It's always the independents who do it. So we-, we definitely don't use our bazooka — our hidden camera — to kill flies. We go after sacred cows and that's a key distinction.

Where is the mainstream media headed financially in terms of revenue?

I think that the mainstream media is eventually going to basically become irrelevant. Because their whole business model is based on the fact that they have relevance. And the fact-, I mean everything they predicted in the 2016 election was-, turned out to be false. *Every prediction*. Every poll turned out to be wrong. And they're just doubling down. They're doubling down on this whole "Russia" stuff. What's going to happen is they're beginning to become-, the mainstream media is going to become a reactive institution that reacts to things that citizens do. They're going to cover what people, who are close to the action, are covering and they're going to recycle that — borrow that.

You can't do journalism without being on the ground in front of your-, of your source. You can't. You have to go. *Vice*'s motto — I saw in Times Square recently, they had an advertisement that said, "We go there." Imagine how bad the media must be that your unique value proposition is to actually *go* to the location. To actually conduct the investigative work. That-, that's actually like a unique thing. We-, we are nothing but if in the field. So the mainstream media cannot-, cannot survive in its current form. It's going to have to just simply aggregate what citizens and independent people do. That's what will happen in a few years.

Why does Big Media, Deep State, and Big Tech seem to be playing on the same team?

Why is the mainstream media on the same page as Big Tech? Why are they all working together? We asked this question when we did the *American Pravda* story. CNN was being defended by *The New York Times*. They're competitors. Why are they defending each other? I think it's an "us versus them" sort of mentality. The Tech Industry doesn't think that they actually are media companies. Sheryl Sandberg [COO of Facebook & founder of Leanin.org] said that, "We're not a media company." I think they're the *biggest* media company.

But there is a sort of alliance between Establishment people against Independent people in this country. Against the *people* — there is an alliance. And there's almost a resentment of these established folks towards the masses and, for some reason, you see a sort of alliance happening between CNN, *The New York Times*, *The Washington Post*. They're all competitors. What?? You'd think that *The Washington Post* would secretly be rooting for me as I take on *The New York Times*. But they're like defending their competitor against me...I don't understand. Well, I do understand. Now, it has to do with the fact that these corporate conglomerates are "us versus them" in these polarized times. And now you have *The New York Times* which is trying to become more digital. They're trying to hire people from the technology world. In many ways, they're trying to emulate these technology companies. They want to *be* a technology company. They must become a technology company for them to survive. Because they're not doing journalism. They're not doing-, they're doing a sort of data aggregation through Internet experience, right? That's-, that's not really — in the scheme of things — that's not really *journalism*. So that's probably why they're colluding.

ALEX JONES INTERVIEW

Who are you and what do you do?

I'm Alex Jones and I'm a radio and TV host who runs a news site, Infowars.com, out of Austin, Texas, and I'm attempting to promote free-market, second-global Renaissance.

What do you think the media has said about you or how do they describe you?

They call me "Fake News." They call me "Alt-right." They call me "the enemy." They call me "a liar." They basically take things out of context and edit it together when I'm talking about a completely different subject, and then project it onto whatever lie they're pushing.

How does that make you feel?

Makes me feel targeted, because when you're one of the main subjects that's been chosen to be destroyed — because they know that what I promote really does symbolize basic American values

– if they can destroy that, they think they can hurt their real enemy...that is, the American people.

Why does the media call you "Fake News?"

The media calls me "Fake News" because that's a term that-, the media calls me "Fake News" because we're so effective at exposing the fact that *they're* Fake News; that they have an agenda. That they lie even when the truth would serve them better. So they're trying to project what they know-, what *they* are – fraudsters – onto me because I've exposed so many of their lies effectively.

What are some of the media lies that you've exposed?

They've exposed the fact that there are a lot of dangers associated with vaccines that they've covered up. And the fact that there is a big liability protection fund that's quasi-secret where they pay out billions of dollars to families that have had their children damaged.

We've exposed that there was an admitted connection between Obama and Hillary funding ISIS and Al-Qaeda groups and the Arab Spring.

We've exposed the fact that smartphones, from their inception in the mid-1990s, were back-doored by the NSA to watch and listen to users.

We've exposed that the Federal Reserve is indeed quasi-private and not a governmental institution.

We've exposed these wars are fraudulent.

We exposed, during the election, that Hillary Clinton's poll numbers were fake and that, indeed, a lot of internal polls showed that Trump was way ahead – that they were fixing the election. We also first exposed, with one of our secret service sources, that Hillary was having convulsions about every forty-five minutes. They just said, "Keep your cameras off her when she's in public and watch for her black ambulance. If you see her near that, it means she's having a convulsion or having some more mild seizures." About a month after we told everybody to follow her and track her, we were then able to catch her falling down.

Yeah, that's interesting — the Hillary's Health story — because that still gets brought up to this day by the media, but I think-, did they really think that Hillary Clinton was *healthy*?

The biggest thing that I've exposed overall — and why our credibility is so high, and why the Fake Media tries to demonize and assassinate our character — is the fact that we have a private corporate world government trying to establish a system where a handful of mega-corporations control the nation states and are basically exempt from taxes, exempt from the regulations that they then get governments to pass, to shut down their competition.

So the fact that world government being a technocratic planetary system known as "globalism" — the fact that that is now-, let me say it better now...my back's out, and then I'll sit here and think of the other deal.

You were asking about the accomplishments, so this is really the best one — oh, here we go, here you go. And then I'll go into health and just say it right there — it doesn't bother me once you do it, whatever. I just uh...but if you guys want to put it out, just make sure if you do put it-, just make sure people know that I had a pulled muscle. It just looks like I'm a crazy person. Which I am kind of crazy already but...let me just start again. Here we go:

Infowars' greatest accomplish is simply pointing out that there is a worldwide corporate government being set up that is tax exempt and has diplomatic immunity.

The fact that, more than a hundred years ago, the robber barons of Europe and the United States wanted to be above the law. And so, this whole globalism project is really a modern form of colonialism — not just targeting third-world nations, but also first-world nations. So my greatest achievement is forcing the reality of this geopolitical unelected tyranny out into the open and that's why they hate us.

And, of course, they really dread the stuff we did during the 2016 election – along with many others – exposing the fake polls. Exposing the fact that Hillary already had the questions beforehand. The fact that we broke a lot of that from our sources enrages them. One of the big ones was Hillary's Health. It was known that back in 2013-2014 she was missing for basically a *year*. The word was that she had had surgeries on her brain for tumors. But, whatever the case, she was clearly in and out of the hospital. And had aged quite a bit in the last few years. She was also very shaky onstage...had trouble speaking...had long coughing fits. And so, one of the biggest scoops we ever got was from the Secret Service at the RNC in Cleveland in 2016 when they said, "Listen, Alex. You're dead on – with Drudge and others – saying, 'Look at her health'. Look for a black ambulance. And whenever she ends up getting into this black van, she's having a convulsion, or is about to have a convulsion. We don't know. Whenever you see her in or around this van, it means she's showing signs of having a convulsion or she's already had a convulsion."

And they said "We don't even know what the condition is. They're very, very secretive. But she's collapsing every forty-five minutes right now. Because whatever the medications are she's on, they've gotta take her off of them so that she can actually present well in public. Because the anti-seizure medications make you look like you're basically drunk. Or have taken a bunch of pain pills. Slurred language, you name it."

So-, so one reason they hate us is we broke the news. Secret Service alerted us back at the RNC back in 2016 to Hillary Clinton's collapsing every forty-five minutes or so. And they simply said, "Alex, put the word out on your show that wherever your listeners are in the country, when Hillary has a campaign stop, look for her in or around this black ambulance. This black van. Because if she's around that, it means she's showing signs of having convulsions or has just had a convulsion. Also, try to catch her when she's going in and out of medical tents that they always set up behind her events now. So that she can basically duck out and get cover when she needs to."

The media jumped the shark. Said that we'd made that up.

And a month later, on September 11th, she was caught on video collapsing. Then the media doubled down again and only showed her wobbling. Didn't show her falling on her face and being carried into the van. And said that we were all Fake News [for] claiming that she had even fallen down. They thought if CNN and MSNBC said that she hadn't fallen down, that no one would go online and actually *see* the video. Well, the video got seen hundreds of millions of times. And the media, again, got even more discredited — right along with Hillary, who they were trying to cover for. So if you want to talk about a hoax, that's the very definition of it.

It's just one of the biggest hoaxes of the campaign-, wasn't the fact that they were staging the debates or any of it – the only person who wasn't in on it was Donald Trump. It was Hillary collapsing in public and then them trying to cover it up.

And then Mike Cernovich is on *60 Minutes* and [Scott] Pelley says, "Well, the campaign says she didn't fall down," or, "The campaign said she had pneumonia." As if because the campaign of a known liar tells us something that we're gonna just supposedly buy into that. It shows where they've got such hubris that the only people they're conning is themselves.

So Hillary Clinton gave a speech because she was so intimidated by New Media.

Yes. About a month out from the election, Hillary Clinton gave her "Dark Heart" speech. Where she said that I was just the most evil, horrible person in the world. She went on to misrepresent what I had actually said. But this really wasn't an attack on me, specifically. It was an attack on the New Media that she was so intimidated by.

Can you talk about emotionally what it was like?

A lot of emotions ran through me as I saw Hillary Clinton on stage saying that I was this evil dark heart. In fact, I was live on television that day when it happened. So we were already carrying her speech. And then, all of a sudden, she goes into how I'm this "Dark Heart." And how evil I am. Then it made me think, "Wow. This lady's really weak. If she thinks I'm the reason she's losing."

But then I understood. She was just using me as a figurehead to try and demonize the New Media.

And it later came out that they were planning — once she got in office — to actually use regulators, lawsuits, the FCC, and others, to censor myself and a laundry list of others. And even despite the fact that she lost, the Democrats are still moving forward with these plans — and have even tried to have Federal Elections Commission investigations on what I'm doing on-air.

They're projecting, though. The reason they're so unpopular is not because of what I'm even saying. It's because the people have broken with them. They've broken with the Republican Establishment. They've broken with the Democratic Establishment. And so, when they attack the New Media, or citizens that are simply speaking out, all it does is make them that much weaker.

Edited versus Unedited TV?

I got into media through local talk radio and through access television. And so, nobody ever scripted what I said or did. It just came from basic research — having guests on — taking phone calls. And really just trying to keep my finger on the pulse of the world. Then you look at mainstream corporate media, where everything is taped — or it's highly scripted. They're reading off teleprompters. And you realize that this is a dinosaur system that has been setup from the beginning, so that corporations and special interests can misrepresent what's really happening.

Live formats just lend themselves more credibility because there's more time. There's more areas to bring in exhibits and information. And it allows people to challenge ideas in [real] time as well. When I'm on Twitter or Facebook or YouTube, doing a live feed, there are hundreds of people commenting a minute who are fact-checking everything I'm saying in real time. And that's wonderful. But when you take somebody like Megyn Kelley — she interviewed me for over eight hours for a nineteen-minute piece, where I only talked for about two minutes. And she would take pieces where I'd say one thing twenty minutes before, on one subject, and edit that into something that was a completely other subject to make it sound like I was a stark raving, babbling, stuttering lunatic.

Would you say that edited TV is an example of Fake News?

By its very nature, highly produced, edited television lends itself to deception. It lends itself to being perfect for Fake News.

Take Megyn Kelley: They spent weeks after they got the interview, cutting it down more than eight hours to nineteen minutes. And out of the nineteen minutes, I was only on-screen maybe three minutes. And what they put out on the other end was unintelligible from what I actually said. They took comments from hours before and then cut it into something I said over an hour later on two different subjects.

That is beyond Fake News. That is fraud.

It's the equivalent of taking say, the *Bible*, and cutting out a bunch of pages, and cutting out each word, and then putting them back together again and saying, "well, in the *Bible*, Jesus says, "I love Satan." Well, Jesus never really said that. What they're doing is-, is taking the words, editing them together, and putting them back together again as a fraud.

But people more and more are seeing through this. And that's one reason that people like Sean Hannity talk about this.

Even before Megyn Kelley's Fake News piece came out-, even before Megyn Kelley did her profile on me — her Fake News piece — I had challenged her, saying, "Listen - you guys have a big website, NBC News. Why not put out some big excerpts, at least of the hours and hours of interviews you admit you want to do with me," and she said, "Oh, yeah-" —

Megyn Kelley and her people got to these studios at nine-thirty in the morning. We weren't done until past ten o'clock at night. I added it up. Together I was on their camera for more than eight hours —

You could write a textbook on Fake News if you just analyzed that day-long interview that Megyn Kelley and NBC did. They got here at nine-thirty in the morning at these studios — and interviewed for more than eight hours on-camera to produce the fraud that they tried to pass off to the American people. The good news is her ratings cratered after the interview. And she was soon basically put on the back bench and her program canceled. And that's not any testament [as] to how good I did in the interview. I looked horrible. Like a stuttering, stammering moron. But people instinctively knew it was a fraud and rejected it. So Megyn Kelley and NBC killed that show. Not me. Though I'd love to take credit for it.

Explain to the viewer the process of editing, how they seduce you when they're doing it.

I knew when Megyn Kelley called me, and was buttering me up, that I knew it was going to be a very deceptive piece that would assassinate my character and the independent media's character. But I still accepted the interview, because I wanted to document the anatomy and fraud for my listeners and viewers, postmortem. And that's exactly what we did. We released — before the interview was even out — the preinterview, where she promised me it wasn't a hit piece. That she didn't even want to get into the subjects like Sandy Hook and things like that. And of course, once she got here, she uncloaked herself politically and showed that she was engaging in a very, very viscous attempt to destroy my credibility.

So let's get into a little bit more detail: They call you up. What do they say? What's the whole process?

From the beginning, I knew that Megyn Kelley was really planning "the hit piece of all hit pieces," because my producer told me that they were being so "sicky-sweet," and she was being so "sicky-sweet" on the phone and just begging for the interview, because they knew that I didn't give Establishment dinosaur media a lot of interviews.

We had had hundreds of TV networks and newspapers call us in the month before Megyn Kelley called. And I'd refused all the interviews, because I knew that there was basically a bounty out to do a huge deceptive hit piece on myself and InfoWars.

And so, when I heard that Megyn Kelley was calling up my producer being "sicky-sweet," saying, "Oh, here's my cell phone number. Please call me personally. I'm really into Alex. He's really cool." That right there was a giant *red flag*. And as soon as I call her: *boom*. She wants to go out to dinner with me. She's obsessed with me. She thinks I'm "really handsome." She thinks men that have a little potbelly like me are "sexy." The "best men" look like me. These are exact things she said. So I got my other phone and started recording it on speakerphone. And she kept pouring it on. And I knew that this was gonna backfire on her and that I was gonna walk my audience, after the interview aired, through the anatomy of a deception. And exactly that happened. But as soon as she actually —

I knew Megyn Kelley was coming here to destroy me. But my entire career has been about putting myself out there to take the hit first — to draw the enemy out so that more people wake up to the larger picture. And so I knew that she was coming here to destroy me. I knew she was coming here to do the ultimate hit piece. And so I understood that I had to basically take her attack on, so that I could use it as a way to educate my listeners and viewers on the anatomy of a hit piece.

I did the Megyn Kelley interview not because I was enamored of another "infobabe" on television. I did it because I turned down hundreds of other establishment interviews in just the few months preceding it. So I knew the order had gone out to "get Alex Jones."

I did it because she was so nasty and so deceptive, I wanted to show the public what she was really like behind the scenes, so other people who haven't had a chance to be through as much as this, as I have, could get a warning upfront on how these type of deceivers operate.

Talk about money and how money influences the news media.

The mainstream media knows that they've been dead for more than a decade. But still, the corporate establishment has to prop them up like a facade — so that they can be disrupters in the culture. And outfits like CNN have become vending machines, where Middle Eastern dictatorships and other groups go in and finance, sometimes one-time shows for four hundred to five hundred thousand dollars, to say, "This Gulf State dictator is great."

People ask me all the time: "Okay, Alex. If the media is controlled, *how* is it controlled?" That's like asking me how the Pacific is *wet*.

Thousands of examples: Four years ago, Congress legalized the CIA engaging in domestic propaganda through media outlets and deceiving the people *officially*. Obama signed the Ministry of Truth piece of legislation into action before he left — to use U.S. intelligence agencies against the American people.

You can go back five years ago when high level CNN producers and reporters went public on the fact that Gulf State dictators were paying hundreds of thousands of dollars per news piece to put out favorable news on dictatorships. Look, if CNN corporate bosses want to worship dictatorships, that's their right. But when they're getting paid by the dictatorships to do it, in my view, that's criminal and it's downright anti-American.

And from there, there is thousands of admitted examples. ABC News and its weekend shows are financed by the Bill and Melinda Gates Foundation. So is the London *Guardian*. It just goes on, and on, and on from there. Corporations are paying billions of dollars of media-, big corporations are spending billions of dollars a year to dinosaur media to put out stories that are prewritten by their corporate boards and by their PR outfits.

So that's beyond Fake News. That's corporate propaganda foisted on the American people and, most of the times, the media won't even tell ya that they've been paid to do it.

So the Establishment propaganda bureaus — so these modern "ministries of truth" — these modern *1984* bureaus of lies know that we're onto them. So they've gone out and financed from the very same people — like George Soros, Bill and Melinda Gates, and others — these so-called "fact-checkers." And some of the worst out there are groups like *Snopes*. *Politifact* is the really bad one.

So now that the corporate media has been caught lying over and over again to the American people, they've gone out and increasingly started financing *Politifact* or *Snopes* or *Media Matters* or *Right Wing Watch*, and then all it is is admitted political operatives going in and basically denying that the sun is yellow at high noon.

The same megacorporations, the same big tax-free foundations that have been financing and propping up mainstream Fake News, have also created and are massively funding groups like *Politifact*.

So now that the big corporations have been caught engaging in massive Fake News and deception of the public, they've moved on to creating and financing all these groups like *Politifact* and *Snopes* and all these other organizations like *Media Matters* that are run by political operatives of the Democratic Party. They then go out and supposedly tell the public what's "real news" and what's *not* "real news." And they have incredibly bad track records doing things like saying, "All seventeen agencies agree that Russians stole the election." And then it turned out, well, it's only three [agencies]. Well, *four*. Well, it was a few guys, you know, basically at dinner, who agreed to it and told *Media Matters* so. So, they just basically used this appeal to authority to say that, "Oh, David Brock over at *Media Matters* says that,

'This isn't true,' or somebody over at this other group says, 'That isn't true.'"

But there's layers of this deception. The big multinational corporations don't just have the corporate media out there lying for them. They create and finance all these so-called "fact-checking" organizations like *Snopes* and *Politifact* and others.

And when you actually research the claims they're making, it is the most crazy upside-down garbage you could ever imagine

Have you ever gotten a story wrong?

I personally have gotten stories wrong before, and every time we do, we retract — because that's part of us being truthful with the audience. And every time we do it, the media uses it and acts like we're admitting that we're Fake News. *No* — when we make a mistake, we *admit* it.

When corporate media makes a mistake, they just quietly change the narrative. And basically *never* admit when they're *wrong*.

Anybody who is reporting on news over a long period of time is going to make mistakes. And I've certainly made them. But when you look at mainstream news, they don't even issue retractions now. Or, if they do, it's buried in the back of the paper. In fact, corporate media has gotten worse now because they used to-, some of them would hold each other to account. Now they're competing with who can be the most deceptive. And they've even had news articles at mainstream papers saying, "Hey, Trump and the liberty movement is evil. We're gonna lie about them. We're gonna physically attack them. We're gonna go after their sponsors. Because this is *war*."

Some people would ask, who were uninformed, "Why is Alex Jones in a movie about Fake News?" In fact, I bet when this film comes out, they're going to have reviews saying, "Oh, look at the filmmakers. To cover Fake News, they talked to the King of Fake News." Even if that were true, you would want to talk to the King of Fake News. So, see, they don't even have logic in their arguments. That's what's so deceptive. If I was the King of Fake News, then I should be the first guy on your list.

But the truth is, we've been fighting the Fake News — they're falling apart. We're rising. And so that's why you came to talk to me, because I'm the *anti*-Fake News. I'm the guy that, when I make a mistake, comes out and tells the world. And then the Fake News media, that never wants to admit their problems, uses that to beat me over the head saying, "Look, he's fake. He's fake." But more often than them finding something I said that's wrong, they will simply *misrepresent* what I've said. And then go after me for the straw man they've created, saying, "Disavow the fact that you hate all minorities." And I say, "Show me, Tom Brokaw, *one* clip of me saying *anything* racist." And they can't even do it.

Because they are the *real* Kings of Fake News.

Could you talk about how the media treats you when you use satire and hyperbole?

A big thing that the corporate media does to deceive people now is to take satire or jokes or hyperbole, that's clearly being done in jest, and take it out of context. And put it out as a quote on television. Or in a newspaper, so it sounds completely insane.

Or if-, if I have a guest on who says something outrageous, they will then put that person's words in my mouth. And it's only getting worse as they-, corporate media gets more and more desperate.

Can you give an example of the media treating your hyperbole as it was literal?

An example of the media taking my hyperbole that's a joke, and turning it into something serious, is "gay frogs." About six years ago, I'm sitting there reading *New Scientist* reports about the majority of frogs being sterile or being bisexual because of [EDCs] and other chemicals, so I kind of fed the trolls and went, "Oh, my gosh! They're turning the frogs gay!" so it would get picked up in the press on purpose. So, a lot of the times, I actually feed into the fact that they take things out of context to get attention on something that wouldn't normally get attention because it was only in a scientific circle.

So that's another example of why I like to hit the barb wire for everybody else. To expose chemicals in the water, I throw in little tidbits out there that I know that the media's going to take the bait on.

So if I'm playing the part of the Joker to illustrate something, they'll say I'm a fraud. Or if I'm joking around about gay frogs, they say that I'm a fraud. But, again, that's what they do. And that's why people should actually go to the source of media to check out information for themselves. And not believe anybody. And that means me. That means CNN. That means MSNBC. That means Matt Drudge. That means Mike Cernovich.

That means you need to do what Ronald Reagan said: "Trust, but verify."

The media says you sell fear and paranoia to sell products. How do you respond?

One of the other big talking points that they have is that I'm this fearmonger. That I'm creating artificial fear so that people will politically do what I want or buy my products...when it's the opposite.

I'm the one trying to stop the Iraq War: I and II. I'm the one trying to stop the Arab Spring. I'm the one trying to stop the destruction of our borders. I'm the one trying to get people self-sufficient so that they're not living in fear. So they can't be controlled by the globalists. I'm the guy telling people that we don't want a race war and that we should love each other and come together.

They're the ones promoting the division. They're the hatemongers. They're the fearmongers. They're the ones that are negative. And that's why they're losing their viewers and listeners. And that's why they're panicking.

And that's why they're now calling for Chinese-style censorship or Russian Soviet Union-style censorship to come in and control what we're doing.

Where do you get your news from?

One of the most common questions I get is, "Alex, if the media is fake, where do *you* get your news?"

Well, I get it from eyewitness reports. Live videos that are shot. I get it from the actual legislation. I get it from what the UN documents actually say. I get it from whistleblowers and people inside corporations and the government.

And even mainstream media, a lot of the time, is telling the truth if they're reporting on just a dry subject. The lies tend to be when you get into the political realm and understand what's happening there. I go directly to the source documents nine times out of ten.

How do you vet your sources?

People ask: "Alex, how do you vet what's *real* news?" And it's over time doing research. Knowing what sources are good. Going to the direct source documents. The legislation. The police report itself.

And it's also, again, having journalists' trust — like Sy Hersh, or Mike Cernovich, and others — that have been proven, over and over and over again, that they got the sources and they're reporting on what's really happening.

Do you consider yourself a journalist, a commentator, a radio personality, an activist...*all* of them combined?

Folks are always asking: "Alex, are you for real? Are you a radio host? Are you a filmmaker? Are you a commentator? Are you a journalist? Are you an actor? Cause the media says you admit you're an actor." Well, I look and then I say, "Absolutely, I'm an actor."

And the corporate Fake News will probably take that clip out of context and say, "See? He admits he's a fraud."

I wear many hats. But 99% of the time I'm a father. I'm an American. I'm a patriot who wants to simply research the facts and present them to the public so that we can live in a better, more productive, safe world.

But absolutely! I wear the hat of a journalist. I wear the hat of a pundit. I wear the hat of a comic trying to have some gallows humor.

And occasionally I wear the hat of an actor when I illustrate a point I'm making via fiction. And when I am involved in fiction, it's always incredibly obvious that I'm engaged in a *joke*. The media tries to blur the lines there and use those different distinctions to confuse the audience that they're preying on.

Could you talk about your YouTube being censored?

There was massive censorship going on in the campaign in 2016. It's admitted that Hillary was talking to Google in live time managing her search results. So that's confirmed.

But since Hillary lost, the corporate media has chastised Facebook that they haven't done *enough* censorship.

So now, in 2017/going into 2018, we are seeing North Korean-, Soviet-style, Communist Chinese-style/level censorship of anybody that is off the mainline political reservation.

And we see the social networks with the big TV news networks and others altogether pushing that censorship isn't just *happening*, but that it's a *good* thing. We're seeing a perfect storm of dinosaur corporate media losing audience. Scared political elites losing constituents and supporters. And scared corrupt corporations all coming together in an attempt to bring in massive unprecedented censorship here in the United States. Also in Europe. Also in Canada. Also in Australia.

[Editor's Note: YouTube has since deleted all of Alex Jones' associated YouTube channels, which had between 1.5 and 5 billion views across platforms.)

Could you give a specific example of Google Search Results?

One example is: for the last eighteen years, if you typed in "info", "*Infowars*" came out number one or number two in the search result. Now it's not in the first five pages. And the examples just go on from there...how we've been delisted. How we've been restricted. How we've been dialed back not just by Google, but by other major search results.

And then, during the campaign, people would search, "Hillary criminal," and they would only get bills she introduced back in the 1990s that had *nothing* to do with current things and scandals she was involved in.

Earlier this year, it came out that Google had put out a multi-million-dollar contract, to outside PR firms, to go in and vote down the news and information posted at *Infowars*.

And once we got the actual document from whistleblowers, Google admitted that, indeed yes, it was true. There was a program to censor me. And that it was ongoing. And that it was a mistake. And that they were going to stop it.

Now, why did they do that? Because Google has advertised itself as this "utility" open to the public. And if a Christian couple has to bake a cake for a gay wedding, then certainly conservatives, and Christians/others should have access to the marketplace that is YouTube/Google. And they certainly shouldn't have their own search results from their own personal, private websites artificially voted down by an army of trolls hired by those companies to basically put our information into a black hole.

And how does that affect your pocketbook?

Here's the great news: I don't want to just single out Google. But they are just the biggest shark in the ocean.

But their subsidiary, YouTube, first demonetized our YouTube videos – and my reporters' videos – by about 50%, six months ago. And said, "You better watch what you do or we will curtail more."

Then it was 75%.

It's now almost 100% of our videos are demonetized as a punishment for what we are politically doing.

And they've gone from six months ago denying they were doing this, to now publicly admitting they're doing it.

And Google even reached out to *Forbes*. And told their magazine, "You better watch what you do supporting certain policies, or we'll list you as a 'hate group' and not let you have advertising as well." That's how far this has gotten.

And that's why you sell products, right?

Well, exactly. So simultaneously the corporate media demonizes us for direct-selling products, so we can fund our operation, while Google had us banned off Google Ads, and while they have demonetized us 95% for our political views.

So they want me to just go to the Gulag. Shut up. Go bankrupt. Shut down. And stop having my speech. And I'm not gonna do it. And our listeners and viewers understand that. And in the face of this unprecedented censorship, we've only seen our support go up.

So now they're in the news calling for criminal investigations into me — claiming I'm a "Russian agent." So that's their last bastion. Because they can't beat us in argument after cutting off our funding. Censoring us. Sending out hordes of people to physically attack us. With scalding coffee...you name it.

Because that's not enough. Now their last refuge is cold hard political imprisonment.

When is the dinosaur media going to die?

So when is the dinosaur going to finally give up? When are they finally going to die and go into the dustbin of history?

And the answer is: "Never!" Not as long as big corporate money is financing them. You know I coined the term "dinosaur media," but really they're not dinosaur media. They're the *zombie media*. They're the *undead media*. Who everybody hates. Who almost no one trusts. With a 7% approval rating in *Gallup*. Who just keep coming on. Because they're artificial. They're not real. They're propagandists in a rearguard action. Because we've taken the media over, but we haven't yet taken over the Jeff Bezoses and the Zuckerbergs who still have their big fraudulent systems in place.

You talk about brazen Fake Media. We have billions of taxpayer dollars being spent, before Trump got in, financing major U.S. newspapers and major television networks. We saw massive amounts of money in stimulus packages, under Obama, given to NBC — back when they owned MSNBC — to engage in political warfare against the American people.

And now we have Jeff Bezos, one of the richest men in the world — close to one hundred billion in wealth — with his oligopoly, Amazon, getting a six hundred-million-dollar contract from the CIA to house their servers, while he uses *The Washington*

Post — that he owns — as a warfare machine against President Trump and the American people.

This is beyond a hoax. This is a giant organized *fraud.* This is political warfare through the news media...against the American people.

Fake corporate news media is nothing new. It's just more financed today and a lot bigger and a lot slicker.

Operation Mockingbird — which is a declassified admitted case – Operation Mockingbird, a thirty-year-plus secret program for the CIA to control our media and take control of our country, didn't end in the 1970s when Senator Frank Church exposed it. It simply went underground and changed its name. And got boosting in its funding.

Gary Webb faced this modern mockingbird operation in the 1990s when CIA operatives at the *LA Times* published Fake News stories about himself and his family to destroy him — even down to breaking up his family.

And later, it all came out.

Folks ask, "Why did you start *Infowars*? Why did you go on air? "Why did you get politically involved?" "What was the trigger for Alex Jones?"

And that's because early on, in junior high and high school, I saw police dealing drugs in the school — and at parties — who would then be running the anti-drug programs at the auditorium a few weeks later.

So my skepticism began there. And then I saw Waco and Oklahoma City and the whole Clinton era. I knew I had to get involved.

And that's why, since the time I was twenty-one years old, I've been on air because I've known there's been a war on for our minds.

Mainly because I was a history buff. I played sports and was involved like everybody else in normal activities. But, early on, started reading historical books that were around the house, because my mom has a degree in history. And I found it so entertaining that I read hundreds of those books.

But then I began to see the parallels of history with what was currently happening. So there is the old saying that goes, "Those [who] don't know history are doomed to repeat it." So the *Infowars* really owes itself to the fact that I'd read so much history. I saw all those patterns repeating themselves and decided to get politically involved and we've now had quite an effect.

That's another testament to the fact that even if you don't have all the answers — and even if you don't have all the skills — if you simply get involved, and take action, you can change the world.

CASSIE JAYE INTERVIEW

Who are you?

I am documentary filmmaker Cassie Jaye.

What kind of films have you made?

Well, the majority of my work focused on women's issues and women's rights and LGBT rights. But my latest film, *The Red Pill*, focused on the men's rights movement.

How long have you been doing films?

I started making films when I was twenty-one years old. I'm now 31, so a whole decade.

What got you into filmmaking?

Oh, that's a roundabout story. Well, I-, I'll try to summarize it very quickly — but I grew up doing theater, musical theater, and acting in plays in Seattle, and then I moved to Las Vegas, and I started acting in films and commercials there. And then, when I was eighteen years old, I moved to L.A. to try my shot at being an actress in Hollywood. And so, from eighteen to twenty-one, I was doing that in L.A. and then the Writers Guild strike happened in 2007-2008, and the town kind of went into a slumber and everyone was growing beards protesting the writers' strike. There was no work in Hollywood. And I started watching a lot of documentaries. And I really gravitated to the rawness of documentaries — that it's real people's stories. And, you know, told in a cinematic way and I thought I could do this. I wanted to try it. So when I was twenty-one, I-, I enlisted my mother as my producer and camerawoman and we hit the road filming and made our first film, *Daddy I Do,* which looked at women's rights.

How have you experienced Fake News?

And I think people who have been printed in the media a lot can start to identify who is Fake News, because they know their true story more than anyone and they can see who is not telling the truth.

It's horrible. It's horrible. But at least you know that your close friends and family know the truth of who you are before the whole media storm happens. But it is difficult when someone you don't know [sees you] in a grocery store and they think they know you because of what they read.

And yeah, I-, although I live in kind of a pocket of the San Francisco Bay area that's pretty disconnected from most mainstream news, but have had some people-, have heard about me, like my dentist — he hadn't seen the film, but he heard about it, and he heard or he thought he knew this story about me because of what the mainstream said about me. But yeah, I just try to win him over with a dental appointment I have. So he knows I'm not the monster that the mainstream try to make me out to be.

Have you ever been recognized in public?

I think I have. But they usually don't come up and say anything to me. And, you know, I think oftentimes they don't want to come up to me because they think something poorly of me or what they've heard about me. So that's about it.

You did your first documentary [in] 2010. What was it?

It was called, *Daddy I Do*. And it was about sex education in America and it specifically looked at women's issues regarding reproductive rights and single motherhood, and we had a rape story and...it just looked at a lot of different women who have been affected by bad sexual education. And that film was really embraced and supported by Planned Parenthood. They funded Northwestern screening tour of the film and flew us out and we did a bunch of screenings and had dinner parties and it was wonderful and it was really-, it was really supported in feminist circles. And so, yeah, that was my first film and we went to ten film festivals, won six awards, and that kind of got the ball rolling for me to continue filmmaking because we did get so much praise for *Daddy I Do*.

How'd that feel to have good media coverage?

I mean, I felt like we were so blessed and we hit the jackpot as far as instantly getting really positive press. Film festivals loved our film. I mean, it was featured on Upworthy — which at the time on Facebook, Upworthy — whenever they featured something, got tons of views, and so that was a big boost in our reputation as filmmakers to have it on Upworthy, and so we have a lot of success. And-, everyone was saying that I had a bright future as a filmmaker because of that film and it was good.

Debut film…media talking good about you…must be nice.

Yeah, and I think maybe I took it a little for granted at the time because, obviously, not all filmmakers or whistleblowers or activists or people who work on political topics and expose corruption in politics…not all of them get that much positive response and accolades and recognition for their work and so I immediately had it out of the gate with my first documentary.

The first documentary I directed was called, *Daddy I Do*. Or, the first documentary I made was *Daddy I Do*.

So what happens after *Daddy I Do*?

So my second feature documentary was called, *The Right To Love: An American Family*, and it was about gay marriage before gay marriage was legalized across the nation. So, I followed a gay couple and their two adopted children and they were legally married in California before Proposition 8 passed and then same-sex couples' right to marry was revoked. And so-, but they were a legally married gay couple with two adopted kids and-, and that film also did really well. And I was invited to GLAAD — which is one of the big LGBT organizations — one of their big fundraisers as a special guest and walking the red carpet and being recognized there for what I did with *The Right To Love*. And we had a big premiere screening in the Castro-, at the Castro Theatre — over two thousand people attended and it was a great-, a great film and at the right time. And we got a lot of support, and it kind of kept in line with my theme of documentary filmmaking, which always kind of focused on gender in some aspect or another, where my first film was about women's issues and reproductive rights. And so then my second big feature film is about LGBT rights. And then I made a slew of short films about-, mostly about women's issues. I made one about the need for more girls to get into STEM education. And that was called, *The Story of GoldieBlox*, and it featured a female CEO who made a new kind of Lego-type toy for girls to get into engineering. And I made a film for the International Museum of Women that focused on single mothers and was raising awareness about maternal death rates, which is roughly eight hundred women per day around the world die from pregnancy or-, or childbirth-related causes. And so I directed a film for the National Museum of Women and and that was kind of my brand and that was my reputation. And-, and I had a lot of support and that...

Act One: Cassie Goes to Hollywood. Act Two: Everyone Loves Cassie.

Yeah, how do I say it? I got a lot of positive favorable press and I never had anyone question my credibility or my intentions, wondering if I was a good person or not, I was always just really embraced and accepted as a reputable, you know, filmmaker... which, of course, I believe I am. So there was no reason for them to question that. But, you know, I just had a lot of support and a lot of praise — especially in my friendship circles and my family and because I live in the San Francisco Bay Area and I was working on women's rights, mostly, and LGBT rights and so I had a lot of support.

What happened next?

Oh, okay...where did I start? And so in 2013, I was looking for my next big feature documentary to make and I was considering making a film on rape culture because it was blowing up my social media feed around two-, a couple-, two friend-rape cases and, around the world, where in India there was a gang rape on a bus and another one at Steubenville-, and there was a Steubenville rape case. And so I was starting to research these rape cases and just getting really angry and fired up about, *what is this rape culture that we live in?* And there hadn't been a film — a documentary — in recent years about rape culture, and so I thought I was going to be the filmmaker to make this film about rape culture at the height of the discussion around this topic. And as I started digging into rape culture talking points — the most common kind of, I guess, accusation of what was fueling a rape culture was people who are rape apologists or blame the victim. And all of my feminist sources pointed to the men's rights movement as being the rape apologists and the victim blamers, and so I started to research what is the men's rights movement and I came across the largest and fastest-growing online hub of men's rights activists which, at the time, was A Voice For Men. It was-, it was a blog and kind of forum website. And so, I started looking into Voice for Men's articles and I was triggered. And I was put off by what I was reading. I had never heard these talking points before because I was a feminist of about ten years, at that point, with my work focused on women's issues. And they were posing the devil's advocate argument on rape culture, but as well as all these other topics regarding gender politics, and I was fascinated that I never heard of them before. And I was afraid of them. I felt afraid of them. I didn't know if they were actually women haters or not. In my feminist circles, and also feminist blogs and websites that I read, they would say that men's rights activists were violent and they were misogynists and they-, they're trying to turn back the clock on women's rights. And so I thought, *all right, if we have a war on women these are the people perpetuating it.* And so I shifted gears [from] making a film about rape culture to making a film about the men's rights movement and then, over a period of three-and-a-half years, what came out of it was *The Red Pill* movie.

Initially you wanted to do an expose on the men's rights movement, yes? What did that look like preproduction for you?

So initially I thought I was going to be making a film exposing men's rights activists as misogynists, rape apologists, women haters trying to turn back the clock on women's rights. And that was the film I thought I was going to make.

And then I spent one year interviewing forty-four different people, anywhere from two hours up to eight hours on camera with each individual person. And I interviewed men's rights activists as well as a few very prominent academic feminists high up in kind of their notoriety and-, and in feminist circles. And-, and after that year of filming forty-four people, I realized that the film I thought I was going to make was not the truth of the story I got, and the story I got on-camera after a year of meeting all these people and really getting to know them and doing the research to check their claims. I thought that's what-, that story was worth telling. And I also knew [it] wasn't on-brand with who has supported my films and political correctness and the whole kind of air of-, of what documentaries were being put out at that time. And-, and I was kind of going off-script with the story. I found that I wanted to tell them...

So initially, then, would it be fair to say your view on the men's rights movement was Fake News?

Yeah what I thought of men's rights activists before I started making *The Red Pill* movie was purely based on what I read online and saw in the media. And now, looking back, I can absolutely say it was Fake News. I mean, no doubt they were cooking up stories and putting together these lies hoping that the snowball would keep rolling and getting bigger where it's-, it's too big to squash. And, I mean, and there's no stopping it once it's that big of one...once it's been repeated that often, people don't question it. And journalists don't question it, which I think is, like, this crazy thing is, you *should*. Even if it's been reported in those words or printed time and time again, you still have to check the credibility of that statement or that claim. And so, often what I would find in these articles falsely reporting about the men's rights movement — or falsely reporting about myself — they would hyperlink a claim that they would make-, they would put a link to it. As if to tell the reader that, "Here's the source of this claim." But if you clicked on that link, it goes to another article they wrote. So they're using *themselves* as the source of their own lies and it's just shocking to me that none-, none of these Fake News articles — [nor] the shows that are putting out these lies — they don't have proof of these claims, but they just tell their audience or their reader, *it is fact*. And people don't question it.

So I found that journalists use themselves as the source of their own lies.

Do you trust the media?

I don't trust the media anymore. I used to. I thought the media's purpose was to be the whistleblowers on corruption — to tell the public, "This is what we need to know to effect change." And now I see the media as the-, I don't even know how to explain it...the "Chatty Cathy" hairstylist that says, "Well, here's what I heard in the nail salon and it's got to be true." And if you want the source, well look at what I said last week — that's the proof.

I mean, there's no actual research happening and I don't know where journalistic integrity went. I want to believe we used to have that. I think we did. And I think when we used to have subscription-based newspapers, where a paper would be held accountable if they lied, where they would lose subscribers — I think that was possibly the last time we had true journalistic integrity, because there-, there were repercussions for lying. And now there are not. And actually, in a lot of circumstances, they actually make more money and get more job offers if they don't tell the truth, because then they have to continue the story and keep printing new articles and making corrections and now having, you know, more clicks and more commenters. So the incentives have changed, and the motivations have changed for that as well.

What are the specific lies the media has told about you?

The biggest most damaging lie the media has has told about me is that *The Red Pill* movie was funded by men's rights activists. Quick little sound bite to suggest to the reader/their audience that it's a propaganda film that can't be trusted. And there's no credibility to Cassie Jaye's name or the film itself. And it's just this little sound bite in an effort to discredit my entire last four years' work and why it's so frustrating to have this lie printed over and over again and said on TV. And like an Australian weekend sunrise in the project, why it's so frustrating is because the truth of the matter isn't a snappy sound bite, so it's a lot more difficult to come back with. Here's the truth — but I'll try my best to make it very quick:

The truth of the matter is the film's filming production was self-financed by myself. My now fiancé and my mother, who's my producer at the time, were three self-identifying feminists making a film about men's rights activists. We put tens of thousands of our own savings and earned income into making this film. And then when it got to the point of having to go into post-production, which is far more expensive than the filming process for a documentary, we had exhausted our funds. Every single film grant that I apply to for *The Red Pill* movie, we were declined from-, were rejected from all those film grants I applied to — over a dozen. And I was actually offered a large sum of money from a feminist organization to complete the film — with the caveat that they would have creative control — that they would have the final say in how the film was completed and released.

And I did not want to give up creative control to *anyone,* no matter their political leanings: not to MRAs, not to feminists. not to any kind of organization. I wanted full creative control because I knew the story I had and only I could fight for that story to be told. If anyone else had creative control, they would have made it into an activists' piece for their cause...and I didn't want that.

So I only had one option: to try to get post-production funding for *The Red Pill* movie. And it was a crowdfunding campaign, so I turned to Kickstarter, and it's the most transparent way a documentarian can raise funding for their film, because not a single Kickstarter backer has any creative control over your film. They don't even have a stake in your film. They don't have equity stake or anything. And that was the only way I [could] retain *full creative control,* make the film I wanted to make, and not be locked into promoting any kind of cause. And I said that in my Kickstarter view: I said, "I'm turning to Kickstarter because I don't want to give up creative control." I think if people really want to look into documentaries and try to say that they're propaganda pieces and yet there is no information about how they are funded-, funded, there is no information about how *The Hunting Ground* was funded, or how *[The] Invisible War* was funded, or how Michael Moore's films are funded, but people don't raise the question of, "Well who funded *that*?"

So I did a Kickstarter. You know where the funding is coming from. I wasn't getting, you know, backed to where a sack of money from an organization-, to make them the commercial. I did a Kickstarter campaign. Everyone knows no one has creative control if you're a Kickstarter backer.

And the media used that against me and it was the most transparent way for me to raise the funding I needed to complete *The Red Pill* — the most transparent way. And that was the only thing that the media could use to try to discredit me — to say that it was a "propaganda piece" and it's this little sound bite: "a film about men's rights activists funded by men's rights activists."

Were the Kickstarter backers men's rights activists? They're a minority of men's rights activists, a minority of feminists, and mostly people who don't identify as either. And the reason I know that is because they wrote me private messages, or commented on the Kickstarter page, saying, "This is why I backed your Kickstarter campaign." But I know that feminists also funded the Kickstarter campaign, because they wrote blogs explaining, "I'm a feminist. I backed this Kickstarter campaign because I want to see this film made even if I don't agree with it."

But *The Project* in Australia, they wanted to just say-, well in their video package before my interview aired...my edited interview aired...they put together a video package setting me up as a monster, and in their graphics they said-, they showed the figure "two thousand seven hundred thirty-two," which was the number of-, how many Kickstarter backers I had. And then, underneath, they put the text and graphics MRAs and the voice-over said, "All these people are MRAs that funded *The Red Pill* movie," and that was probably the most atrocious kind of outright lying that I saw from a mainstream media source. Because, I mean, they made it into this edited video package right before they show my interview and I didn't know that they were showing that. So I couldn't even respond to that lie. And you know their biggest fan base is young millennials. So all eighteen- to thirty-five-year-olds are thinking, "Oh, it's a propaganda piece funded by the MRAs." And I wasn't even offered the ability to counter that/to debunk that lie.

So, anyways, my point is that this is the most frustrating lie that I've seen repeated over and over again. One is-, one of the worst I saw was *Vice:* they wrote an article where the title was, *Why Men's Rights Activists Had Their Bullshit Documentary Banned.* And within the first paragraph, it said *The Red Pill* movie is a documentary examining men's rights activists, but it was funded by men's rights activists-period. And, immediately, if you're a reader and you only read the first paragraph, you immediately think it is propaganda.

So-, so they won't even watch it. And I continue to see on forums — on, like, even mother/mommy blogs — I see people saying, "Have you seen *The Red Pill* movie? Really changed my life. You should watch it. I'd love to talk to you about it." And then there'd be twenty people below her, saying, "That film is bullshit. It was funded by men's rights activists. It's an MRA propaganda piece. I'm not going to watch that shit." All that kind of stuff. And it's just so frustrating to me, because I think-, I think it would be educational for anyone to watch the film — if they're feminists — even if they don't want to agree with the film. But I think it's an important film for *anyone* to watch. And so many people aren't watching it because [of] that one lie being repeated over and over.

At least they're repeating the lie. At least they've heard about it.

Yeah.

See, you haven't transitioned to the post-fact world that I live in.

The *what*?

The post-fact world that I live in.

"Post-fact?"

They construct a narrative about me and I just construct my own alternative narrative and their narratives fight it out and hopefully mine wins and theirs loses.

Yeah.

Because you're still attached to the truth, still.

Yeah.

You have to release that emotional attachment to the truth about your film.

I do see, though, that there's two different worlds: There's the mainstream media and there's alternative media...or "New Media," or whatever you want to call it. But this kind of-, still semi-kind of "underground world" on YouTube and Periscope and Twitter and Facebook and the conversations that [they] are having there, I think, are really important conversations. And I love the comments section on any YouTube video, because I think that's when really interesting ideas are brought up. And, of course, you have *trolls*. Of course, there is a minority I think most-, for the most part, a minority of trolls that are just there to trigger people and write something outrageous, and you just gotta create your own filter to not let that affect you. But there are some really interesting conversations happening there, or on reddit, or even on 4chan, as-, as much as you know people want to demonize those kind of platforms, there are some really interesting conversations happening there. But they're-, I think they're still underground and-, and the mainstream media, unfortunately, does have a stronghold on the people who only have a TV — maybe have their phone, but haven't figured out how to use all the different apps...probably aren't going online as much... maybe work, you know, extreme long hours...70-hour weeks. And the only kind of news they get is Friday night on Trevor Noah or, you know, something that they think that's their news source: "That's The Daily Show, or that's MSNBC, and that's going to give me everything I need to know and I don't need to question anything else." And there's a lot of people only getting their information from those sources. And I used to only get my information from those sources. And I believed it. I thought, *That's all I need to know about that topic,* until I became the subject of a smear campaign and realized that the sources I used to trust cannot be trusted with my own life story. And how could I trust anything you say now?

How did you feel when the media went after you?

Oh, I think when I started to see the media going after me — personally, on direct attack — trying to take down my credibility and my reputation, I felt cheated and lied to for my entire previous life before I became this public figure with the smear campaign. I feel like, *how can I have trusted anything they've ever said about all these other people who I've seen smeared in the media before?* And I believed what the mainstream media said about them. But-, but when you're on the receiving end, then you don't know what to believe. And when people are telling the truth — when you see bloggers or YouTubers actually telling the truth — and then their reputations are being smeared, you feel like you can't win, because any time someone does try to correct the lies or tell the truth, then they become the next target. So when does it end? And I don't know...I don't, at this point, see how it's going to get better — which is scary.

So, in your own life, you were affected personally?

Yes. And I still have friends and family who refuse to see *The Red Pill* movie because of what they read in the media — and they *know* me. They've known me my whole life. And they refused to see the film because the mainstream media said, "Don't pay attention to it — it's not worth your time." And they're my *family*. But here's where I feel like I understand where they're coming from, because it is a tall order to ask someone to "trust me." And admit that the rest of the world is lying. And when I say the rest of the world — the mainstream media — is lying, and all the people that are leaving the mainstream media are eating the lies, that's a tall order to ask someone to believe — just one person, *me,* saying that — "*Vice* is lying. *The Guardian*'s lying. *The New York Times* lied. *The Village Voice* lied..." That's a tall order to say that all these different institutions and companies that aren't being punished — that aren't being held accountable — [lied] because we would think that if-, if there is injustice happening in our country, then the justice system will take care of that. But it's not happening.

What do you do if you can't trust the media anymore?

This is-, this is the hard part, because...so if you can't trust the media anymore, then how will you find the truth? Most people don't have the time to be their own researcher and to fact-check everything they read. But there are some people that do take the time. I try to take the time, obviously, in my own life's work, to fact-check anything I read from the mainstream media and alternative or New Media — fact-check *everything* — and it takes a lot of time. I know a lot of YouTubers who are kind of becoming the New Media reporters, or anchor people on YouTube. I think there's a wonderful, growing movement of-, of people who really are trying to be the researchers and fact-checkers and get that information out to their following. So I think those are great sources. So if you hear about something in the mainstream media, then go to the New Media and figure out what they say about it, and then go to someone on the left, and then go to some on the right, go to the whistleblowers. Go to people who their reputations have been smeared and see what they have to say about that topic, because they don't have much to lose anymore. So, "They're going to tell you what it is," and, "They've already been spared, so they're not." "They're not risking their reputation anymore." "They've already been smeared, so they're going to tell you, 'Look, this is the truth of that story and what's happening.'" — but do your own research still.

Biggest difference between mainstream media and the New Media?

Well, I see the difference between the mainstream media and the New Media — or the "alternative media" — is, well, the mainstream media, or *corporations*, they are: Bottom line numbers...How do we get more money rolling in?...We have a big staff-how do we keep them on payroll?...How do we, you know, keep a legal team, because I'm sure there are lawsuits coming their way and they have to have, you know, money set aside for that. Whereas, New Media and alternative media...a lot of it, that I see, is funded by the people through crowd-funding platforms — whether it be Patreon, or a Kickstarter, or GoFundMe, or Indiegogo, or just a "donate" button to PayPal. And I think that's really great, because it is kind of a new sub-scription-based model, where if-, if you start reporting bad news, you're going to lose your donors. So-, so I think, you know, there's a different incentive in the New Media personalities and-, and I...because they're not beholden to a corporate higher-up kind of chain of command that they have to keep in line with, politically correct, or on-script agendas, I think they have more freedom to share the truth and go off-script, because they don't have to answer to the CEO of some big paper. So, I think it's all worthy of being out there.

Can you tell us your experience with *[The] Village Voice* and New Media?

Okay, so let's see. So, for *The Red Pill* movie, I was going through the process of getting the film qualified for the Academy Awards — the Oscars. And, for a documentary feature film, in order to get it qualified, you have to have a weeklong screening in L.A., a weeklong screening in New York, and you have to have a film review in one of three popular New York papers and one of three popular L.A. papers, as well as a very small advertisement placed in one of those three New York papers and one of those three L.A. papers.

So these are just some of the requirements to get your film qualified for the Oscars. But it had to happen in order to get qualified.

So, for *The Red Pill*, my publicist set up-, set up a film review with Alan Scherstuhl of *The Village Voice*. And *The Village Voice* is one of the three in New York papers you have to have a film review printed in. So my publicist started up with Alan Scherstuhl.

And my theatrical booking agent also set up that a one-inch-by-two-inch advertisement would be placed in *The Village Voice*. And so, all this was ready to go and we're getting ready to premiere in New York. And Alan Scherstuhl gets a screener copy of the film one week in advance before *The Red Pill*'s worldwide premiere.

The first strange incidents that started happening was: I started to see Alan Scherstuhl live tweeting about *The Red Pill* movie – a film that hadn't yet been released to the public. So there is a series of tweets where he is talking about his distaste and disgust of the film.

And then there's a Twitter account of someone who's had it out for me ever since the previous year when I did a Kickstarter campaign for *The Red Pill* Movie — it was a Twitter account called, "Takedown MRAs." Obviously, you know their agenda... so this Twitter account, Takedown MRAs, tweeted to Alan Scherstuhl, saying, "You should talk to David Futrelle of We Hunted the Mammoth. And We Hunted the Mammoth is a rabid, radical feminist blog, that's sole purpose is to cherry-pick any kind of bad-sounding articles or comments written by men's rights activists. And, basically, to smear men's rights activists.

And David Futrelle is the head of We Hunted the Mammoth, and he's actually written blogs or articles for big papers and online websites: Salon.com, *New York Post*, *The New York Times*-I think he wrote for...I mean, he has his connections.

So TakeDown MRAs told Alan Scherstuhl to talk to David Futrelle before writing his review of my film, *The Red Pill.* So, sure enough, Alan Scherstuhl's film review of *The Red Pill* was released two days before the film premiered and it wasn't a *film* review. It was a rant, and he was furious about the film. He was furious to have been asked to review the film, and he gave a commercial sound bite piece for David Futrelle at the end of his film review, saying, "Thank you, David Futrelle, for his invaluable site We Hunted the Mammoth," and did a little plug for him there.

So that was the first and only article or film review to be written about *The Red Pill* movie. And where it gets really crazy is that we had to have this one-inch-by-two-inch advertisement printed in *The Village Voice* during the week of our New York theatrical release of the film in order to be qualified for the Oscars.

Alan Scherstuhl was apparently so angry about watching *The Red Pill* movie, that my publicist talked to someone at *The Village Voice* that worked there, and the person at *The Village Voice* said that Alan Scherstuhl threw a fit in the office. He refused to let the paper publish our one-by-two ad in their paper. And he was going to write his review, but it was in the effort to take this film down and take me down.

So this was communicated to my publicist. And now we have less than forty-eight hours to figure out: Where are we going to publish our one-by-two advertisement in the papers so that we can still be Oscar-qualified? Everything else was fine. We had all the dozens of qualifications that we needed to have to get the film pre-qualified. We had it all set in stone. It was perfect. Everything was going well.

But *The Village Voice,* because of Alan Scherstuhl, refused to run our paid-for advertisement in their paper. And this is one of the papers that the Oscars demands that a filmmaker have an ad published in.

So, now we only have two other papers at our option. It was either the *New York Post* or *The New York Times*. And the *New York Post* was past their deadline of when they would need artwork in order to be published in that week's paper. So we didn't have the option to use them. So *The New York Times* was our only option and they were willing to basically cut a deal with my booking agent to let us get last-minute artwork-, artwork into *The New York Times* to run that ad.

But it was *thousands* of dollars more than what *The Village Voice* was charging us, and I didn't budget for that. So we had to scramble up the money to do this one within forty-eight hours.

And in the moment of all this happening, I was flabbergasted. I had no idea that a paper could do this. That a paper that the Oscars requires a filmmaker to have-, either have a review or an advertisement in that paper, that that paper — *The Village Voice* — would have the power — *and this film reviewer* could have the power to not let my film get qualified for the Oscars. That *one person* has that kind of *power.*

And, I mean, looking back now: it's a year later, since this has happened, and I'm still I'm thinking *this can't be legal.* I didn't have the money to file a lawsuit at that time. And I think, you know, a lot of people in my situation — a lot of struggling documentary filmmakers — wouldn't have the power to fight that.

I'm just so grateful that *The New York Times* was friends with my booking agent and they cut a deal, but I just can't believe that, you know, the amount of power that one film reviewer *with an agenda* could have over the success of my film.

And piecing together a couple other suspicious things here: His main source of his film review was David Futrelle, who has had it out for me the whole twelve months prior to my film's release. Because he started going after me during my Kickstarter campaign. He was the first person who had, I guess, power. I mean, he does have power. Now-, now I realize he has power at the time it-, and realize how much he has. But he was the first person with power to really start going after me and creating the script of how to discredit me and-, and planned this full-on smear campaign.

And he's fed the lies to all the different sources. And so, Alan Scherstuhl's initial film review that was published-, it was published in *The Village Voice* and also in three other papers. And his film review is now used as the *source* for anyone trying to discredit me or the film. They all link back to his film review and then his film review-, review rant. He says that *[The Red Pill]* was funded by men's rights activists. That's the origin of that lie. David Futrelle fed him that lie. Alan Scherstuhl printed it. And now everyone else prints it.

And, I mean-, and there's no way to stop that snowball from continuing to roll down the hill. I mean it's just gotten out of control. And as often as I try to dispel that lie — that the film was funded by men's rights activists — it never seems to stick, because no mainstream source is willing to print that.

How was your experience with the alternative media versus the mainstream?

I have a special affinity for the alternative media because I especially love that they do interviews with me that are live or completely unedited. And so, I've done interviews with Dave Rubin and Stephen Crowder and Alex Jones and Stefan Molyneux and TheRalphRetort and all these different kind of fringe alternative media sources online. And they've always presented my story truthfully and honestly and that's all I can ask for. And that's what the media *should* be — is reporting the truth of the story and let the audience and reader decide for themselves. That should be what the media is. But that's not what the mainstream media or the Fake News is doing. They are-, they may try to get the truth of the story — I don't think they always do try to get the truth of the story. But, say they do actually get the truth of the story and they do their research and find all the information. But that's not what they're going to print or air. They're going to spin it into, "What-, what do we think the public should know?" That's the story they're going to put out there. And I, as a documentary filmmaker, you know...you could say I am a part of the media — I'm a documentary filmmaker. But I have faith in my audience that they can think critically for themselves, and I allow them that what should be, I think, a basic human right: that you should be able to be given truthful information, critically think about it for yourself, and make your own opinion. And whatever your opinion turns out to be, you can go write a blog about that or an op-ed about that. But that's not the media's role to be the op-ed, or to be the *opinion*. And there are very few sources that are presenting the truth in an objective, factual way to let the audience come to their own conclusion. There are very few journalists that do that now.

Do you think the mainstream media is pushing a left-wing narrative?

Okay, let's talk about the left-wing bias in the mainstream media — because I am a *liberal.* I'm a registered *Democrat.* I have always been my entire adult life. And it wasn't until I became the subject of a smear campaign that I started to see through the liberal bias of the mainstream media. And now I see it everywhere. *Everywhere*! I mean, it's not just the news. It's the TV shows you watch and it's commercials and it's everywhere. It's the music videos that are being put out...it's the VMA Awards...it's *everywhere.* It's not just news television shows.

So, yeah, I absolutely see the left bias in the media and our pop culture programming that we get. And, you know, I guess because I'm a liberal and a registered Democrat, I was kind of the fish that couldn't see the water that I was swimming in. And, so I believed it *all*, back before making *The Red Pill* movie. I believed what SNL would joke about. I believed what Rachel Maddow would say. I believed it all and didn't question it. *Until I became the subject of the smear.*

And I was targeted by Fake News. So...and that's what's so upsetting, because I think when it's your own family and a label that you identify with and you hold proudly...I can't say I hold it proudly anymore. Not proudly. I still hold the label of "classical liberal," but not *proudly* anymore. And I think other people like me who do identify as liberals and are Democrats should call out the radicals. I mean *any* group should call out the radicals. And when you're putting tribalism over truth or ethics or integrity, your tribe is not going to have a very long existence.

How do you think we'll be able to heal the divide?

I think the people that are actually being smeared the most are the people in the *middle*. It's the conservatives that are willing to talk to the liberals, and the liberals that are willing to reach out to the conservatives, and there is a lot of discussion happening in the middle. And creating that bridge and wanting to challenge ideas and say, "If you give me an argument that is better than my own, I will change my position," — I think that's where we all need to be is willing to reach out across the aisle and talk to someone with a different label than your own. Those discussions are happening in the middle and they're being attacked by the mainstream media the most. And I don't know what is the cause of that. Do they want to keep this divide? They don't want people in the middle talking? They don't want people to find solutions and work together? They want to keep us on opposing teams — at *war* with each other? I mean, it looks like that. That's how it looks right now. But it is the people in the middle who are willing to-, I mean...and when you go on New Media or alternative media sources and see what they're doing, they are talking across the aisle. And there's Dave Rubin who's a liberal, talking to Alex Jones or Dinesh D'Souza and they are having those conversations, and it appears that the mainstream media is fearful of those conversations the most. And we need to ask, "Why?"

Why is the media going to all this trouble?

So why is the media going through all this trouble to smear outliers? I think that may be the age-old question. I hope it's not age-old. Maybe they just want sheep. They don't want independent thinkers. They don't want honest conversations about these difficult politically polarized issues. Maybe they see independent-thinking people as a powerful position and they don't want people to have that power. I don't know. Do you know?

It's scary times we're living in.

I'm trying to think of, like, what I could say to people who may encounter what I've been through. Because I do have a feeling that when there are people that are the target of a smear campaign, it's a warning to others to not do what she or he did.

But I think why smear campaigns happen to people like me is to send a warning to other people to not go off the reservation and do something like what I did. So the mainstream media-to-Fake News having the smear campaign against me was in an effort to make me an example — a warning — to: *Don't do that or we're going to do to you what we did to her.* And, I mean, you can see this — on even the most simplistic level — is like a classroom, where someone's acting out and/or asking too many questions. Now the teacher decides, "All right — that person — we're going to punish them and we're going to make a mockery of them and we're going to embarrass them and shame them." And now all the other students know: *we've got to keep in line*. Don't talk up, don't ask too many questions, don't fidget like he was, or whatever he was doing that got him in trouble. And it's a fear-mongering kind of tactic. Or it's a way to incite fear in people to keep in line with how they want the system to be. So I don't want people who are coming up who haven't yet had a smear campaign against them, but maybe have really good ideas on how to get out there-, I don't want them to be afraid of what's happened to me or anyone else like me who has been smeared and lied about in the media and dragged through the mud and completely had their what once was a wonderful reputation, now tainted and disparaged and blackened. I don't want people coming up to be fearful of speaking out because of those examples. Because there's also a lot of support in, maybe, E-mails...or whispers of saying, "Thank you for doing what you do." It really impacted me wonderfully. "You saved my family...you saved my life." I've had so many e-mails of people saying that they didn't take their life because they saw my film and they finally felt like their story was spoken up for. And that's what keeps me going is knowing that there are people — they may be in the shadows, they may not want to be public, they may not even want their name to be signed at the bottom of the e-mail, because they're that fearful of being attached to something with a stigma — but there are people that *need* it. And so, if there are courageous people that are willing to step into the limelight and take the tomatoes being thrown at them — or whatever kind of analogy you want to use for what happens to people that do that — it needs to be done. We need whistleblowers. And we need whistleblowers who aren't afraid of being smeared, because it's going to happen. It's a given. You are going to be smeared. Just take that as a badge of honor that you're doing something important if you're smeared, because obviously there's something — some forces at play that don't want you to speak up — and that means you need to speak even louder.

What are these forces?

Well, I think there's many different ways to silence people. You can silence them by affecting public perception that they shouldn't be listened to and efforts to discredit them. To assassinate their character. And that's definitely an effective way that works with-, if you want to know the-, *why*, you should follow the money. I think a lot of it leads back to where money is exchanging hands. Oh, if you want to know who's in power, look at who you can't criticize. And I am not going to take credit for that quote, because I think that's Winston Churchill — or someone like that said that. But I do think that's true. If you want to look at who is in power, look at you who you can't criticize.

Talk about your experience with Wikipedia.

One of the biggest "aha!" moments throughout: my time being the subject of a lot of lies being put out there about me. Something that was really disheartening to realize was how much you cannot trust Wikipedia. And I hate to say that in a lot of ways, because I also don't want to get in trouble from them. I don't know how powerful they are. But I've definitely started looking more into how Wikipedia pages are created. And, honest to God, I've never edited *anything* on Wikipedia. I still don't know how to do that. But I know that people can create a Wikipedia account and make edits and then those edits can be challenged. So I've watched how *The Red Pill*'s Wikipedia page has evolved over the past few years, and it's very apparent there is a war between Wikipedia accounts who are against me and my film and people who want to share the truth and print the truth on Wikipedia, and it's this back-and-forth battle. And every other day, I could go there and see a new-, either something that's truthful having been printed and then someone who wants to take that truth out that may make me or the film look good. And one of the most, I think, clear-cut apparent examples of this is the awards that my film has won — that *The Red Pill* has won. So we've won...let me just remember exactly...so *The Red Pill* movie has won six awards at four film festivals and this is shown on our IMDb page. It's shown on our website, but there's only been two different mainstream articles that wrote about our awards. One was an article that was written about our Idyllwild Film Festival award wins and they said that we won three awards at the Idyllwild Film Festival. And Wikipedia accepted that fact about the film that we won three awards at the Idyllwild Film Festival because there was an article that I wrote about that so they printed that. We won two other awards — won one in the Louisiana International Film Festival — we won Best Documentary. And also the Fly Film Festival in Oklahoma — we won Best Feature. But no mainstream source has written about those award wins. And apparently Wikipedia will only publish what has a mainstream source having written about it.

But here's where it gets strange: We won the Women in Film award at the Hollywood Digifest film festival. And there was one mainstream source that did print and publicize that we won the Women in Film award at the Digifest [Temecula] film festival. And the source was *Breitbart*. So someone on Wikipedia tried to publish on Wikipedia saying that *The Red Pill* movie won the Women in Film award at the Digifest [Temecula] film festival with the source being a *Breitbart* article link. So that was removed from Wikipedia with the argument that *Breitbart* was not a credible source. But, anywhere else, you can go to that film festival and ask them, "Did *The Red Pill* win this award?" and they would tell you, "Yes, you can see on our website, you can see on IMDb, you can see on your Facebook page, but Wikipedia's rules is that only a mainstream source can allow you to print this on the Wikipedia page." And they said that "*Breitbart* was not a credible source." Which, all the times that *Breitbart* has printed about me, every single article was *accurate*. And they've contacted me for exact quotes to put in their articles about me and I would write a paragraph for them, send it to them, and they would print exactly that. I've only seen — at least about my story — I've only seen *Breitbart* print the truth about my story, but Wikipedia wouldn't accept them as a *credible source*.

How has the mainstream media smear affected your career?

So how has my life been affected by the mainstream media's false portrayal of who I am? Well, it showed me who my true friends and family members are because they stuck by me. They knew the truth of who I am and that my intentions have always been pure. And the entire *The Red Pill* movie, and everything I've said in interviews since the release of that film, has always been accurate and consistent. But I did lose some friends, and some family members continue to refuse to see my film because of what the mainstream media has published about me. And, you know, moving forward with my career as a filmmaker...I don't know how this smear campaign will have impacted my future opportunities.

Do you regret doing it?

Oh, gosh, this is always one that gets me. I mean, I come from the mentality that *you get one life*. And tomorrow is not promised to you. And so I'm so grateful and I do feel very blessed in a lot of ways for all-, all the people who needed to *The Red Pill* and wrote to me saying that this film saved their life. And so, for that I am so happy that I made this film and I'm glad it's helped people. But I do, once in a while, wonder what would've been the trajectory of my life if I "zigged" instead of "zagged" — if I didn't complete *The Red Pill* — because I don't think I would have made a feminist propaganda film with *The Red Pill* footage I had. I don't think my conscience would have let me do that.

Knowing the footage I had and knowing the journey that I went on, I don't think that film would have ever been made in any kind of alternate universe. But it very well could have happened that the Kickstarter campaign wasn't successful. I didn't have the funds to complete the film myself and the footage was just shelved and I moved on and no one would have known about the film I would have made. And I could have still-, have written my own future and I think I've lost a lot of opportunities in the mainstream because of doing this. Do I regret doing it now having lost those opportunities now-, now also knowing that the mainstream isn't necessarily a place I want to be invited into now? But-, but I wouldn't have known that because I had to go through releasing the film and having the smear campaign against me to see how messed up the mainstream politics are. But I would have had a more quiet and peaceful life without having so many people really adamantly believe that I'm the devil. I mean, there's a whole country that I flew away from — Australia — that the majority of people there probably would have physically harmed me if-, if they had the opportunity to.

Could you talk about that Australian experience?

So...probably the most backlash that I've received, and my film has received, was in Australia where there are multiple theater chains that were planning to screen *The Red Pill* movie. They even had sold-out screenings. Every seat was purchased and paid for. But — protesters intimidated the theater owners into pulling the film and they succeeded in doing that. They created petitions where they gathered thousands of signatures from people who had never seen *The Red Pill* movie to say that *The Red Pill* movie should be banned from Australia. There was even a petition to ban me from ever entering Australia. And there were two different theater chains — Dendy's and Palace Cinemas —that removed *The Red Pill* from their screens before they had screenings ever get to take place. And they were sold-out screenings and the theaters chose to pull the film and essentially banned the film from their screens. And then the mainstream media in Australia all took on the same agenda-driven scripts that we are going to make this woman out to seem like she is a wolf in sheep's clothing. And that she's a paid-for MRA propagandist and that she-, I mean, even some of the interviews I did on Australian news that the lower third, where they would say the title of the episode they're doing, one of the titles was: Filmmaker Changes Her Views On Gender Equality. And that was the lower third title when I'm doing my interview. And the thing is, I did not change my views on gender equality. I actually *expanded* my views on gender equality — that we should consider men in the equation when we're talking about gender equality. But they wanted to make it seem like I was against women's rights. So they would say that "she changed her views on gender equality" to infer that I'm now against women's rights, which couldn't be further from the truth.

What are your thoughts on censorship?

I think there's a lot of different ways that censorship takes place in under-the-radar kind of ways. One of the big ways is funding. If you can exhaust someone's funding or refuse them funding or take away their funding source, you are going to effectively silence their voice. And I experienced that with *The Red Pill* where I submitted to over a dozen film grants and I was denied from *each and every one*. And...well I don't want to get into the Kickstarter thing again...

You could take away their funding. You could dismantle their Patreon which is what happened to Lauren Southern. That was her main funding source. You could deny them film grants like I was. Or another way to censor is you deny them a platform. And this is very effective and it's very difficult to fight, too, because I was denied a platform for *The Red Pill* movie when multiple different theater chains chose to pull the film from their screens. And many people who were against me, and promoting the ban of my film, would say, "This isn't censorship. She doesn't have an innate right to be able to screen her movie in a movie theater. Go somewhere else." But all the other theaters were fearful — they didn't want to invite protesters. They didn't want to incite the kind of rage-filled people with pitchforks going to their theater doors saying, "How dare you screen this misogynistic film?" They don't want to invite that kind of attention. So there weren't other platforms that we could go to. The theaters pulled the film and then all the other theaters cowered. So it was censorship, but there are people saying, "Oh, it's not censorship. You don't get an innate right to have your movie screened in a theater." You don't have a voice as a filmmaker if you don't have a theater to screen your film in. That is a take-, that is taking away your microphone. That is taking away your voice and your free speech. So if you're a YouTuber, and you have your YouTube channel banned or suspended for some reason...if you-, if your main following is on Facebook and you have that suspended for however long...if you're on Twitter — look at Milo: his biggest following was on his Twitter, his fan base is narrow, and he was banned from Twitter. He was pulled from Twitter forever...I see that as an attack on free speech. It is censorship and there's many different ways to censor, whether it's through funding or denying them funding. Pulling them from their funding source. Denying them a platform. If you're a filmmaker, that's a theater, that's your platform. If you're a public speaker, and different universities de-platform you, saying you cannot speak any more — look at Richard Dawkins. He was supposed to speak at the atheist conference and he was de-platformed for something he said against feminists. I mean, how many times have-, have conservative speakers been de-platformed from college campuses. I see that as an attack on free speech.

So...okay. You know that saying that, "If a tree falls in a forest, and no one's there to hear it, did it really fall?" If a film is made and there's nowhere you can release the film, is there really a film? There's only one platform that declined releasing *The Red Pill* movie and it was Netflix. And my distributor was in discussions with them for at least two months and they seemed positive that they were going to go through with releasing *The Red Pill.* And at the last minute — the 11th hour — they decided to decline the film...shut the door on us...locked it. No discussion moving forward. They didn't give us a reason why. They didn't say if it was political reasons or topic-based. We were the bestselling film on YouTube — in multiple territories — in Sweden, in Australia. And this was the bestselling film — not just documentary, but film — ahead of Moana and Guardians of the Galaxy and Rogue One, the Star Wars movie. We were the bestselling film. And Netflix *declined* it. I don't know why they would decline a bestselling film on multiple platforms in other countries. Unless it's political. And I know that a lot of the documentaries that they screened on that platform are feminist-leaning and that my documentary *The Red Pill* doesn't go with that agenda.

What is the mainstream media going to say about *Hoaxed*?

What is the mainstream media going to say about *Hoaxed*? Well...I don't think you should be anxious to hear what they're going to say. I don't think you'll want to hear what they're going to say. But, hey! Whatever they say, it just proves the point of your film. And I think they know. That's-, that's the difficulty of where they're in right now, is if anyone tries. Like I said, if you want to know who has the power, look at you can't criticize. We have free speech in this country or we should we believe that to be a value that we want to uphold. Do you have the free speech to criticize the media? I mean, I would think that the media says that the backbone of the-, the backbone of what they do is they exercise their free speech. But do we, the people, have free speech to criticize the media? We'll find out.

STEFAN MOLYNEUX INTERVIEW

Could you state your name and what you do?

My name is Stefan Molyneux and I'm a philosopher.

So, I have been debating and thinking and reasoning since I can barely remember, and I have sort of taken those skills and refined them. I've had some fairly good formal education in philosophy through a graduate degree, but I have really been inspired by Socrates. Who did not seal himself off in an ivory tower, but went among the people, spoke about philosophy, attempted to bring the rationality of reason and evidence to their daily concerns, and their hopes and aspirations and their fears. And so, I do a call-in show. I get a lot of questions. And I really strongly engage with the public. I rely on donations. There's no advertisements. And most of my books are free. So I really try to bring my talents and abilities as a philosopher to daily concerns, whether it's politics or personal relationships or professional ambitions or anxieties. There's a lot that philosophy can do to serve humanity, which, unfortunately, it's kind of been separated from doing because we take people good at this kind of stuff and we often bribe them with tenure in academic positions, and four months off in the summer, on the condition that they do not say anything that really changes the world. I'm aiming to try and reverse that trend and bring philosophy down from the clouds into the marketplace of ideas.

I'm the host of Freedomain Radio at Freedomainradio.com. And it is a show really devoted to philosophy, from first principles, and examining their impact on personal events. On world events. On families. On careers. Because reason and evidence has to be, how are we going to guide the future — if we're going to have a future that's civilized. And that's been my mission as a public intellectual for about a decade, and for a long time before that — in a much more private capacity.

The mainstream media are the newest incarnation of the ancient enemy of philosophy which is sophistry. Sophistry is using every emotional trick in the book to make a terrible argument appear compelling. And they appeal to your sentimentality, and they appeal to your fear, because they will attack you if you step out of line. They serve their own lust for power. They serve their political masters' lust for control, and it is the enemy that philosophers have been fighting for over two thousand years. But now we have the ultimate weapon, which is a direct connection to the people. And we can bring our case — I can bring my case directly — to the people, without interference. And let's see who wins.

You mentioned that you cover world affairs. What would that include?

Well, politics. You know, there's an old saying from Plato that you can choose not to get involved in politics, but the net result "is that you end up being governed by your inferiors." And so, I critiqued politics for a long time before I got into the political arena. But ever since demographic winter and immigration issues and cultural dilution, and so on, I have waded into the political arena particularly with the Trump campaign and my interest in that. And so, I do a lot of politics. But I also do metaphysics — [the] nature of reality. Epistemology — the study of knowledge.

Ethics, in particular — like, why should we be *good*? If you don't accept that the government just has to order you to be good, or if you don't accept that there's a sacred text that orders you to be good...if you want to be self-generated in your virtue, what are the reasons behind that? And also, if you don't believe in a transcendent consciousness that runs the universe, how do you have meaning? How do you have virtue? How do you have truth? And what is its value? And that — really, I think — is the job of philosophy.

Have you ever had any experience with the media?

I have, in fact, had personal experience with media and media outlets. And because, when you're on the receiving end, you read all these stories and you say, "Oh, well, there's this and that. It's interesting." Or, "Sometimes I agree with this, and sometimes I disagree with this." But I think most people — and Michael Crichton talked about this as well — is most people, if you have expertise in a particular subject and you read what the mainstream media talks about, you're like, "*Whoa*. That is *not* correct." Like, I'm really good at computers — been working with computers since I was eleven. And whenever I go to a movie where they talk about anything to do with computers, you know, like, "Hey, let's take this USB drive and disable this Alien operating system." And it's like, "No, that's not how it works." And it's the same thing with the media. When you have expertise in something, and the media writes about it, it's wrong. And then there is this kind of belief that everything else they write about this is just an anomaly. This is just a blip where I happen to know stuff.

But my dealings with the media were mostly about ten years ago, and I found that it was very much distorted from the questions that were asked to me directly, versus what sort of came out the other end. And I realized that it is very much a driven agenda. The agenda is not driven by the pursuit of truth or illumination or exposition or explanation. They're not there to *educate*. They're there to propagandize. They're there to control people who step out of a particular social set of rules. And they are there, sort of like the whipmasters, to discipline people who don't follow the correct narrative. And they're really there as a whip-arm of, a lot of times, political elites. But other economic interests as well.

Have you been personally lied about in a news story?

I'm actually trying to think of a time when I haven't been personally lied about in news stories. So, I think the answer to that would be, "One hundred fifty percent *yes*." And I think that's-, it's a shame. But it's one of the things that's a lesson that you can learn brutally and you learn early. It's like being bullied. You know, like, you have to fight back hard, whether verbally or physically. You have to create the space where people don't want to mess with you. And I think that I may have spoken to the media three times about ten years ago, and the output that came out was just so unrecognizable from the conversations that we had, that it's like trying to dictate your life story to somebody who doesn't speak your language. They're just going to write whatever they feel like, because they don't really understand what you're saying.

How did Fake News impact your life?

Well, it made me very committed to what it is that I do. I came out of the entrepreneurial world. Like, some of my background is: I actually went to theater school and then I got a graduate degree in history. Really focused on the history of philosophy. And then I got into the IT world as an entrepreneur.

So, how has fake news impacted me *personally*? I would say that it's made me very committed to what it is that I do. Because, I sort of started in the theater world, while I did half a degree in English literature, went to the National Theatre School [of] Canada, then got a graduate degree in history — really focusing on the history of philosophy. And then I was an entrepreneur for quite some time. Co-founded a company. Grew it. And was involved in the sale and it going public through a parent company.

And then I just started podcasting, because I had a long commute, and I was like, "I'm tired of audiobooks." I just, you know, I've had these ideas. I would have, actually, debates and arguments *out loud* in my car. You know, it's good that there were cell phones back then, because I didn't look completely insane. And I just started publishing stuff.

And I was like, "Yeah, maybe I can find a way to blend these two things." I really enjoyed the-, the world of software entre preneurship, and maybe I'll just sort of do this a little bit on the side. But then when the media sort of got their hooks into what it is that I was doing and to create, in a sense, a firewall between me and, you know, the business world, because back in the day-, because things are moving so rapidly now. It's hard to comprehend how quickly things are changing. Back in the day, when the media would write negative things about you, I mean, it was there. You know, people could search for it. It was there. And there was no real capacity to respond. Because, you know, the alternative media and allies and other places — where you could put out a response — really wasn't available. So they had a lot of power back in the day. More so than they even had in the past. Because in the past, you know, this old saying that, you know, "Today's news is tomorrow's fish wrapper." If they publish something mean or untrue about you, people have got to go to like microfilms and stuff like that to find it out and nobody really bothers. But there was a time when they could publish stuff. It would be burned into people's brains, available in a search, with no real capacity to respond. Now that's, I think, been diminished a lot.

So, what happened was — when I was first attacked — I was, like...two thoughts were in my head. Number one is like, "I've got to be close to something," you know, "I've got to be close to something really important — if these kinds of guns are coming out." And number two: Given that it's important, and given also that you know people search, and so on, there's really no going back. And, in a sense, it was enormously helpful to help me know where I was relative to the important issues in society. And also to overcome any temptation — which, I think, we all have when you have a new direction — to say, "Well, maybe I can just blend these two. I can balance these two." It's like, "I know I'm close to something important. And I better be all-in, because there's no turning back."

How did they find you? It's always interesting to me how they choose their targets.

Well, I did shows that were just me speaking out about abstract topics. I love economics, and so on. And then I do a call-in show, where people call in and ask me, sort of, questions related to philosophy. And some of those are very abstract. Some of those are more personal. And when you talk about abstract issues, you get a lot of latitude, because nobody can really trace the impact of what you're saying into their own personal lives and changes that might happen. When you talk to people about their own personal issues, then the traceability of philosophy-to-personal impact is very close.

So, I think that somebody was upset with something that I was talking about — maybe somebody in my call-in show — and then roused the media that way. And now, looking back, you know, it's the old thing: *Life would be a lot easier if you had the hindsight* boomerang. Now, looking back, I really do understand what it was all about. But, at the time, of course, it was really quite bewildering and surprising. If you've never been part of that kind of targeting, it's really quite a surprise when it first happens. And you do, of course-, and the fascinating thing is: When enemies emerge, so do friends. And that is something... there's a little bit of a lag, and that little bit of time can be quite exciting psychologically. But when you get targeted, you also get allies. And that's *really* worth it in many ways.

Let's talk about it psychologically: What was your experience, like, with public shaming when you experienced it for the first time?

Well, I certainly felt some fear, because when you want to be a good person, you want to have a good reputation. I mean,

I'm very aware of that. I think that old saying, you know, "A reputation can take-, takes decades to build and five minutes to destroy." But what I think was a saving grace for me was because I have such a strong foundation in reason and evidence and virtue and philosophy. First of all, I know philosophers are publicly shamed on a regular basis. The whole point of being a philosopher is not to tell people things they already know. You know, you don't take an advanced course in physics for somebody to say, "Hey, let go of the ball. It falls down." You want to be told things that are surprising and unusual. You know, "The speed of light is constant." "There's no such thing as ether." "The sun and the moon are different sizes." "The earth is flat." You want to hear all those things. And, so, the job of the philosopher is to push the envelope of what people find acceptable. To move that Overton Window to areas that are surprising. You know, "Hey, we've always had slavery." And then certain philosophers came along and said, "Maybe that's not a good idea." We've always had aristocracy. "The King is planted there by God to rule over you." And people are like, "Well, maybe not."

And that's very unsettling, because there are existing power structures that rest fundamentally on belief. Not on empirical reality. Certainly not on rationality. They rest on belief. And philosophers throughout history who come along and say, "Maybe what you think is true — what you accept as the physics of your environment — is nothing more than historical era reinforced by inertia." And reinforced by power structures such as the mainstream media.

So, I kind of knew that that was part of the game. The topic that erupted was more around voluntary family relationships, which was a little bit more surprising to me. Because what I thought about I was talking about politically was much more, quote, "radical." But what saved me, and what's helped me to build a stronger organization and a stronger public presence, was a simple refusal to internalize it. Right? Because it's one thing to be shamed as, "You're bad," from the outside. And if you don't allow that to pass into your inner-, like, if you don't allow shame to be transferred to guilt, then it's a growing experience. If you internalize it: "I did do something wrong. I am a bad person. I am doing horrible things," then they have successfully implanted that, sort of, superego finger-wagging into your own mind. And then you are in a great deal of trouble. Because then you're not fighting error. You're not fighting liars. You're not fighting the world and evildoers in it. You're now fighting *yourself*. And that's almost always a losing battle in the long run.

How have these structures changed over the last few years?

Other than maybe the invention of the printing press, there's not been a bigger change in human communications. And if we look at, of course, the invention of the printing press — I won't go into all the details — but, it did fragment a monolith of thought, which was Christendom at the time, into a bunch of different sects. And the result was a lot of social conflict. Some of it verbal, and, of course — given the primitive nature of the political structures at the time — often very violent. And so, when you have a monolithic structure of thought, and people have the capacity to pass the gatekeepers...

...You know, when I was in graduate school, I had thought, to some degree, about a career in academia. Because there was no real Internet back in the day. And so, the idea of like, "Well I'll just take my case directly to the people," was not a possibility. So I found, though, of course, that you really are swimming against the current. And it's a very-, kind of soft censorship. I think what goes on in the mainstream media, when somebody who's not on the left comes and tries to apply for a job, they're all like, "Well, thank you very much for your time." The person leaves. They're like, "Can you believe that guy tried to get a job here?" It's a very soft kind of pushback. They don't say, "It's wrong. It's written down here. You can't do it." It's all soft bigotry.

So what has changed now is that it's become a real meritocracy in the public sphere. Because before there were all these gatekeepers: the publishers, the editors, the academics, the boards... whoever. You name it. Where if you didn't please the people who were there, you couldn't get through to the audience and hope to please them. Because there were these people who stood between you and the audience.

Now with the Internet, like, I started with a twenty-dollar mic and a ten-dollar webcam and you can speak directly to the people. And it's interesting to me that the same thing happened with the software industry, which revolutionized the communications industry. In the software industry it's a meritocracy. If you look at the people who are at the top of the software industry, very few of them have — what? — PhDs in computer science. They are all-, it's a meritocracy. They had great ideas. They willed it. They pushed forward. They got their products out.

And the meritocracy that occurs in the software field is mirrored by the meritocracy that they then facilitated in the communications field. Where — if you are good, if you have intelligence and you have new and interesting things to say, if you're willing to be charismatic and be vulnerable and make jokes and whatever it is that you do to engage your audience — it's you and it's the audience and nobody's in between.

Like, before you had the texts of Christianity, you had the clergy. And the clergy was the ones who told you what was in the text. And the clergy spoke it in Latin, after which the common people didn't speak. So, if you had a question, you went to the priest. You couldn't go to the text itself until the printing press. And Martin Luther. Now there is no cadre of thought blockers between those who wish to engage with the public and the public. So, it's turned into a real meritocracy. And because you are fighting hard to establish credibility.

You know, something comes out from-, I don't know... *The New York Times* or whatever. And people are like, "Well, you know, it's the paper of record. It's the old gray lady. It's got to be pretty solid." But if you're just some guy out there, how do you build your credibility? You have to work extra hard. You've got to work *really* hard. I remember this from the entrepreneurial world: You go up against a company like IBM, you got to offer something, say, "Well, we're going to work harder." "We're going to be more innovative." "We're going to be more nimble." "We're going to," you know, "charge less." Whatever it is that you do, because, you know, nobody ever gets fired for buying IBM. And so, the same thing: You're up against these giant monolithic structures that still have so much credibility to so many people. You've just got to work that much harder to engage people and to gain credibility. And I guess I'm just prejudiced. Maybe it's the Protestant in me. The sort of...maybe I'm prejudiced towards people who are just willing to work harder. But I think that's the biggest change. It's you. It's the audience. And it's a conversation without interference.

What would you say are the biggest differences between new media and old media?

Well, I think-, I mean...this is going to sound kind of prosaic in a way, Mike, but to me the biggest difference between new media and old media is the funding structures. The funding structures. The media is-, old media doesn't have the goal of delivering newspapers to you or news to you or entertainment to you. It has the goal of delivering you to their advertisers. And advertisers *rule*. Advertisers *dictate*. And advertisers are pretty conservative in many ways. We can see this with some of the demonetization stuff. Advertisers are pretty conservative. They don't want to rock too many people's boats. They don't want to be associated with a "negative brand." So there is a kind of, "Don't upset people," from advertisers. And, of course, the wiring in of the mainstream media with leftist politics has also created that kind of unity, whereas so the relationship with the mainstream media is often with the leftist politics — leftist politicians — and with their advertisers. And it's not primarily with the audience.

The new media — you have to appeal to the audience. I mean, nobody is going to say, "I am starting up a podcast. Hey 'company,' do you want to advertise with me?" They'll be like, "Forget it." Right? So the goal, of course, is to connect with the audience and the funding models that people use. You know — donations. Or you use it to support book sales or speaking tours or something like that. It's very different. Because your money is generally flowing from the audience themselves. Because you don't have-, even on-, on YouTube, when people monetize, you don't have a direct relationship with the advertisers. They're just kind of thrown into the mix by some algorithm. So the fact that...

Everybody follows incentives, right? Basic law of economics. And if your incentive is: *I must be able to provide value to my audience. If I can't provide value to my audience, I don't have a business.* Whereas the mainstream media is: *I want to get leftists elected and I want to provide value to my advertisers.* The audience is secondary or tertiary to the fundamental equation. And I think that direct relationship is one of the reasons why the new media, I think, is fundamentally more honest in terms of being responsive to the audience.

What's the difference between news and propaganda?

So, the difference between news and propaganda is very blurry in many ways, because there's no such thing as "objective news." I mean, I'm-, I'm fully onboard with that. I'm no postmodernist, but, as far as that goes, when I choose to do a story — you choose to do a story — we do so for a particular reason. There is a near infinity of stories that you could do at any point during the day. And the ones that you choose are because it fits into a particular goal. And I think as long as people are open and honest about that — that's one of the differences between the new media and the old media: The new media say, "Yeah, I've got biases. Yeah, I've got preferences. Yeah, I have got a goal. Yeah, maybe I even have an agenda. And I'm up front about it." Whereas the old media has all of this pseudo-objectivity camouflage designed to cloak what they're really up to.

So propaganda, to me, is when you have a goal and you work backwards from there, saying, "What do I need to say to achieve my goal?" Like, you go and buy a car — you're going to a [car] lot. And maybe you buy a car — maybe you don't. So, you know that the car salesman wants you to sign on that line so he can get his commission. Now, he probably also wants you to have a good experience buying the car, say, so you'll bring your friends and come back or whatever. But he is working backwards from that signature saying, "Okay, here are the steps that I need to take in order to get you to-," and they say that openly: "What do I need to say to get your signature on the dotted line? What do I need to say to get you driving out of here in a new car?" Right? I mean, they're very open about that. They have a *goal.*

Propaganda is when you have a goal that you want people to do: X, Y, or Z. Propaganda is like a yippy dog in a way. So, propaganda is when you want people to do something *specifically* and you work your way back from that. And when you *don't say that*. Again, you watch an advertisement and people show you some tasty beer. They want you to go put your money down and try their beer. All right — fair. Everybody knows that. Everyone knows it's not an objective beer analysis. It's, you know, "Buy this beer."

But when you do have a specific goal — which, for the mainstream media is *vote Democrat,* or *support some big giant government program,* or *don't control immigration because immigration is a source of leftist votes* — when they have that as a goal, and they don't state it either explicitly or implicitly, but they claim to be objective, but they are as driven as the used car salesman in getting you to do something, that, to me, is where the real propaganda is. The moment somebody says, "Okay, here's my agenda. Here's my preference. And I'm going to try and lead you to the truth, because I believe my own agenda and the truth are, you know, mostly united." That, to me, is not propaganda, because you are being open about what the goal is. You're transparent about your methodologies. And your goal is to try and enlighten people, rather than get them to do something that serves your interest without telling them that's your goal.

Fake News is a recent term, but has a storied history. What would be a prominent, catastrophic example of Fake News?

I measure things in terms of headcount. The biggest headcount for Fake News is communism as a whole — communism as a whole. Lots of people have done a lot of research and they can't really narrow it down within the five to ten million range of the headcount. But reasonable estimates are close to a hundred million dead just in the 20th century from communism alone.

And there are still people out there with Karl Marx buttons. You know, you try and wear a Hitler button. Hitler's head count was far lower with communism. You go out there with a Karl Marx button and people are like, "Oh, that's edgy." Or, you know, Che Guevara T-shirt and this proselytizing and pumping up of communism that happens.

And we see this recently: "Women had better sex lives in Soviet Russia." I mean, like, "Okay, so, sure. It's a hundred million death count, but at least I get a toe-clenching orgasm out of it." It's like, that's horrifying and horrible kind of weighing in the balance. So, covering up, to me, the crimes of communism, which was done very explicitly. And we know that Walter Duranty of *The New York Times* got a Pulitzer for his reporting on the Potemkin villages under Stalin. When he was toured around and they're all, "Look at these fat, happy workers." And they were just taken out of the Gulags, stuffed full of chicken, and thrown in front of his eyeballs. And this has never, to my knowledge, been disavowed nor rejected.

The infiltration of Hollywood — this is more controversial to people who have not been red-pilled in this area — but the infiltration into Hollywood and other media outlets of open communists...this occurred in Hollywood. This occurred in the State Department, who virtually served up China to Chairman Mao, who then proceeded to slaughter tens of millions of people.

Starve them to death. Brutalize them. Torture them. Murder them. Kill their children in front of them. Throw them into Gulags. The whole nightmare. This was handed over by the State Department, who were full of communists. Some of them were directly taking orders from Moscow.

And then, you know, the two big media hit pieces over the last half century — for those who are a little older, two big media hit pieces, where Joseph McCarthy, a little more than half a century ago, and Richard Nixon, and both of those people were involved — Richard Nixon originally got Joe McCarthy started on looking at the communists in Hollywood and in the media. And you had these two great hit jobs because these guys were exposing this toxic and murderous ideology embedded within the American political system, the entertainment system, the media system. And that brutality of: "Don't disturb my murderous ideology. Don't disturb my murderous intent." That is where the most blowback occurs: When you are directly threatening the interests of extremely vicious and immoral people. And that's where the biggest blowback occurs, I think.

I believe it was *The New York Times* who went to Cuba and covered Castro. He had just a few guerrilla soldiers. He had them march one way and hide — and then put on a new outfit and march the other way. And *The New York Times* did a big write-up...Castro has this huge amount of support. And that was actually a big morale support for him. A lot of people said that was a big tipping point towards his taking over Cuba.

Well look at Augusto Pinochet in Chile: One of the great demon overlords in the leftist pantheon is Pinochet. And Pinochet was begged by the Chilean government to stop the communist takeover under Allende. Because they had seen what had happened in other countries. And he ruled as a dictator for, I think, more than a decade and a half and ended up relinquishing power. Was he a great guy? I don't know...but compared to *communism*?

The fact that North Korea started as a communist state is very much overlooked. And this artificial split again between these two warring groups — like the National socialists in Germany in the 1930s and the communists. You know, there was an old saying about Germany in the 1930s: They said that a communist is a beefsteak red on the outside/brown on the inside, for the Brown Shirts of the Nazis. And the idea that these were two vastly opposing forces is also not honestly reported. Even the word, "Nazi," because they don't want to say, "national socialist," because then that word, "socialist," falls under disrepute. So they had to invent an entirely new word.

What other group has that kind of cloak — that kind of linguistic cover? So there are a brutal number of Fake News stories about the hideous nature of communism. And given that the facts are so easily available — given that the data is so easily available — I really do more than question. I have nothing but bottomless contempt for the people who cover this stuff up, because they are aiding and abetting some of the greatest genocides in human history.

Could you talk more about Walter Duranty?

So, with Walter Duranty, there were stories coming out of Russia in the 1930s. A hugely closed system/massive propaganda wall between what was going on in Russia and what was going on outside of Russia. But lots of questions about it. One of the big problems that they had — and this goes back almost 100 years now — that in the early 1920s, an Austrian economist, by the name of Ludwig von Mises, published a whole series of takedowns of socialism. In particular, he focused on this issue called the "price issue." Which is that, when you have a free market, you have a price which signals supply and demand and signals where resources should be best applied. When you have a kind of push centrally planned economy, you don't have prices, so you don't know where to allocate resources.

This was completely counter to the received wisdom at the time, because capitalism for the free market was-, because...*it was chaotic!* It was random. It was unorganized. It was unmanaged. You know, when they say the word, "unregulated — 'It's an *unregulated* market.'" People think it's crazy. They're throwing babies off buildings! And it's like, "No, it just means *free.*" They say "unregulated" when they mean "free." And it very much went against the wisdom of the time to say that a centrally planned economy cannot possibly work. It doesn't matter the intentions. It doesn't matter the virtues. It doesn't matter the processes or procedures that go in place. You simply *can't* make it work.

And this is very much what happens with the lefties. When they lose an idea war, they escalate the propaganda war, which then results in the actual physical war. The physical combat. The Civil War. This happened in the 1960s under Khrushchev and when the crimes of Stalin came out — which we can get to — but in the 1920s, these continual takedowns of socialist ideology, of central planning ideology, where somebody's confidently predicting it can't work...it cannot work. No matter what you want out of it. And so, because they couldn't reply to it-, they tried, but they failed. They couldn't reply to it. So, of course, did they give up their ideology when it's proven false? No. They're ideologues. They're cultists.

So, what they do is, they escalate the propaganda war. And what that meant was taking a whole bunch of reporters — Duranty was just one of them — taking a whole bunch of reporters out of the West, and putting them behind the Iron Curtain in Russia, and saying, "What do you mean it doesn't work? Look around you. You know, this is wonderful." And you can see this in North Korea: They put these Potemkin villages out there in North Korea, as well. We've got these happy peasants who we see smiling and so on, because, you know, they get shot if they don't.

So they brought all these intellectuals and reporters over and they showed them — in a very tightly controlled environment — they showed them how socialism was working and how "happy" everyone was. And it really didn't take a lot of skepticism to say, "Okay, this is what you're showing me — I want to see stuff that you're not expecting me to see. I want to go to this random village today." And then you actually see how it goes. Because you can manufacturer sets. You can manufacture statistics — your "Five-Year Plan." You can type whatever you want into that. But the intellectuals were very keen to provide empirical information that they felt was going to counter the anti-communist theories of the Austrian economists — the free market economists — as a whole. You know, they pull all these people over and these people all came back and said, "Oh, no, it's working beautifully." It was not an argument — it was just manufactured evidence.

And that helped stretch out the communist regime for another couple of decades. And it helped to spread the communist regime to other places in the world: Korea, North Korea, North Vietnam, Cambodia, China. You know, there was a time when a third of the planet was under communist dictatorship. That had a lot to do with the intellectuals who came across and spewed the propaganda that they were fed. And they were happy to do it, because they wanted to save the system — not deal with the facts.

Didn't Walter Duranty cover up the Ukranian famine?

The Holodomor: One of the unbelievable, brutal, and overlooked genocides, in many ways. They had horrible stuff going on. So, this is typically the way that it works, which is: Very few people are actually competent in the world. I mean, it's one of the sad-but-true things. And, you know, I'm not competent in most things. There's a few things I'm good at. Very few people are competent. And, in a free market, resources tend to accrue to the people who are the most competent. And that's better for everyone. Because you want to have enough to eat. So, you want the land to end up under the control of the most productive people. But what th-, and this is because of the bell curve of IQ and all that. And just the bell curve of ability. But the communists come along and say, "Okay, you're working for this guy. Not because he's smarter. Or works harder. Or takes more risks. Or studies more. But because he's *exploited* you. He has stolen from you. And we're going to get back what is yours. We're going to get back that land. We're going to split it up among you..."

So, what they did was, they went into the Ukraine, which was formerly called, "The bread basket of Europe." The soil is so rich. I mean, it's just astonishing. You can, you know, spit out a hayseed — you come back, and you got like 12 loaves of bread the next day. It's insanely productive land. And, what they did was, they took the land from the most productive people, called the "bourgeoisie." The "kulaks." The most productive farmers.

And then they shot or imprisoned or drove off those farmers, and handed it out to the people who were incompetent. And the same thing, of course, happened whenever they collectivized the farms. And the same thing is happening in Venezuela now.

Because there's a wild thing that happens between the farms and the cities: If the currency is undermined, farmers don't want to send their goods to the city, because you don't hand over an iPhone for a Monopoly [game] dollar. It's not real money. And, of course, there were all these problems with currency under the communists, so the farmers didn't want to send their goods to the cities. And so, of course, rather than improve the currency, they just send troops around to try and round up the food from the farmers, and so on. And the starvation then resulted.

And exactly the same thing happened under Mao, where you had people-, they would rip open their pillows and eat the goose feathers trying to get nutrition. They would eat bark hoping to get something — some insects — something under the bark. I mean, unbelievably horrifying stuff.

And this was all covered up. The reports were coming out. Just like the reports were coming out about the Holocaust. The reports were coming out and people were frantically covering it up. Now, of course, they'd say, "Well, this is just counterrevolutionaries spreading disinformation." But they did not examine it as much as they should have. And millions and millions of people starved to death as a result.

And the reason why it's so sinister — which you've talked about before, Mike — is that they want us *dead*. If you openly cover up for a regime that the first people targeted are people like you and me, I can't view this as a merely ideological dispute. This is not an academic difference in opinion, because if the system that they want gets in power, myself or my friends, my family, everything will be the first to go. And this is what happens, because they can't win the argument. They keep losing the argument — ideologically, empirically, factually. They keep losing the argument, but they won't let go of the ideology. And so they have no choice but to escalate.

You know, the moment you pull out either: slander, abuse at a social level, or a law, or a gun, or a concentration camp, you have lost the argument. And the regularity with which the left escalates to violence is, to me, an indication of just how badly they have lost the argument. They will not accept that what they want *cannot* work and is not only inhumane, but anti-human. And so, they have to continue to escalate. And anybody with any knowledge of history knows exactly where that leads. And if you can see the bodies in the language, you fight the language ferociously — because you know where that language leads us.

That leads us to Antifa violence. Why do you think the media won't give them coverage?

Well, the reason that the media covers up the Antifa violence is they want it. Because they don't want open conversation in the public sphere. They do not want open competition. They do not want a marketplace of ideas. Because they *lose*. Every. Single. Time. They lose. Facts, reason, evidence — with the accumulated weight of the 20th century — anybody who's out there defending leftism, socialism, communism...is anti-human. And they know that they're going to lose.

If conservative arguments-, if non-leftist arguments were so terrible, bring them on. *Bring them on.* Invite them to come and speak to your audience. Bring them in. Advertise. Broadcast. Have everyone come. You know, I had a guy at my show: I spent an hour talking about the "flat earth" with him. Great! Bring it on. I'm curious. You know, I take *nothing* for granted. You know, tell me all about it.

And so, if these ideas are bad, turn the light on. Turn the light on. If the painting is so ugly, why do you keep turning it to the wall? Turn it around! Let us embrace and see and understand and reject how terrible these arguments are. But they don't do that. And why don't they let in on leftist speak? Why do they use violence? Why do they oppose? Because they cannot overcome through language. They cannot overcome through reasoning. They cannot overcome through debate. And, therefore, they must smash the mouth whose words they cannot reply to.

Here's what they say — they say: "This Fake News thing, when it comes to Pizzagate, it leads to a guy shooting a gun in a pizza store." But they don't acknowledge the deaths that result, for example, from the second Iraq War.

Sure, sure — so the question of hypocrisy. It's not always a winning strategy to use it in a debate. But it is a very important thing to understand the genesis of how this all comes about. And so this criticism is generally that: The left — whenever there's a tragedy that involves a non-leftist, you know, like Stephen Paddock shooting in Vegas — they will politicize it immediately. *Immediately*. It's about "white male privilege." It's about... you name it. They will politicize it immediately. When another tragedy or act of violence occurs, like the recent attack in New York City by the Muslim, [it's]: "Hey! You can't politicize it. It's *wrong* to politicize."

And it's-, of course! To expect non-hypocrisy from most people in the intellectual realm is a fantasy. In my particular-, I can't prove this, but I think there's strong reasonable arguments behind it: Language, philosophy, ethics, universality was invented by and for hypocrisy. Because if I can create a moral rule that says, "Don't use violence," and then except myself from that moral rule, I have disarmed you, and I'm now elevated and powerful. If I go into a boxing ring, and I've convinced the guy verbally to not fight back very hard — or not fight back at all — but, look at that!: World Champion.

So, of course, you want to create these universal rules and immediately except yourself from those rules. That's where you get your power. So, to me, trying to make universal ethics and to oppose this kind of Saul Alinsky "exceptionalism" and all of that — it's kind of taking a weapon that was designed for resource exploitation for grabbing things from people. For making people feel guilty so that you can continue to inflict verbal abuse on them. Like, you're punching them, so they say, "Okay, here's five hundred bucks to stop punching me, okay? Here's money to stop attacking me. Here's money to stop calling me a 'racist.' Here's money to stop me from being called 'homophobic.' Here's money to stop me from being called 'xenophobic.' Just stop pushing my *horror* button. Stop pushing my *guilt* button. Stop pushing my *shame* button. I'm going to cough up."

You know, in the old mafia example, it's like, "Hey, nice pizza restaurant you got here. Be a shame if something happened to it." It's like, "Hey, nice self-esteem you got there. Nice view of yourself you got there. Nice reputation you got there. It'd be a shame if something happened to it. So, maybe you better tow the line and pay the hell up. Otherwise, we're going to burn your reputation down to the ground." This kind of shakedown has been going on from the beginning. Hypocrisy is why universals and ethics are invented, and the fact that the left uses it merely confirms that thesis.

Now, there are those of us who want to close that loophole and say, "Okay, universality is what you claim. We're going to hold you to that standard. And we're going to try and close this loophole of hypocrisy." And that is a very ferocious battle, because people live and live and survive and thrive on that hypocrisy — on that loophole. Trying to close it is very volatile.

So, the fact that leftists create rules, and then except themselves from those rules, that is the standard! That is why those rules were invented. To disarm you and to arm themselves. Like, when people say, "Oh, we've got to get rid of people's guns in society." Well, you've got to have a very well-armed government to take people's guns away. So they want themselves to be armed and you to be disarmed. That is the whole point. It's the same thing with ethics.

So, the fact that the left creates loopholes for themselves is entirely to be expected. And the right does it sometimes, as well. Trying to close those loopholes — this is what people live on. This is where they get their meat and their rent money and their milk and their survival. So, trying to close that loophole is extremely volatile.

So, you have facts and fallacies. It seems that fallacies are more persuasive in the culture. What advice do you have for people to discern between the two?

So, the question of, "facts versus fallacies?" is something that I have been deluded for a lot of my adult life. Everybody has this fantasy. This fantasy is that someone comes up with an idea or an argument and they're wrong. The facts go against them. Their reasoning is fallacious. And you point this out. And you say, you know, "The facts don't support what you're saying. In fact, they support the opposite. And, by the way, your reasoning is incorrect here, here, and here. You've made a mistake here."

And then the fantasy...ooh, wouldn't we all love to go there? I don't know what you have to smoke to get there, but it probably has something to do with time travel to the future, hopefully. But the fantasy is: People say, "Wow...thank you. Thank you *so* much!" You know, if you're driving the wrong direction, and you stop and ask someone, and they say, "You're going the wrong way." And you're late for something: It's like, "Thank you! Thank you so much for putting me in the right path."

That's the fantasy. But that's not what happens, unfortunately, in reality at the moment. In reality, people don't make their decisions according to reason and evidence. They have emotional preferences often programmed into them by culture, by families, by state schools and government schools. So, they have these emotional preferences. They wish to have the approval of their peers. They don't want to step out of line. They don't want to think for themselves. We're not evolved to think for ourselves. We're evolved to breed, and breeding requires social cooperation.

So, the fantasy is, "Oh, I got this great reason and evidence. Beautiful. Now we can all agree." The reality is that when you bring reason and evidence to oppose people's emotionally invested identity — this is their self...this is their identity — they say: "I am a socialist." "I am a Democrat." "I am a communist." And if you oppose that, they feel like you're undoing their entire personality. Truth, reason, and evidence — to most people — appear as a very dangerous predator. It's a fin in the water where you don't expect even dolphins to swim. And people get really freaked out by it. So, it is a great challenge, because people don't listen to reason and evidence — so why do they change their mind?

So, people don't listen to reason and evidence. The question is, then: "How do they change their minds?" And the sad truth is that they change their minds based on how certain you are. They can't judge your ideas. They can only judge how you judge your ideas. And if you are all-in, and you are certain, and you are willing to go to the wall in the advocacy defense and spread of your beliefs, that is the only thing that will change people at the moment. You have to be committed. You have to be all-in.

The left understands that. I mean, they have terrible ideas, but they spread because they're all-in. And the non-leftists. And, again, this left-right paradigm is all kinds of problematic. But the non-leftists — they still hope for the world where reason and evidence will change everyone's mind. The studies are very clear: It doesn't doesn't change people's minds at all. In fact, when somebody has a fixed belief, and you give them opposing reason and evidence as factual, it hardens their belief. It reinforces their error. You're actually making your enemy stronger by bringing reason and evidence to a sophistry fight.

And so I do-, you know, reason and evidence still-, you've got to be right. You've got to be truthful. You've got to be correct. And you've got to be good. But thinking that alone is going to win you the future is a great error. And people need to work more on their communication skills. They need to work more on their body language. They need to work more on their own certainty. Once you assert yourself, then you can step into the public arena and, hopefully, sway some minds. That's been my experience. But thinking that reason and evidence will do it? You can learn how to box. But if you don't train, and get big and strong, you're still going to lose.

Why are these media people — who are well-off — why are they so interested in income redistribution?

So, the question around why the elites tend to lean left — when they are themselves, wealthy — is a very interesting and powerful one. I think that the answer goes something like this: If you have the choice between political power and money, you are wiser to choose political power. Because political power takes away money. They can jack up your tax rates. They can foreclose on your property. They can gin up stuff through the tax code. They can do asset forfeiture directly. So political power trumps mere immediate material resources in terms of wealth or property.

I mean, if you look at 1917: It's the 100-year anniversary this year. The 1917, quote, "revolution," which was a criminal takeover of Russia. Well, you had all these people who had all this property. And then you got a new-, the Mensheviks came in. They were overtaken by the Bolsheviks. The Bolsheviks gained power over the police and the military. *Boom*. Your property rights are meaningless and everything gets taken away. So who won there? Your property rights or your political power? And so, the fact that people who have wealth gravitate towards political power is because they're smart enough to understand that if political power expands, they want to be on that side of the gun. Not on the side of people waving a piece of paper, saying, "But it's my property." Because that won't be enough to allow them to retain it if political power goes the socialist route.

What are the different types of Fake News?

So, there are a number of different types of Fake News. To me, what I've seen, they most often break down into abuse and sentimentality. Those are, sort of, the two big ones. So the typical example is: They want a particular government measure to go through — socialized medicine or Obamacare. They want some particular government measure to go through. So, what they do is, they will-, and it's the soft piano stuff. You know, like, that it makes you, like, almost weep instantly if you're a sentimental kind of person. So, they have somebody who's sad-faced. Who's a victim. Who's facing hard times. You get the soft piano going. You give them a very detailed backstory. And then, you paint some shadowy, nasty corporation — or group, or insurance companies — denying them. And then, they're sad and their children are sad. And so, you appeal to that sentimentality. And then, by appealing to that sentimentality, you hope that people will throw aside — or crush or destroy — universal principles like property rights and freedom of association, because these people need to be "saved."

Now, of course, the reality is that-, I get this question all the time. I get: "A free society, without all of this massive government redistribution of wealth — who's going to take care of the poor? Who's going to take care of the sick?" And it's like: "I know they're going to be taken care of, because this piano, sad-eyed people, coughing weakly into a silk handkerchief — or whatever — that works! It works for people. They're willing to throw aside constitutions and property rights, because they just want to help people." So you don't need the state to do it, because people will do it of their own accord. Nicely, voluntarily, charitably and, I actually argue, much more effectively in the long run. So, there's the *sentimentality* button, which people hammer a lot.

Now, the sentimentality button, you know — to maybe frame things generically, gender-based — the sentimentality button tends to work a little bit better with women. If you look at the Olympics, right? The figure skaters — you get that. You know, she used to get up at four [o'clock] in the morning when she was six years old. And the mom, proud, and all that kind of stuff. And it's effective. It's very powerful.

On the other side, the people who aren't quite as moved by sentimentality: The people who are like, "Well, no, we've got these universals. We've got these property rights. We can't keep making exceptions to these rules so there are no rules. We have no society. We have no laws. We have no civilization." Those people who don't respond to the soft, tinkly piano, sad-eyed, you know — people who are doing poorly and are victims and need help against some big shadowy monster corporation — the people who don't fall for the tinkly piano? Well, they need to be smashed.

And that's where you get the "Deplorables." You know, that famous statement, that in some ways really cost Hillary the election was: "Half of Trump supporters are what I call the 'Basket of Deplorables.' The racist, sexist, xenophobic, homophobic..." That's not tinkly piano, sad-eyed people. That's just smashing people who stand between you and your political goal. And it's designed to chase people out.

And you can see this when non-leftists come to speak at college campuses. There are people who, like — in a weird way in their mind — they're like, "I'm so upset. There should be soft piano music and a deep voice narrator to tell everyone how sad my story is, so that people will stop triggering me." But that doesn't work. So they escalate from the sentimentality and the self-pity... self-pity.

Sentimentality is the flipside of brutality. They're very close psychologically. Because sentimentality is: *Give me resources, because I'm sad.* And if people don't buy that narrative, then you flip to aggression. And everybody who's tried to comfort someone with tough love, when they're going through a self-pity phase, has seen that in viper strike of kickback and blowback.

And so, if the sentimentality doesn't work — if people are standing firm against that, and saying, "I'm not going to let giant political decisions, involving billions or trillions of dollars and essential human freedoms, to be driven by pianos and sad eyes," well, then, you have to smash them. And the media, sort of, plays both sides of the fence. And then, you get the attacks. The bike locks come out. You get people threatening to throw acid in the vents of a peaceful social gathering for non-leftists. And that's, you know, "good cop and bad cop." The sentimental cop and the truncheon cop. That's the role, I think. Those are the two poles that Fake News and the mainstream media, in general — of years between, when facing down a foe — that they can take down through reason.

How do we stop that escalation?

In the "lovely world of the future" and of what I want to get to — oh, I think what we all want to get to, if we're reasonable — you point out that: *Piano is not an argument. People being sad is not an argument.* That you cannot build universals off emotions. For a couple of reasons — that emotions are not tools of cognition. They don't tell you what's *true* or *false*. They just tell you what you like and don't like, which can be very varied, you know. I mean, to some people: "Oh, this group is terrible!" To some people: "Oh, this group is great!" You can't run a society based on emotions, because they're subjective.

And so, when people do this tinkly piano, sad-voice stuff: *Sorry — that's not an argument.* We cannot overturn moral universals. Like, things like property rights and sovereignty of the individual and freedom of association. You can't just overturn that because someone is *sad*. Because it's not an argument. And also because it means that people's emotions then become their tool for getting things. That's not good. That's not right. You wanted your tool for getting things to be either because people love you, you know, and they'll take care of you, because they know you've done wonderful things. You get old. You get sick. Your kids will pay your bills and come visit you, because they love you.

Or, because you're providing some value to people in the world. That's why you want to get stuff, because you're providing value to people. If it's just, like, "Well, if I sit here and I'm sad...or, I'm angry...or, I'm having a tantrum," we all know this with kids: Your kid goes to the store, and they always have those, like, candies at eye-level, strategically placed by the dentist, or whatever. And, you *know* that the kid [is]: "I *want* the candy bar! Ohhh, you're *not* going to give me the candy bar?!" and they *blow up*. You don't give the kid the candy bar! Or you're just buying peace at the expense of rewarding tantrums with *candy bars*. "Hey! Feel like having a tantrum? Here's a candy bar!"

And it's the same thing with emotional manipulation and sadness and rage and all these things. They can be good motivators. They can set you on the journey of trying to develop an argument. But they themselves are not an argument. So, in the ideal world, you say, "Sorry. Being sad is not an argument. Having a tantrum is not an argument. A bike clock is not an argument. Pulling the fire alarm is not an argument." And, because it's not an argument, it is a *confession of loss*. You have just lost the battle.

You know, you don't show up for a sports game — what happens? You lose by default. If you don't show up and play baseball, when you're supposed to show up and play baseball — if you show up in hockey gear, or you show up with a howitzer, or you show up with a video game controller of some-, it's some hockey, golf, or some baseball game — *you lose.* You lose, because you're not there playing the game. And, in the ideal world, people who don't engage in arguments have confessed to losing. Have said: "I'm not able to handle the basic requirements of this intellectual realm." And people ostracize them from that realm...as they should.

You know, I go on audition for the American Ballet Company, or wherever — they're going to ostracize the hell out of me because I have the flexibility of, well, this *chair*. Well, not even this chair... this floor that we're sitting on. So, they should ostracize me, because I'm not competent in ballet. So, it's my goal. I wrote this book, *The Art of the Argument,* with the idea, partly, of saying to people, "You need to know who's not competent in the realm of ideas, so that you can shuffle them off to something more productive." You know, it's better for me to be doing what I'm doing, than trying to be a ballet dancer. I mean, the market says so and aesthetics say so... and how I look in a tutu. Well, that's different. Actually, that's just-, I'm going to leave everyone with that mental image — with everyone — for the moment. Should we just pause there?

So, I would say that the way that you have to push back against this kind of Fake News now is simply point out that *it's not an argument*. We still do have enough of a vestige of respect for the philosophical traditions that we've inherited — all the way back to the pre-Socratic/some twenty-five hundred years ago — we still have enough vestigial echo-based leftover tan from a vacation six months ago. We still have enough respect for reason and evidence that this is why I'm sort of famous for this, "Not An Argument," thing. Because I want people to know what's not an argument, so that they can know that someone who thinks they're making an argument — when they're just being manipulative or abusive — they've lost. That's all you need out of that entire situation.

So, this brings up an interesting question, which is: What is our relationship to sophistry in a world where bland reason and evidence is not going to change people's minds — at least not at a rate that we need? My relationship to this is a strong case to be made. Sophistry itself is amoral. It's a tool. It's like a gun. You can use a gun. You can shoot someone — you're a bad guy. You can use it to defend yourself — you're a good guy. It's the same tool — different moral standing. Given that we can't win the battle with bland reason and evidence, to me, I have a very friendly relationship with sophistry. Plus, you need to use it in order to be able to recognize it. So, to me, if you are serving the cause of truth and you use sophistry, fantastic. You know whatever helps spread the ideas. And also, because people mistake confidence for truth, sophistry can give you a lot of confidence if you know how to use it. If you combine that with truth, I think, you're taking a weapon from the enemy and using it in the service of the good.

So, then, is the mainstream media justified in using sophistry? After all, they believe they are on the side of truth.

Well, there you raise an interesting question: Is the mainstream media justified in using it, if they believe that they're in the service of truth? Well, belief doesn't have anything to do with philosophy. Belief is, in fact, the most dangerous countercurrent to the pursuit of truth. The fact that somebody believes that they're right — this goes all the way back to the ancient story of Socrates. He was told by a friend that the Oracle of Delphi, who cannot lie, said that Socrates was "the wisest man in all of the world." And Socrates said, "Well, that's nuts. I don't know anything." So, he said, "Well, the Oracle can't lie, but I don't really know anything, so how can I be the wisest man?"

So, he went around and he questioned everyone - all of the leading sophists and philosophers and thinkers and teachers and politicians and artists, and so on, and he said they all came up short. The artists would produce the most astoundingly beautiful, deep, melancholy, and hilarious work. But when you ask them how they do it, and what it means, they have no idea. Like, these weird empty vessels that pour out this language with no conception of where it comes from. And the teachers didn't know. The politicians didn't know.

And he said, "I finally understand, at the end of this process, I now know what the Oracle of Delphi meant." Which is that: "I don't know anything, really. But at least I know that I don't know anything. Whereas everyone else thinks that they know something, but they're wrong."

That process of starting from skepticism. Of starting from doubt. Of the blank slate. Wipe everything you know — clear. And say, "How do I even know whether this is real or not? How do I know whether my face, my hands, the chair, anything...how do I know any of it is real?" And, "How do I establish certainty, given that my brain is encased in this skull prison of biology? How do I achieve certainty? How do I go from the study of reality to the study of knowledge to the study of virtue?" It's very hard. Now, it's easy when it's explained, but it's hard to come up with to begin with. And that's something that I've worked on a lot. So, the fact that the media believes that they're *right*, you know, well, beliefs are like assholes: *everyone's got one.*

Could you talk about the relationship between the media and the military-industrial complex?

I think it's impossible to understand the relationship between the media and the military-industrial complex, without understanding that the leftists, again — to reiterate the point — have lost the argument. So, what do leftists do when they lose the argument? Well, they did two things in the 1950s to the 1960s, which play into the current military-industrial complex postmodernism, or the idea that there's no such thing as, "objective reality." Reason is the enemy of everything human. And the focus on emotion. To focus on subjective experience. Why did leftists see fit to discard twenty-five hundred years of reason, metaphysics, and epistemology in the Western tradition? Why did they feel the need — the desperate desire — to discard reason and evidence? Because reason and evidence had disproved socialism and communism. This also occurred in the late eighteenth century, when science was beginning to overturn some traditional ideas of religion. And along comes Immanuel Kant, and other thinkers, who said, "Well, we have found it necessary to get rid of reason in order to save religion." When rational ideas begin to undo people's view of the universe, and of what is good, they sometimes take the mature road of reexamining everything that they had learned, and striving for something better. But, a lot of times, they just roll the grenade into reality and say, "Well, if I can't have the truth, there's no such thing as truth. If I can't have reason and evidence on my side, reason and evidence is terrible." You know the old thing of, "If I can't have you, no one will!" You know, and so, they turned against reason and evidence.

It's so important to remember — people don't remember this as much anymore — communism was sold as *scientific*. It was scientific. It took all of the prestige and good repute that science had accumulated — because of its successes since Francis Bacon first started it — the modern iteration of it in the sixteenth century, but they sold it as scientific. They made specific predictions. I won't go into all of them here, but they made very specific predictions, all of which not only didn't come true, but the exact opposite came true. They said communism [was] going to inevitably arise in capitalist countries, but communism was violently imposed on very primitive countries relative to-, they thought it was going to rise in Germany and England and all of these late-industrial economies. It didn't do any of that. So, doesn't work. They thought it was going to be inevitable, but it turned out to have to be willed into existence. That didn't work. They said it was going to be more productive than capitalism. Infinitely less productive, virtually. And so, all of the predictions that they made were falsified. Now, when you put forward something as rational, empirical, and scientific — when the reason and evidence goes against you — what do you do?

Well, what they did was, they put a giant bag of TNT under the concept of reason and evidence. So that's why this sort of postmodernism and relativism came about. Because the reason and evidence were undermining and destroying the very concept of centrally planned economies of the hierarchical oligarchies of communism and socialism. So, out with reason and evidence, because it goes against what we *want*. Which is power. Political power. Communism, statism as a whole, socialism, it just covers-, it's the grass that the tiger of the thirst for power hides in. All this ideology that masks the simple thirst for power. They want the power. Therefore, if something stands between them and their power — in this case, the accumulated evidence of history — out with reason and evidence. So they did that.

And the second thing they did was that they recognized that people from the Third World are much more likely to vote for the left. For a variety of reasons. And so, they got rid of reason and evidence and they opened up floodgates in the 1965 immigration bill to Third World immigration. While, of course, making the claims, "It's not going to adjust demographics. It's going to be very small." And, of course, it turned out to be a massive flood. And it's the only thing that has sustained the left.

Because the undertow against the left is all of the facts that are coming out repeatedly in the '90s. They even own a project: The decrypted cables of the Soviet Embassy to various embassies around the West conclusively proved Senator Joseph McCarthy was right in almost every one of his estimations, in almost every one of his accusations, about hidden communists in the State Department and in Hollywood and other places. The decrypts proved him almost universally correct. Again, a huge blow to the narrative. And so, every time they lose the fight, they find some other way to get the power that they want. I mean, because they're addicted to power. Power is physically addictive and, like any addict, they don't care how they get their drug. They'll lie. They'll cheat. They'll finagle. They'll steal. They'll kill, sometimes. So they want that power...they want that drug. So, in terms of the military-industrial complex, the question is: "Why was the left anti-war in the '60s, and why were they *not* anti-war in the 2000s?" Particularly when an unbelievably unjust and immoral and vicious and destructive war against Iraq was being proposed by a Republican.

Well, in the 1960s, of course, there was a draft. And so, because there was a draft, when people went off to war, an equal number of leftists and non-leftists got killed. And so, the leftist were like, "We're very much anti-war now." And, of course, they also had sympathies for the North Vietnamese regime — a lot of the people on the left — because it was a communist regime and they were big fans of communism. So, the combination of being pro-communist and there being a draft meant that they had a very strong anti-war message.

Now, one of the things that happened in the Vietnam War was it ended shortly before the complete command structure and implementation of the war collapsed. I mean, you had soldiers fragging their officers. You had massive drug addiction. You had alienation. You had people just going AWOL. It was really falling apart. So they did pull out before that.

And the military recognized something that is very important, which is that people don't like to kill people. You know, in an extremity of self-defense, it's one thing. But being shipped thousands of miles to a war you don't understand, to a purpose that is not clear to you, it's really, really hard on people. The majority of soldiers in the second World War never fought with their weapons. They never even pulled the trigger. And they recognize that the draft was not giving them the kind of military that they needed, for the kind of wars that they wanted to fight, so they switch from the draft to the volunteer army. Draft was in abeyance, so they switched to a volunteer army.

The military in America is predominantly a phenomena of the South. Not a lot of people in Manhattan signing up as grunts. So, when it switched to a volunteer army, then the left could get involved in wars, knowing that it was going to kill off people on the right.

So, it's very hard to restrain the military-industrial complex. The left used to be good on American imperialism. They used to oppose American imperialism. But that's when American imperialism was going against communists, right?

— In the great-, the grand chess game of, "Here is how the world works..." you know, communism is going to spread. There was this whole "domino theory": They take one down country one next country one next country. I did "one down country" which wouldn't make any sense. Let me start over again...

In the grand chessboard that people talk about, there was the thing, of course, called the, "domino theory," — largely discredited now — but the domino theory was, well, a communist is going to take over this country, and then this country, and this country. And so they were against American imperialism when American imperialism was targeting the communist countries that they lived. But, since they have not been targeting communist countries anymore, but instead of targeting other groups — other kinds of countries — the left has gone very lax on their anti-imperialism. And it's something that happens when you look at political groups. This stuff that aligns with stuff that is virtuous.

Yeah, okay, imperialism is bad. It's the initiation of force against usually far weaker opponents. And the left is against imperialism.

That's a good thing. But, then you realize the deeper motivation behind this, which is the desire to protect communist countries from Western aggression. Then the whole veneer of virtue falls away and it's, you know, a bit of an ennobling but embittering experience as well to realize that it's easy to get fooled by surface motives and miss out. So, the right is more keen in many ways on imperialism. The left has lost its opposition to imperialism since America stopped opposing communist regimes. So now who stands between America and imperialism? Well, there may be some libertarians. There may be some others. But I think one of the great barriers has fallen away and this is why the empire is very hard to contain.

If you were the head of a major news organization, how would your coverage of military conflicts and wars differ from theirs?

How would I cover a war if I had control of headlines? "The beginning of wisdom," as the old saying goes, "is to call things by their proper names." And "war" has been associated with so much propaganda in history that it is almost a term that conceals more than it illuminates, at this point. Certainly, with something like Iraq, you have a sovereign nation that had not done nothing to directly threaten the United States. That was invaded. That invasion was the international crime of aggression, which is about the worst crime that you can pull, internationally. Which is invading a sovereign country without any immediate pretext or justification of self-defense.

So, you have to call that by its name. It's an invasion. It is an overthrow. And the people who fought against that had some significant ethical justifications on their side. That they were being invaded. And this is very brutal to bring up in a modern context. Because it sounds like, you know, when you-, whenever you talk about injustice in Iraq, people somehow flip to, "You think Saddam Hussein is a great guy." And, of course, he wasn't. He was a dictator. But the question of who was going to be in charge in Iraq was not up to the Americans. Most Iraqis chose to live under Saddam Hussein than to revolt. Than to have a revolution. To take on those risks. That is their choice. That is not a choice that can be imposed by outsiders.

So, I think you need to start calling things by their proper names. We're not talking about war. We're talking about unjust invasions. We're not talking about regime change. We're talking about uncorking the bottle. Or uncorking the hellish genie of saying, "We don't like something. We can kill people until we get what we want." And that is a very, very dangerous — in fact, horrifying — precedent to bring into the sphere of international affairs.

And, of course, given that Saddam Hussein had done a lot to disarm — just as Gaddafi in Libya had — what you're doing is, you're saying to people that you want to disarm, "Hey, disarm. Disarm and everything will be great." And then, when they disarm, you invade them. And you end up hanging Saddam Hussein from a noose. You end up with Gaddafi being dragged through the streets and sodomized with bayonets. And then you go to some new country. Maybe you go to North Korea and you say, "You've really got to disarm." Well, they have a view of disarmament that is not generally as available to the American population, and they say, "Absolutely not." Like, "You have to kill me to disarm me, because I know if I disarm, that's what you'll do. You'll kill me."

So, it is just about telling the *truth*. And if you tell the truth, though the skies fall, people can make better decisions. But you can't drive blindfolded and you can't run foreign policy by pretending things are somehow other than what they are. Which is, America and other countries have a lot of power. And people in power like to exercise their powers. No point having a whip if you never crack it. There's no point being paid to defend something, if you never get to pretend to defend it. So...you need to start calling things by their proper names. And when we do that, we have a chance. A chance to make better decisions, but not *until*.

Let's talk a little bit about Fake Financial News. For example, in 2008, "Everybody has to buy a house, because, if you don't, you're gonna miss out on this deal."

It's very costly to listen to people, because we have this belief that there are people out there who are just giving us the impartial facts with no agenda. And there are a number of scams that are going on that are incredibly destructive and dangerous to people. The scam of higher education: Where you get seventeen- and eighteen-year-olds to sign these documents that put them in debt tens of thousands of dollars or more — and have them defer going into the marketplace — and learning skills, getting contacts, making money, for four years or more, and then you dump them out into the marketplace. Often they know less, according to tests, than they knew before they went in.

They are now in *debt*. They're embittered. They've been programmed with a hatred of the free market system. Which is not going to give them the very best attitudes in any kind of job interviews, or any enthusiasm to start their own business. "Ah, U.S. business owners. They're corrupt. They're exploitative. They're mean. They're nasty. They're big, fat guys with monocles and cigars and someone walking on the skulls of the poor." How is that going to make you an entrepreneur at all? It's like saying, "Oh, you could be an entrepreneur the same way you could join the KKK." It's like, *nobody wants to do that.* So the higher education scam is brutal and it's, in a sense, lying to kids. They're kids when they make these decisions. Lying to kids, and through that kind of deception, in a sense, forcing them to fund their own economic crippling and their own propagandizing. It is brutal. And so, that's one.

The Bitcoin thing: I mean, Bitcoin is to money as the Internet is to books. It is an unbelievable expansion of the potential of exchanging value. And, of course, people in the established framework — in the established financial industries — don't want Bitcoin. Bitcoin can lower transaction costs to the point where a multi-trillion dollar industry around the world could go the way of the horse and buggy. Bitcoin can publicly record contracts, and other dispute resolution mechanisms, to the point where lawyers will have much less to do. And, of course, fundamentally, given that countries around the world — with very few exceptions — rely on these central banks to create money out of thin air in order to buy votes from the population and pass the debts down to the next generation. Although it may not be the next generation by the time these final debts come due. Fiat currency, which can be created at will and at whim, is in direct opposition to the intrinsically limited nature of the Bitcoin universe.

And so, while fiat currency loses value, as we've seen — I first talked about Bitcoin when it was seventeen cents; today it went over seventy-five hundred bucks, U.S. So, Bitcoin has gone progressively *up* in value, whereas fiat currency has gone *down* in value. And most people have their transactions — their fortunes, their savings — in fiat currency. And those people are in control of the media empire. So, do you think they want to talk up Bitcoin? Every dollar that goes into Bitcoin is a dollar that's not going into fiat currency — that's not going into government debt instruments. It's not going into a bank.

And so, of course, they don't want you to buy Bitcoin. Of course they're going to keep telling you it's a scam, because it's a win/lose. They're in direct competition. And we don't seem to understand that. I mean, if you listen to one sugar-bottled water manufacturer talk trash about another, you know that they're in competition! You buy this drink, you're not buying that drink. So, of course, you don't expect them to be objective. "My beer is better than your beer." "My bathing suit's better than your bathing suit." It's a win/lose. And you buy one, you don't buy the other.

And the fact that there are financial powerhouses out there in the media, and elsewhere, constantly trash-talking Bitcoin, of course! Their entire revenue stream — their entire basis of their wealth management — is predicated on people staying in fiat currency. I mean, how many people really want to be in the stock market? Maybe-, maybe one in a thousand people should be in the stock market. You know the industry. You know the business. You know the players — the competition, both domestic and international. It's really complicated to buy a stock with genuine knowledge. But the stock market has been swollen, like some cancerous tumor blocks out the sun, because everybody's money is being forcibly herded into the stock market. And so, you say, "Okay, well I can give my money to the stock market, or I can give it to the IRS. Or I can give it to whatever tax department is local to your jurisdiction." And it's like, "Okay, well, I'll throw it in there, because there it's gone for sure, but here, maybe I'll get something."

And so, massive amounts of money get poured into the stock market, which completely distorts what goes on at the CEO level — what goes on at the executive level. And I've seen this from up-close. And people, then, they chase the next five minutes of stock value and shareholder satisfaction. They don't look down the road as long as they should to build viable, sustained business. So you get a lot of random walks in the stock market.

And Bitcoin is invested in by people who know what they're doing for the most part, at least at this stage, and who want to be there. And so, the knowledge base of Bitcoin is far greater than the knowledge base of people who — either are voluntary or involuntary — end up in the stock market. And I prefer financial instruments where people know what they're doing, versus: "Well, I had to hand this money to some guy or the tax man was going to take it," which creates a very unstable environment. I prefer financial instruments where the people who have their money in it, or their resources in it, have a good deal of knowledge about what's going on versus people who are jammed in there by force and crossing their fingers with very little knowledge.

And then, meanwhile, the people who said that Bitcoin is a scam — was going to crash — the media keeps putting them on as "analysts."

Well, there's two issues: One, to me, is sort of financially practical and the other one is moral. So, to deal with the first one: The fact that they're scaring people out of Bitcoin has a great deal of value to me, because it means that only knowledgeable people stay in Bitcoin. And understand it. And know what's going on. Which produces a certain amount of not only stability, but upward growth. That's the practical aspect. The moral aspect is they are standing between people and financial security. You know, in America right now, seventy-eight percent of workers are living paycheck-to-paycheck. If they had heard the truth many years ago about Bitcoin — about its potential — and you can compare...it's interesting. Compare how the media pumped up the dot-com bubble in the '90s compared to how much they're trash-talking and throwing shade on Bitcoin at the moment — that is a fascinating difference. Because the financial behemoths, the financial industry, was benefiting and gaining from the dot-com bubble. So they were like, "You got to get into the dot-com bubble. People are really going to want their toilet paper delivered by Internet. And you know they're going to want their pets fed by the Internet." Everything was Internet-based, because then you would say, "Oh, I got to get in on this bubble. I got to call my stockbroker." And they made lots of commissions. So, I mean, man, they loved that dot-com bubble.

But Bitcoin is a different matter. You don't need to go through a stockbroker. You don't need to pay exorbitant transaction fees. There's no fifteen-minute delay on prices. None of that crap that keeps people at a regulatory arm's length distance from direct involvement in the stock market. So now, of course, it's interfering with their profits, so they're saying that it's a scam. And they think that that is going to somehow prevent it. But can you imagine? Physical booksellers saying, "Oh, this Internet. It's a fad. It's going to pass. It's not real." Well, sadly, they're just going to end up taking money from the gullible and transferring it to the wise. Which is the way of things in the economic world.

When Bitcoin was at about twenty dollars, you went on TV to defend it, and people treated you as a kook.

Yeah. Oh, I just-, direct evidence, way back in the day, that I was talking about Bitcoin going to thousands of dollars, and part of that, of course, is my knowledge of fiat currency. But part of it is the fact that I have a very strong software technical background. So, I can understand the code. I can understand its purpose. I can understand how it's going to change things. I did a presentation on Bitcoin — the truth about Bitcoin — back when Bitcoin was running at about one hundred and forty bucks each. And it is, of course, my hope — you know, I love my listeners, and I love the people who love philosophy — so, it's my hope that people went out and invested. And that they gained value — not just emotional, not just moral, not just relational, not just professional — but direct financial benefits from understanding the world and knowing the truth about these big strategic inflection points in society when things fundamentally change.

There is no long-term future for fiat currency. There never has been, in the entire history of the world. All fiat currencies fail. The longest it's ever lasted is the British pound sterling — about 400 years. But it's lost ninety-eight percent of its value over that time. There is no long-term future for fiat currencies.

And the future is in whatever can't be manufactured on a whim. Now they're always finding more oil. They're always finding more silver. They're always finding more gold and stuff gets taken out of circulation. There's kind of a rollover. But that is subject to some instabilities. Now they are, of course, producing more Bitcoins, but at an ever-diminishing rate. And, at some point, the electricity required to power the processes to get the next Bitcoin is going to be far greater than the value of a Bitcoin.

Although that seems to be a race with no upper limit at the moment. So it was not hard to figure out that Bitcoin was like a super-gold. It was limited. But it doesn't have the difficulties of gold in terms of governments grabbing it. In terms of fiscal transfer. In terms of storage and costs. And so, the idea that Bitcoin was as superior to all former forms of currency, that the Internet was to all former methods of information storage and transfer, was not that difficult to make at the time.

Could you talk about ownership of the news media and how that affects coverage?

The ownership of news organizations is highly concentrated. In, really, over the last twenty or thirty years, it's gone from hundreds to about half a dozen or so major players. That is very significant, because when the media is diversified, then gaining control of any one of the hundreds of media companies or media outlets is not that significant. But when the media concentrates at getting one of those six, that's a big deal. And so, people will bid up the price of those media companies. But, like any investor, you want your money back — you want return on your investment. Now, anyone who buys that sort of fixed, mainstream, physical dino media company, at the moment, is probably not looking for a massive payout. If they wanted a massive payout, they'd go out and buy some Bitcoins.

So, what they're doing is, they're trying to influence a worldview. They're trying to advance a political agenda. And this, to me, is clear in organizations like *The New York Times*, where Carlos Slim — one of the big telecom monopolists in Mexico — bought out a lot of their data, and ended up owning a significant portion of the company. And they are very, very pro-open borders. They're very, very pro-immigration. And one of the reasons for that is very, very simple: It's that when Mexicans come to America, they make money or they're on welfare. They get money *somehow*. What do they do? They send it back to Mexico. And then people in Mexico buy cell phones and cell phone plans from Carlos Slim. It's not that complicated.

And all of this other stuff is just kind of like a cover: "Diversity and richness and cultural enrichment." No, it's bank account enrichment. It always has been. And this is not discussed at all. It is not talked about. Obviously, you wouldn't expect it to be talked about by *The New York Times,* but are *other* outlets talking about it? Well, no, because they all have their own compromises. And if you want to know why someone has a particular opinion, the first thing you do is you *follow the money*.

I had read that Carlos Slim — who, by the way, is a terrible person and monopolist — has extracted so much value from the economy that if he hadn't, Mexico would be like America's economy in the 1960s. They wouldn't want to even come in from Mexico. That's the tragedy no one talks about. Because *The New York Times* covers up for this guy and flooding the borders. If they had just put him in check and regulated him, because what he was doing was *theft*, then Mexicans would prefer to live in their own country and would be prosperous.

The disaster of South and Central America could be an entire other show. Argentina, up until the 1920s, had the same economy as America. Same GDP per capita and aggregate. And it got progressively more left-wing over time, I mean, for the Mexican government having people flood to the United States and send remittances back.

And remittances are huge in the Mexican economy. Bigger than their oil revenues. Remittances are a foundation of the Mexican economy. What a great deal for the Mexican government. People leave the country, send massive amounts of money back, they don't have to provide education, health care, services, roads...you name it. They don't have to provide these things. Which means that the government gets all this free money without having to be responsive to their citizens. And then we wonder why there's so much corruption and indifference to the needs of everyday citizens in Mexico. It's viciously corrupt. The way to stop it, of course, would have been to have a border. Why do you have to have a wall? *Because you didn't have a border*. If you have a border, then people don't come across, take the money under the table, often, and send their remittances back. That's number one. And number two, of course, is do not allow illegal immigrants to get welfare. Because if you allow illegal immigrants to get welfare, they send their money back, which creates a vested interest for the government to push more people over the border, and hollows out any vestige of democracy in the originating country.

And it prevents the Mexican people from rising up against their own government.

It prevents-, it lowers the marketplace for more honest people to gain any traction. And, of course, what happens is, you know how bad it's gotten with the cartels and the corruption in Mexico — that is very hard to undo. Because honest people with that kind of power structure are being allowed to grow and faster. Honest people, you know how it goes: "Silver or lead." You get the money or you get the bullets. And honest, decent people find it too risky, I think, to go into politics in Mexico, which means that, unfortunately, a soft reform seems less and less likely and a hard crash seems more and more likely, which is going to be absolutely brutal to the most vulnerable people in Mexico.

Imagine that you're talking to a person of good faith who perhaps works at *The Washington Post*. Imagine they said, "What could we do to fix the media?"

I would suggest that if their goal is to tell the truth to the people, then they need to keep trying to do that within their existing structures. You know, like, if you're blindfolded, and you're going through some room, you go slowly until you meet resistance. And that's how you navigate. So they want to keep trying to get the truth out. Like the Weinstein story: It popped up regularly for the last couple of decades in the mainstream media. And then, for some reason, a couple of weeks ago, *The New York Times* pulled the trigger on it. And we've seen all of the dominoes cascade down from there. Keep trying to get the truth out. Find out where the resistance is.

Now, when you come up against resistance when you want to get the truth out, you can find a way to overcome it. To bring the other person into the mindset that you have about bringing the truth out. You can even chain them. You might be able to threaten them peacefully, saying, "You know, it's going to be bad for your career if we have to go somewhere else, or some other news organization breaks this story." You find the resistance and you try and find a way to get around it. Now, either you can, or you can't. If you can get around it, then you have a new way, a new skill set of getting information past the resistant gatekeepers. Fantastic! If you can't get around it, then your basic choice is to give up trying to tell the truth. Or leave.

What's the future of news?

By God, I hope the future of news are facts. I hope that the future of news is illumination. I hope that the future of news is humility. I can't imagine what kind of mindset it takes to openly and directly *lie* to people against their own self-interests. Against the self-interest of their culture. Their history. Their culture. Their future. Their children. To lie to those people for the sake of the mere pursuit of political power. The mindset that is involved in that is almost beyond comprehension to me. Because I've never been an addict, so I don't know, like, *why* you would burn your entire world to the ground to get five more minutes of the drug that you want.

So, the future of news is up to us. The future of news is up to those of us who produce quality content. *Factual* content. Reasoned content. Primarily through the Internet. But, most importantly, the future is up to the consumer. Where do you put your eyeballs? Where do you put your resources? Where do you put your focus? Who do you share? Who do you get behind? Who do you advocate for? If you're advocating for liars — if you're putting your resources and support behind liars — you're going to get more lies. Whatever you subsidize, you get more of. If you put your resources behind those who are really working hard to tell the truth — who are really working hard to fight falsehood, injustice, and propaganda — then those people will flourish. We who bring facts of the world, all we can do is be present in the conversation. How much people listen. Whether they share, whether they get involved, whether they get behind us, is up to them.

The spread of truth is a collective enterprise. It is a conversation. And, if you flee towards the pseudo-security and pseudo-credibility of those who've been proven to repeatedly lie — year after year, decade after decade and, in some cases, century after century — if you flee towards those people, you may gain a small amount of social approval. You may not have people thumbs-down whatever it is that you post. But you need to look. It's a very personal conversation that people need to have with themselves. Everyone is involved in the propagation of truth in society. There is nobody who is excluded from it. And people need to look deep in their own hearts and say to themselves, "Who am I with? Who do I support? Who am I putting my energies behind? Who do I wish to join?" And it's that commitment that determines where the future of news goes.

How would you respond to people who say, "Mike Cernovich is Fake News," or "Alex Jones is Fake News"?

Not an argument. It's not an argument. The term, "Fake News," is not an argument. It's like saying, "You're wrong." Okay. Saying it doesn't make it so. "Hey, look! I have a mohawk." Does that change anything on the camera? I don't think it did. So, "Words are easy proof," is hard. Words are easy. Facts are hard. Saying that you love someone is easy. Acting in a manner consistent with love and respect can sometimes be hard. Saying you support someone is very easy. Acting in a manner that is hard to support that person, or that cause — that is hard. Calling someone a liar is easy. Finding and telling the truth — that is hard.

So, Fake News. People use the label. There are people out there trying to define it in some manner. No. The whole point of free speech is that people get to lie, and people get to tell the truth. And may the best man, or woman, win.

Could you talk about the manner in which the media covered the European migrant crisis?

Well, yeah. So, the European migrant crisis is wrong in every conceivable syllable. First of all, it's becoming less and less *Europe*. Secondly, they're not "migrants." And thirdly, it's not a "crisis" if it's self-manufactured. You know, if somebody runs into my car, okay, that's a bad thing. If I regularly drive a shopping cart into my own car, that's a different situation. Self-manufactured problems cannot be put in the same category of crisis.

So, it's less Europe. Most of them are not migrants. And it is not a crisis. It is something self-inflicted. This is a known goal on an ancient and noble civilization. So, yes, of course, there have been horrible disruptions in the Middle East and there has been imperialism and the destruction of Syria and of Iraq and of Libya, and so on, by Western powers. But the remedy to that is to deal with things politically, domestically. If you have warmongers and people who've unjustly invaded and destroyed and undermined and helped to overthrow other governments, you deal with them in your own political system. You try them. You throw them in jail. You apply the death penalty if that's what is justified in your legal system. But when you have leaders who are acting unjustly in other countries, to take in all of the people who no longer are happy in those countries, and then inflict those people on the taxes and on the living spaces of the domestic population is saying that "two wrongs make a right." And that's not the case.

If Europe is at war with the Middle East — some could argue that it is — if Europe is at war with the Middle East, you don't take refugees — young fighting-age militarily refugees — from countries that you are at war with. Can you imagine this? England, 1940: Young fighting-age Germans pouring across the channel of the white cliffs of Dover, and the British people saying, "Sure.

Here's some welfare." I mean, this would be incomprehensible. If you're at war, you don't take refugees from your opponents. If you're not at war, you are under no obligation to take refugees. There are legal definitions of what a "refugee" is. And recently, in Italy, less than three percent of the people arriving on the shores from other countries — and, particularly, from North Africa — only three percent of those people met the legal definition of "refugee." A refugee is supposed to stay in the country they land in. There's none of this welfare shopping across the continent of Europe. But it happens. People who are supposed to be deported do not show up, do not exit. They disappear into the no-go zones. They disappear into the underground networks in Europe.

It is, to a large degree, a manufactured hysteria. It is an inevitable and predicted result of, particularly, the destruction of Libya. This is what Gaddafi said very clearly: "You take me down — I am the barrier between Africa and Europe — you take me down, and you will have floods of migrants." And they are economic opportunism migrants. I don't blame the migrants. It is a perfectly rational resource acquisition strategy to spend a couple of thousand bucks or a couple of hundred bucks, or however much it costs, for various people to get in. It's a perfectly reasonable acquisition strategy. To say, "If I invested this amount of money to get into Europe, I get this amount of money in resources through the welfare state. Through free health care, free dental care," and so on. The manufacturer of sentimentality — because we've talked about this earlier, when I talked about the two main varieties of Fake News being sentimentality and brutality — playing upon the heartstrings of the emotionally hypersensitive or attacking people for resisting a narrative, well, the boy who was supposedly drowned, well, the father was not a refugee. He was trying to get to Canada. He wanted dental work, and so on. The boat was overloaded. It was a complete clusterfrack from beginning to end. And then they show a picture of this boy drowned upon the beach. It is a tragedy what happened to him. Is it the fault of the European taxpayer? Pretty hard to make that case. And if you compare that to the bodies regularly strewn across the streets in Europe from terrorist attacks, some of which are committed by these migrants or their descendants, those bodies you can't see. Those bodies will not show up. Sharing pictures of those bodies — of the children mowed down by trucks in the streets of Europe — showing those bodies can get you censored on social media.

And this is the kind of manipulation that is occurring, and I sadly think that one of the reasons why it's occurring is that Europeans — native Europeans — are just not really having many babies. If you're not really having many babies, you tend to-, like, your maternal/paternal instincts tend to spill over, kind of randomly and kind of wildly. If you have your own children, then you have a culture and a history and a set of freedoms, specifically, to protect and hand to your own children. If you don't have children, it's easy for those wild, unattached parental instincts to attach to anything. Oh, there's a kid on a beach. There are some sad-eyed people in a boat. They're kind of like my children now and that's convincing people: "Don't have kids. We need zero population growth. Children are environmentally disastrous to the planet. Don't have children." This is a message that was generally only applied to white people. Only applied to Europeans and North Americans. Nobody, to my knowledge, was out there in Africa saying the same thing, or in the Middle East saying the same thing. Nobody was proselytizing among the migrant populations in Europe saying, "You're having way too many children." No. Environmentalists who are so concerned about the environment were saying, "Well, we're taking people from a low-resource consumption environment in the Third World and we're moving them to a high-resource consumption environment in the First World. This is disastrous for nature. This is disastrous to the environment." None of them are saying that. And some of them appear to have been directly bought-off, these environmental groups. Saying, "We'll give you this money. Don't you dare talk about immigration." And this horrible lie: "Don't have children. Don't have children. Don't have children... Oh, we don't have enough children. We need to import people from the Third World." It's one of the most horrifying and, I think, eventually, very brutal bait-and-switches that has ever occurred in human history.

You brought up a point that I like: Assad allegedly gasses his own people. We're told that you can't post pictures from the Nice terrorist attacks. But when Assad does, we see those images everywhere.

Sure, sure. I mean, because they know how powerful the sentimentality button is, in particular for the childless, and I do wonder the degree to which some of these stereotypical lonely cat women who dress up their cats in little human outfits and baby them — or, you know, you can see-, I was at the airport the other day flipping through some magazines, and at the back of these magazines there are always these lifelike babies you can order that coo and move and it's like, *why do you need lifelike babies*? Don't you have babies? Don't you have grandchildren? But the yearning is still there. You know, somebody on a diet will still salivate at looking at pictures of food and they know how powerful the sentimentality is. They also know that they do not want to trigger in-group preferences among Europeans.

Out-group preferences is the way things have been going for the longest time. Now, the left has relentless in-group preferences. They don't hire people not on the left. They don't promote them. They don't review their books. I mean, I think, what? Ann Coulter has never had a book reviewed by *The New York Times*. Despite that, she's been a number-one bestselling author, repeatedly. So the left has a relentless in-group preference but, of course, if you're on a team. Let's say you were on a soccer team. If you can convince the opposing soccer team to pass to you, and pass to themselves — if they want — but to pass to you while your team only passes to yourself: Guess what? You just won the game. So, if you want to win the war of ideas, you relentlessly oppose and attack any in-group preference from your enemies, while relentlessly promoting in-group preferences among yourselves.

If you really want to see a microcosm of how manipulative the media is — and this is a little bit older but you can still find it online — if you look at what were used to be called, "Soweto," in South Africa — Southwest townships — these were ghettos populated by blacks. They were poor. You know, the usual tin roofs, and cardboard couches, and so on. And I've actually visited there and it was horrible. This was relentlessly portrayed in the media to evoke — and, I think, legitimate and genuine — sympathy for the blacks caught up into those circumstances. Since the ANC took over from [F. W.] de Klerk's government, since the end of apartheid, whites have been progressively displaced within South Africa. And now you have, I think, upwards of a quarter of a million whites in their own squatter camps. Very little access to medicine. Very little access to fresh water. Virtually no opportunities.

Now, if we care about people who are forced to live like dogs in the street, then why is it so relentlessly promoted in the past that the blacks had to live this way? But now there are whites living this way? It's not mentioned. If violence against a minority is so terrible, why are the South African farm murders so relentlessly covered up? Buried. Never discussed. Because it is all a Kabuki theater with some very, very bloody puppets. It is all about hitting your emotional buttons. Getting you to succumb. Because there are concerns that people have. Looking at how South Africa changed over the past couple of decades — looking at what is happening to the economy, what is happening to the food supply, what has happened to the whites. If we care about the unjust treatment of minorities in the world, why is South Africa *never* mentioned? Why has it completely vanished from the radar once apartheid was ended? Because there is a warning in that for people that the media does not want you to see, and does not want to activate your "fight or flight" and make the looking at that a possible tunnel of time where things might lead.

Another example of truly catastrophic fake news was the DDT panic that came out of Rachel Carson's book in the late '60s called, *The Silent Spring*, wherein she said that DDT — which is a chemical that is used to control mosquitoes, in particular — DDT would cause a thinning of the shells of bird eggs. And then you would have a silent spring. There'd be no birds left. And because there were no birds, there'd be no this, that, and the other, and so on. Right?

And there was this massive panic. And DDT was banned around the world. Now some very credible scholarship has been poured into this to try and figure out what has been the fallout of this ban. And some fairly conservative estimates put the death count that resulted from the increases in malaria and other mosquito-borne diseases that came out of this DDT ban — because if you didn't have the DDT, you got a whole lot more mosquitoes — at about 60 million people. About *60 million people* have died as a result of this DDT hysteria. And it has actually been reintroduced in certain areas because it is simply the most effective way of breaking the breeding cycle of mosquitoes and reducing the prevalence, not just of malaria, but lots of other mosquito-borne diseases.

So there's an example. Have people circled back? Have they realized what went wrong? Have they tried to fix the processes? No! Just keep going. Keep going. Keep going. Never circle back. Never look at the death count. Never look at the bodies. Just keep going forward. It is intellectually criminal in every conceivable dimension.

Well, they promoted this kind of hysteria. The relationship between the left and environmentalism. It's the way that the left hijacks things like equal rights for men and women. Or equal rights for various races and ethnicities. Or our natural, healthy, and legitimate concern for the sustainability of the environment. Equality? Fantastic! We are all interested in these things and they have very strong philosophical justifications which we should pursue and expand. Equality before the law, care and preservation of nature, are all good and wonderful things. And then the left puts their hooks into these sympathies. Oh, a boy drowned on a beach. You know, we feel terrible. We want to do something about it.

So, when it comes to the environment, the question is: Do they want to protect the environment? *Deep down.* There's an old joke about environmentalists: That they're watermelons — they're green on the outside, but red on the inside. Do they want to protect the environment? Well, if they wanted to protect the environment, the first thing that they would do is they would make sure that the governments did not spend more money than they received. Because when you spend more money than you're taking in, you are going into debt. When you go into debt, you're consuming more resources in the present than in the future. So, if I borrow a thousand dollars and go and buy a computer, well, that's a computer that, in a sense, has been created to service my needs now, rather than in the future. Now, in the future, I'll have to cut back my spending by a thousand dollars — plus interest — to pay that back. But national debts are massive consumers of nature's scarce and precious resources in the here and now.

Also, if you care about the environment, you should not want future unfunded liabilities, which, in America, are well north of a hundred and fifty trillion dollars — or close to ten times the national GDP. So if you make massive promises to people for huge amounts of spending in the future, then you are guaranteeing more stripping of nature's precious resources, because of these unfunded liabilities. So government debts, government deficits, unfunded liabilities should be the first thing that environmentalists should concern themselves with when it comes to protecting the environment.

You care about global warming. Well, how about stop government's borrowing money? Stop government's printing money. Because that provokes massive consumption in the here and now, which ends up in the air, which provokes global warming — if that's your approach. This is the most logical. This is not *brain surgery*. It's basic math. If you can count to twenty without taking off your shoes, you can understand this. So, the question is: What is the relationship between environmentalists and national debts and unfunded liabilities? They don't care. *They don't care.* The government borrows a trillion dollars more than they spend. They print a trillion dollars more. That is a trillion dollars' worth of natural resources converted into consumable goods. Give or take, in one single year. That is a huge amount of environmental damage. Do they care? Do they ever talk about it? Have you ever seen or heard of an environmentalist saying, "We got to get this national debt under control, because it's really bad for the environment"? They don't care. They don't care about the environment.

They care about opposing the free market. See, they used to criticize the free market, because it was exploitative. Turned out, the workers were pretty happy and made a lot more money. Then, what they did was, they said, "Well, the free market is not very productive relative to socialist or centrally planned or communist economies." Turned out, that was completely false. Then, and now, they say the problem with the free market is it's too productive. It consumes too many resources. It converts raw materials into consumer goods too well. People like it too much. They're consuming too much. It's too efficient. It's too great. Prices keep going down. People are consuming more.

I mean, it's a moving target. Doesn't matter. They just *hate* the free market. Because they can't compete in the free market. Because their sophists. And they're manipulators. And the one thing that is very true, in my experience, of people on the left: Nothing spells, "rational pragmatism," like working with your hands *once* in your goddamn life. Work with your hands. Do you know how dangerous it has been? People don't grow their own food anymore. Try having a tantrum because your watermelon didn't grow. Try screaming at your tomato plants. "*More* tomatoes! I *need* them!" But, you can scream at the government. You can scream at guilty people and they'll give you resources so you'll shut up and go away. Try screaming at a cow — she'll just shit on your hand rather than give you milk.

So, the fact that people are embedded in this urban environment where they can have tantrums and nature doesn't care about your tantrums. Animals don't care about your tantrums that much. Pets, maybe, but...you can't scream a field into producing your food for you. You can't attack a tree randomly and then have it fall into a perfect log cabin. You can't do these things. So, the fact that we have this incredibly rarefied, champagne-socialist, urban elite that has never worked a hard job in their life, it's an old Charles Murray question: Have you ever, for a year, worked at a job where a body part *hurt* at the end of the day? I sure have. My feet, as a waiter. My back, as a gold panner and a prospector. My legs, I mean, it's *hard*. And when you interact directly with natural reality, not out there manipulating people. If you are a woman, you can put on a nice, hot dress, you are an attractive woman, you go to a bar and drinks appear in front of you. If you are out in the wilderness — I don't care what kind of push-up bra you've got — there's no water that's going to *jump* into your mouth because Nature thinks you've got "nice boobs." You have to interact with natural, bare, bald, prosaic, fundamental reality in order to be cured of this temptation to constantly manipulate other people into giving you resources.

And my experience has been that a lot of the people who are non-leftists have done some damn physical labor in their life. They have done something where manipulation and sophistry doesn't get them what they want. But if you've grown up, and you've gone to a nice school, and you've never had a particularly tough job, and your parents can get on the phone and get mad at people who stand in your way, and then you can wordsmith your way into a degree program at a university, and then you've got those contacts, so they know you. So, you can go and get some job at a think tank. It's, like, you've never had a single callus in your life. You've never dealt with a reality that does not respond to manipulation.

And I love the fact that there are cities, but I'm mourn the basic pragmatism that comes out of working with nature. We come from a culture that developed its philosophy, particularly its metaphysics, like, "What is reality?" I mean, if a bear is chasing you through the woods, you don't have a lot of metaphysical questions on your mind. Like, you can argue with race. A construct is gender. But that bear will kill you if it gets a hold on you. And, so, you have a bare, basic reality that you have to work with. It will not respond to manipulation. And the fact that our elites are so disconnected from physical labor, are disconnected from reality that they can't weasel, that they can't control, that they can't manipulate — it's a great tragedy. We've inherited this civilization that came out of a very commonsensical group of people who had to work very hard dealing with basic reality. And now we've abstracted and urbanized ourselves to the point where we become these, like, effete snobs who think that-, who think that reality, by itself, is open to manipulation, because we live in a world of ideas and people, not a world of based reality.

So, after high school, I ended up working in Northern Ontario — gold panner, prospector, and so on. And that's pretty real. It's *very* real. And you can get into some very hairy situations if you're not very careful. You can get injured. And if you get injured out there, man, you are a long way from any kind of help. It could take days to get you to a hospital. And I worked out there with a bunch of men and women and we all had this particular goal. I won't get into all the details, but we needed to get samples to figure out where gold was, in the hopes of finding a mine.

So, you got these big giant drills. You've got flamethrowers to get through the permafrost, sometimes. You have snowshoes. You have-, it was so cold in the prospector's tent that we stayed in in the winter that we had to add jet fuel to the propane that we used to heat the tent, because otherwise it was too cold. Like, you wake up with your breath fogging, and so on. And it's invigorating. And I liked the work very much. And I got a chance to do a lot of reading, because you can't work after dark, and it gets dark pretty early in the winter up there.

So, we all had this goal to achieve a particular material end. Whining was not an option. And there was nothing more annoying than somebody who wasn't willing to pull their weight. And when you've had that kind of teamwork to achieve a practical, tangible, material goal, you realize how unifying reality actually is. If you and I are both writing our interpretations of John Fowles' novel called, *The Magus,* or whatever — if you and I are both writing our interpretations of that, we don't need to meet in reality. We don't need to join forces. And neither of us really is objectively right or wrong. We can make a case. Maybe it's better. Maybe it's worse. But if you've not done practical, tangible teamwork of things in reality, it's really hard to deeply understand how unifying reality actually is. And how you end up like salmon in a strong current. You are all swimming in the same direction. You are all trying to achieve the same goal. And shirkers are immediately evident. You know, "Ahhh, my back." You know. "Well, your back was fine this morning." So people who don't carry their own weight are evident and they either pick up the slack or they get gone.

Let's say you're building a bridge: Well, the laws of physics and tensile strength and material strength — they're not open to a lot of subjective interpretation. They are not open to your manipulation. There's no committee you can go to to make sure that they write the correct paperwork in triplicate and make sure the bridge stands up. The bridge stands up or it falls down, according to the laws of physics, and the rigors of your engineering approach. The number of people who have influence in this world who have not gone through any of that process of realizing that to work with a team with the goal of achieving something tangible and measurable in the world, very few of our athletes have done that in any practical way.

When I was in the software field, I was a programmer, and then I was Chief Technical Officer. I ran a group of programmers and kept programming myself. Well, either the program works, or it doesn't. It doesn't have to be, like, tangible. Like, either what you wrote as a software programmer compiles and runs efficiently, or it doesn't. It either achieves the business goals that you have set out for, or it doesn't.

Do you think the mainstream media is pushing a postmodernist worldview?

It's a complex question and I'm going to give a very simple answer. But, it's interesting to me, because postmodernism is postempiricism. It's post-rationality. It's post-objectivity. So, therefore, it should be post-ethics. If there's no "is," how can that possibly be a "not"? If you don't even know whether reality exists, how on earth can you nag people about what to do and how to be good and how to be right and how to be just and fair, if you don't even know whether human beings exist, how can you nag people about racism?

It makes no sense from a philosophical standpoint. Which is why they oppose philosophy, of course. But it makes perfect sense when we talk about competing animal groups who wish to dominate. Because, if you can convince the most logical and rational among you that reality is a concept, then they're off fussing with that crap, rather than opposing your creeping political agenda. So, you know, you want to go rob a house and there's a big guard dog? Reason and evidence? You've got to get that dog out of the way. What do you do? You put a drug on a piece of meat, throw it off to one side, the dog passes out and then you can go do your business, unopposed. Or, if you want to be a good criminal, get some gun control for your victims. You're good to go.

So, to disarm your opponents is *essential.* If the leftists genuinely were post-rational, then they would have no ethics. There would be no identity politics. There would be none of this virtue that they consistently claim to represent and appeal to. And that's not the case at all. What they do is they take away rationality and objectivity so that the contradictions in their own syllogisms can be brushed away as well. "Well, it's true that I make no sense. But really, what is the sense anyway? Sure. I guess at some level you could call my argument irrational, but, hey, what is reason anyway?" You know, I mean, this is all nonsense. I mean, it's-, you're caught with a smoking gun over a dead body, and your defense is, "Well, how do we know that that body even exists in an alternative dimension?" It's all just weasel crap.

It's like when people are finally cornered: The last thing they ditch is reality. And because the left has been so relentlessly just proven wrong time and again, they have to reject reality. But they don't want to reject the consequences of rejecting reality. Which is: They should shut the hell up about truth and virtue and goodness and rightness, and they should stop complaining about other people who have different moral perspectives from theirs, because they don't even really believe those people exist. So why would you bother? I don't spend a lot of time lecturing puppets because puppets don't exist as conscious entities.

What is truth?

So the best way to explain truth is that there exists outside of your mind an objective universe independent of your subjective impressions. Now, when you say something is true, you're saying that your mental construct matches what is out there in the real world. So, if you have four coconuts and you say, "There are four coconuts," you have a statement that is in language that translates to the objective reality of four discrete and independent coconuts on a table, or wherever. Reality outside of your mind is universal, consistent, objective, empirical. And, so, when you are making a truth claim, you're saying that my mental construct, my argument, my perspective, matches what is going on out there in the real world. And, so, when you're talking about personal preferences, you can have a truth about your personal preferences. They're not universal. If you say, "I like ice cream." Good, that can be measurable, you're probably telling the truth. But, if you say, "Ice cream contains dairy," well, then, you're making a statement that is universal. That is outside your personal preferences. And makes the claim to identify something tangible in the material world. Now, when you've done that successfully, that is what they call, "truth." Rightly so.

JAMES DAMORE INTERVIEW

So how are you doing today? Please introduce yourself.

I'm James Damore. I got fired by Google for writing a document that was critical of our culture and our diversity practices. I'm a victim of Fake News.

So, it must be weird for you to be a media personality when you never set out to be a media personality.

Yeah, I was really just trying to improve the internal culture at Google. And I'm a pretty introverted, don't-want-to-be-in-the-center-of-the-universe, kind of person.

You wrote the memo as a way to express your thoughts/share your thoughts with friends. Is that right?

Right. They would point to our numbers, like twenty percent women, and say, "Oh, but look — the population is fifty percent. What's happening? We're sexist."

That strikes me as a simplistic analysis.

Right.

Did they ever talk about how maybe people want to make different life choices?

No, they don't really acknowledge that different people are different in any way.

It's ironic, to me, because your memo, in my view, is about diversity.

Yeah. There's a lot of hypocrisy in the whole program because they say, "Oh, men and women are exactly the same, but we need diversity because everyone is the same." It's not clear why we would need diversity if everyone was the same, for example.

How many of these diversity training things have you been to?

I've been to about five.

How long would they last?

Some would be all day. Others a few hours.

***All day?* Talk to us about that.**

So, one, in particular, was this all-day summit for high-level people in my organization, and it was all secret. None of it was posted online. None of it was recorded like everything else at Google. Normally, we're just really open about everything. But this was really secret. And then they really went down into the details on what specific practices we're doing to try to increase representation, like actually treating people differently if they're a woman, or if they are some ethnic minority, and giving preference to these people.

What were some of the specific practices they recommended? How did they explain you should treat people differently based on their race or gender?

So, for example, in the interviews, if someone doesn't make it in the first try, then they'll give them another interview. Only if they're in a specific category. And then, also, once they get hired, they put them in this high-priority queue so that the managers will quickly hire them. And give them a higher percent chance of actually hiring them.

What specific category?

So, if you're a woman — or nonwhite, nonAsian, then you're in this category.

So, in other words, if you're in this specific category, and you blow a job interview, they'll give you another one.

Right.

A friend of mine told me that he applied for a job at Google and didn't hear back. He reapplied as a transgender and got a callback within an hour.

That could happen.

Would transgender be one of these categories?

I don't know if they've specifically called it out, but they definitely like that category.

When you were at these meetings, were there lawyers there?

Not that I know of. They tried to keep it secret so that-, because I think some of this was actual illegal discrimination.

So, what did you mean by "secret?" How did they notify you that the meeting is going to take place and how did they tell you it was going to be secret?

And they-, they said during the meeting, "Oh, none of this is recorded. Don't really share this." And, so, in that way it was secret.

Corporations have procedures and policies. How did you learn about the event? Where did you show up? What happened when you showed up?

I guess...I heard about it from one of my higher-level people in my organization and they told me where to go.

Then you show up and then what happened?

Then they give you this book about all the biases that we have. And they started giving these presentations about these different practices that we have.

Did they give you any slide shows or anything?

They presented slide shows, but they never actually gave it to us.

Do you still have the book they gave you?

I might.

I would like to see that book.

[Laughs] I'll try to find it.

Okay, so you went to these secret meetings. After you attended these secret meetings, you had a few thoughts. You wanted to express those thoughts on a twelve-hour flight to China. What happens next?

Yes. I wrote it all down. I double-checked it. I did it for quite a while and then I sent it as feedback to this program. And they looked at it, but just ignored it. And then I went to a couple of other programs and I sent it as feedback to those programs, too. And, you know, these programs actually ask for feedback. So I was doing what they asked me to do, but they just completely ignored it. And so I-, during some of these meetings, I would talk to some people and have sort of a constructive conversation, so I would send it to them. And some of them would just be like, "Yes, I totally agree." And others would try to actually have a rational discussion with me. And we would-, you know, I would actually have productive conversations with these people and it was never any of the emotional outbursts that we saw later.

So overall the feedback was, maybe, critical but composed?

It would either be, "Yes I agree," or "About this particular point, do you have a citation?" or something.

How many people do you think saw your memo?

I think a lot of the company has seen it by now.

What about before you were famous?

A few thousand people at Google saw them. Before it leaked to the public.

How did so many people see the memo?

So it became viral within the company. So there is-, the upper management started sending emails to everyone saying, "Oh, about that document — it's harmful, don't look at it. This is not what we stand for." Which just made people look at it, you know?

So, hold on a second. You're sending a memo to colleagues — to H.R. — about working conditions and then it starts to spread within the company. And then management tells people, "Don't look at that memo"?

Yeah, they specifically said, "It's harmful. This isn't what we stand for. This viewpoint is not acceptable at Google."

And this was before the memo had leaked to Gizmodo?

Right.

How long do you think the memo was within Google's infrastructure before it leaked?

It became sort of viral within Google on August 2nd and then it was leaked on about August 5th. I wrote the memo in July. It went viral within the company early August. And my life was changed forever.

When the memo was leaked in August to Gizmodo, was it the full memo?

No. They removed a lot of the citations and my graphs.

Gizmodo, in other words, obtained a copy of the memo. Do you think they unfairly edited the memo?

Yeah, especially since-, so they rewrote all the citations and footnotes, and then a lot of the initial criticism was just that, "Oh the document was completely uncited. So, this is just shoddy work."

I read the initial memo and they even said, "Leaked Full Memo." Is that right?

Yeah.

Yeah, when I read it, it said "Exclusive! Here's the full memo from James Damore." Was it the full memo?

No, it definitely wasn't the full memo.

Would a claim that it was the full memo be an example of Fake News?

Yeah, I think so.

Could you read the headline and describe whether it's a distortion?

So, the initial news report by Gizmodo says, "Here's the full 10-page, anti-diversity screed circulating internally at Google." And, so, they talk about how, you know, it's an anti-diversity screed. And they link pretty much just some of the text, but they remove all the citations and the chart and they actually mess up the formatting in a lot of ways.

Why would they remove the citations?

It might have been because they copy/pasted it, actually. So that that would remove them. So, it's hard to tell.

Do you think it's fair to characterize your memo as an anti-diversity screed?

I definitely don't think that my document could be labeled a[n] "anti-diversity screed." Because I actually state how much I do value diversity and I state ways in which we can increase the diversity without doing some of the illegal practices that we're doing.

It wasn't the full memo and it wasn't an anti-diversity screed, because I actually do value diversity. And I specifically state ways where we can increase diversity at Google.

Do you think it's a fair journalistic practice to frame things in that way? If you were going to write the story of this whole thing, what would your headline be?

I really don't think it's fair to put some label on the document like that, because it really just primes the audience to tell them what to think. And we saw this, even internally at Google, where they would copy my document, and label on top: "Sexism," "Racism," and all these nasty terms. So, yeah, it definitely doesn't let the reader really get what they-, their own opinion about the document. Definitely.

Do you think you are a victim of Fake News?

I'm definitely a victim of Fake News, because they pulled out incorrect quotations from my document. And even said that I said certain things that I never even said.

How has being a victim of Fake News changed your life?

Being a victim of Fake News has really changed my perspective on things. It really makes me doublethink what I see in the news. My life has definitely changed since the event. There's been a lot of social isolation. And a lot of time to think.

How has being a victim of Fake News affected you emotionally?

Being a victim of Fake News definitely stressed me out for several weeks. I lost a lot of sleep. Wasn't eating as much. And it really made me not trust a lot of people, which is unfortunate.

Who didn't you trust?

Mostly, I didn't trust media. I would have these hour-long interviews with some people and, really, I thought that I showed them what my document was all about. But, then they would just repeat in the doc-, in their article, "Oh, he's anti-diversity...he is a bigot." And it really lessened my view on humanity.

What about your family?

My family has been generally supportive. Because they knew me and they knew that I'm not some sort of neo-Nazi. That I actually just want to improve things. They never really took any of the news' claims to be accurate.

How does it feel to be hated?

Being hated is definitely annoying. And I've gotten some confrontations from people in person — that was sort of scary.

Could you tell us about some of these stories?

Once, I was coming out of my car and then someone just said, "F-you." Right in my face. So, I mean, I just walked away, because I'm not really sure there's a good way of resolving that.

Most of my confrontations have been positive, actually. I think most people aren't brave enough to just walk up to you and say, "F-you."

How did you actually get fired?

Now, I got fired over the phone. I was. Yeah, they told me to work from home. So, one thing that happened was someone sent me an e-mail, saying, "Oh, you're a terrible person. You're a bigot.

I'm going to hunt you down." So, either one of us is going to get fired. Yeah, this is an employee.

Tell us about that.

So, there are multiple high-level executives that were sending out these really disrespectful misrepresentations of my document, saying how harmful it is. And then one of those-, reports were, those managers sent me a direct e-mail saying, "I'm going to hunt you down...you're a terrible person. You're a bigot. And F-you." And, so, that was pretty scary.

Did anything happen to that person?

I haven't heard of anything actually happening to them. I sent it to H.R., but I don't really like doxing people, so I never sent it.

Wow, I've never heard any of this.

There's definitely-, most media outlets won't really say my side of the story. And I've been sort of selective in what I share, just because I'm really not that-, I don't want to hurt people, or Google, in general. I just want people to see that the culture is a problem and I'm not some sort of white supremacist.

One of the first media outlets you talked to were Jordan Peterson and Stefan Molyneux, who have both been characterized on the alt-right. Why did you go to them first, rather than an interview with Fox or CNN?

So, I gave an hour-long interview with Jordan Peterson as my first interview, because he's a prominent psychologist in the field. So he would be able to validate a lot of my claims, which he did. And, you know, it was also much less hostile than some of the other media interviews, which I wasn't really prepared to give at the beginning. And-, but one-, the downside was that, because I talked to him, the media started smearing him and calling him "alt-right" or just extremely conservative when, really, he is a centrist. And, so, they just use these labels on people to disregard their arguments so they don't have to actually engage in any truth-telling.

Walk us through your experience doing interviews with the mainstream media.

So, I would give interviews to Bloomberg, CNN, MSNBC, and I would-, I would give these long interviews with them, and the entire time they would just be hounding me and [were] really being hostile. And then misrepresenting the science, and I would have to constantly correct them. And what they would end up showing is just a condensed version of that, sometimes stitching together random parts of the interview. That was annoying.

What was misrepresented and how?

The interviews would usually be about thirty or forty-five minutes long. And they would condense it down to maybe five minutes, where they would stitch together some of my answers to unrelated questions, seemingly to make me seem like I wasn't actually addressing them, or that I was dumber than I am.

Do you think some of the hostility was an act or pretense?

I think some of the hostility was an act. There's definitely a-, it wasn't just individual journalists that are politically biased. There's-, the news organization itself likely has these mandates that you have to act a certain way and you have to propagate a certain narrative.

When I went on these news interviews, they would just propagate their narrative and say these two minute-long questions. Just giving examples of all the ways in which women are hurt and all the prominent computer scientists that are women, and just really try to shame me. For example, with the CEO of YouTube: She has a story about her daughter asking her about, "Oh, mom, are there biological differences between men and women?" And just trying to shame me through that, or with my associations with certain people, and rather than actually addressing some of the concerns that I had.

I don't think the media has treated me fairly.

What is it like to go talk to the media?

Talking with these media outlets is mostly just on Skype and they won't even show their video. They'll only have my video on. So I can't see how hostile their facial expressions really are. And, afterward, they'll just take out random quotations taken completely out of context and try to paint me as some sort of sexist bigot.

How does it feel knowing that people think you're a sexist bigot?

It's definitely unfortunate, because if you just read the headlines, that's exactly what you'll think. And you really have to go through the effort of reading the whole ten-page document to see that I'm not, but at least this is a very good example of how misrepresentative the media has been, because anyone that has actually read the document can see how much distortion there has been in the media.

What would a neutral headline be about your story?

A neutral headline would be: "The Author Of The Document That Criticized Google's Culture And Diversity Practices Was Fired."

Was there any evidence of search result manipulation based on content?

I don't think that there is explicit things that say, you know, a conservative meter, and then they demote things that they think are conservative. But there are a lot of black box machine-learning algorithms, where they give them training data and, based on that training data, they'll either demote or promote some results. And if the training data itself is biased, then you'll start seeing bias in the search results. And we saw this a lot in their attack against Fake News, where all the examples would be pro-Trump Fake News and none of them would be anti-Trump or pro-Hillary Fake News.

What do you think about public shaming?

I think small-scale shaming, it can be fine. But once we've gone into the Internet Age, there's just these huge online mobs and that really distorts things, and our brains aren't really built for that.

Do you think you were slandered?

I think I was definitely slandered. Even some of Google's official statements, where they say, "Oh, [he] made incorrect assumptions about gender." What were those incorrect assumptions? They never really specify. And so, it's really annoying.

Why do you think they are so in favor of the views that they have?

There's a lot ideological bias within Google. And, even beyond that, I think if they took a more objective stance, then they would, perhaps, get attacked by these social justice warrior mobs for not taking the most extreme stance possible. And, so, it's a combination of their own biases and then being constantly attacked by these social justice warriors.

Do you think Google is in a bubble?

I think people are definitely in their own bubble and these bubbles are becoming increasingly common. Their shells are even becoming harder, because, for example, Google is in the center of Silicon Valley, which is in California. So, it's an entire bubble within that. And then employees, you know, essentially live at Google and their livelihood is all in Google. They work, and eat, and make all their friends at Google. So there's a social bubble there. And these company-wide meetings, where they constantly push out the same message, and anyone [who] dissents is shamed throughout the company. That's only consolidating the echo chamber that they have.

Do you think the culture is going to get worse in Silicon Valley?

So, the culture in Silicon Valley is very progressive and it actually is very hostile towards anyone with a conservative view. There's even blacklists shared between companies of people that have conservative views. And, so, they'll get fired by one company for stating something and then they won't be able to be hired by other large companies. And this hostility is only going to spread the two sides further apart. And, so, if they don't address that, there will really be a huge problem.

Are there blacklists at Google?

Yes, there are blacklists where people have huge spreadsheets of names of people with conservative views and those people really can't find jobs in Silicon Valley.

What would the media's reaction be in an inverse universe of Silicon Valley, where everyone was a conservative, and a liberal was fired for expressing their point of view?

There's definitely an asymmetry in the media. So, if Silicon Valley was, for example, mostly conservative and it had the progressive dissenters, then the media would be much more friendly to those dissenters and much more hostile towards the conservative echo chamber. But, unfortunately, it's the other way around. And they don't see any problem with a progressive echo chamber, and they often-, they just label the conservatives as "bigots."

Why do you think we are being fed this narrative?

The media wants to construct a narrative that is just coherent. And, so, they've been pushing a lot of this: "Silicon Valley is just sexist and there's all these tech bros that commit sexual harassment," and they'll actually take out quotations from different studies and say, "Oh, thirty percent of women feel like there is unfair treatment and bias in the workplace. Look how sexist it is." And they don't even look at, in the same study, it says that forty percent of men felt like there was unfair treatment. So, there's complete asymmetry and they just cherry-pick results that fit their narrative.

Google's motto was, "Don't Be Evil." Are they living up to that motto?

So, I think the problem isn't that Google has forgotten their "Don't Be Evil" motto. They've actually clearly internalized it and started mandating it externally. The problem is their definition of "Don't Be Evil" is anything that *they* disagree with. Anything that's *conservative*, really.

What are the tools at Google's disposal for censorship?

Google's main tool is its huge influence on search results and YouTube. And, also, their huge cash reserves. So, we've seen, recently, that there was someone that wrote a piece critical of Google and a think tank that they sponsor, and then they just push on, on that think tank. And now ten people are fired because of that *one* incident.

What is the decision-making process at Google for demonetization?

Many people in the alternate media make their money through monetization of YouTube videos. But we've increasingly seen that YouTube has been demonetizing some of their videos that they see as disagreeable, or potentially offensive, to someone. And these are consistently right-wing videos. So, people's income has really dropped, by sometimes ninety percent, because of this. So, it becomes completely impossible to even have a business.

What is *truth*?

I don't really have a good response over, "What is truth?"

But isn't this a battle over truth?

I was fired for seeking truth. And a lot of people simply are seeking these ideological narratives, and they see any evidence counter to that as just wrong inherently, and they're intolerant to any different arguments.

What do you feel when you think about your own future?

It's definitely depressing to see so many people turn their back on me, and Silicon Valley, in general, being hostile to me, which is where I've been living for four years. I'm hopeful that I'll be able to find something to do, but maybe it won't be a Silicon Valley coding job.

What about the future of the nation?

I see a lot of the media as actually polarizing us and these individual echo chambers that really pit us against each other. And that's been creating increasing partisanship in our politics, which is really damaging for uniting America. And, so, that's something that I'm definitely afraid of.

Do you think alternative sources of news will ever be effectively shut down?

I think YouTube is trying to shut down some of the alternative media. But I think a lot of people have seen what's happening at YouTube, and if YouTube just becomes this echo chamber that doesn't allow dissenting views, then, hopefully, they'll move to a different platform.

Is there a cultural value to free speech that is important?

Free speech is definitely important for our culture. And it's the best tool for creating knowledge and empowering marginalized groups.

JORDAN PETERSON INTERVIEW

Who are you and what do you do?

I'm Professor Jordan Peterson. I'm a clinical psychologist and a professor of psychology at the University of Toronto, and I teach, and I have a clinical practice — although I'm on hiatus right now. I do a lot of business consulting. I have a business online that helps people plan their futures and write about their past and analyze their personalities and-, and for the last year or so, I've been embroiled in a philosophical and political controversy — a series of them, I suppose — in Canada. More broadly, as well.

Why does public shaming work?

So the question is, "Why does public shaming work on the human mind?" Well, it's a good thing that it works. No, I mean, it takes a lot of different emotions to make people properly social, and some of those are positive emotions. We enjoy being around other people. So there's-, that would be a straight positive emotion associated with approach and excitement and fun. We bond with other people, and that's a different emotional system — a number of them — mediated partly by opiates and partly by chemicals like, you know, I won't be able to remember the name — oxytocin. But, then, there is negative emotions too. So, if you're a conscientious person, for example, you feel guilt if you're not contributing to the community. And if you're not sociopathic, you feel shame if you've-, if you've acted in a manner that indicates that you're not a reliable member of the social organization, and you shouldn't feel that way.

Now, of course, the problem with negative emotions — and positive emotions, for that matter — is that they can be amplified beyond utility. That happens in all sorts of mental illnesses. And they can be manipulated. And then, of course, with regards to our current state, which is something we've never encountered before, is that you can be the target of hundreds of thousands, or even millions, of people — suddenly — and it's absolutely overwhelming. So, most of these things are necessary. But, you know, they can go badly astray and they can be manipulated. So, we don't know what to do about that, especially with-, with regards to social media, because nobody — *nobody* — knows anything about social media, really. It's too new, so...

Do you think the media has hijacked shame — to shame people for things that aren't necessarily shameful?

Well, I don't know if the media is — media, per se — has hijacked shame. I think that ideologues hijacked shame regularly. You know what-, you saw this, for example, under the Maoists — in particular, where they used public shaming constantly as an ideological tactic. And, so now, to the degree that the media — let's say, whatever that is now — is complicit in pushing an ideological narrative forward. You know, and maybe the postmodernists would argue that you're always pushing an ideological narrative forward, no matter what you're doing — they're participating in the harnessing of shame for-, for specific political ends. And, well, if you believe like the postmodernists do that the world is nothing but a stage of competition between different groups who are competing fundamentally for power, then there's no way out of that. But I think that's an unbelievably dismal view of the world.

I also think part of the reason that there is an alternative media growing, particularly on YouTube, is because there-, there are ways of presenting information that aren't precisely ideologically motivated. Now, it's tricky, because you have to have a framework through which you look at the world in order to understand the world. And it does tend to be a narrative framework, because narratives tell you how to get from one point to the other. And human beings are always getting from one point to the other. I mean, we're alive. That's what we do.

But, and so, this is something Jean Piaget, developmental psychologist, pointed out. In some ways, the truth is not so much a set of facts — although there are forms of truth like that — as a process. And the people who are popular are on YouTube — Joe Rogan is a good example, as he brings people in and they have a discussion, and the truth is actually in the process of the discussion. And the reason I think Rogan works so well is because he's actually trying to learn something when he's talking to his guests. He isn't driving forward his *a priori* notions. He has them, because everyone does, but he's looking to expand them and transform them during the conversation. And so, the truth of the conversation isn't so much in the conclusions as in the dialectical process by which those conclusions are generated. And people actually really like to listen to that.

So, when I lecture, for example — because my lectures have become quite popular on YouTube — I'm not telling people what conclusions I have drawn, although I can't help but do that to some degree. I'm trying to extend my knowledge of the topic while I'm lecturing. And, so, what that enables people to watch is the process by which-, by which new maps of the world — that's a good way of thinking about it — come into being. And that's very exciting for people. Well, that's what we do in a conversation like this — if it's a real conversation. Now, we're trying to figure out what's going on, rather than to state categorically: This is what's going on and this is-, these are the people behind it. It's like, "Well, no, we can toss out hypotheses. We can try to figure it out." And that's what makes the conversation engaging and interesting.

Yeah, what you're talking about is the unedited news, so to speak.

Okay, so, the unedited issue is like, well...Rogan — Rubin's a good example, too — a lot of these new interviewers, let's say, run very long shows. They're not sound bites. They're not clips. They haven't been run through the production mill and, actually, people on YouTube don't like that sort of thing. They like it-, they like it raw. There's lots of people on YouTube, like "Girl Says What" — Karen Straughan. She just sits at her kitchen table and talks and there's a bit of editing, you know, to get rid of the "uhm"s and that sort of thing. But, you get the whole thing — you get to draw your own damn conclusions.

And I think that's — we were talking a little bit about truth — it's, like, if you're a journalist...see, this journalist came and did a story about me in a magazine called *Toronto Life* last year, eh? And he did quite a bit of background research and the article was actually pretty well researched, but he couldn't resist the temptation to tell his readers what to think. You know, and so, he had some opinions about me and they weren't particularly positive. And so, he lay out some of the background information that he had gathered, and then he'd tell the readers what that meant. And the piece came out and I wasn't very happy with it. And so, I wrote him and I said, you know, "Kudos on your background research. Why the hell didn't you just let the readers make up their own damn minds? You don't have any trust in your journalistic ability. You don't have any trust in your audience. So you wrote a-, you wrote a propaganda piece."

Now, you might say, well, you can't help but introduce your biases and, of course, to some degree, that's true. But you can present — see, the world's too complex to describe completely, and so, you have to lay a structure on it in order to simplify it. And you might say because of that there's no way of getting at the truth, because you have to lay this structure on it, simplify it. But that's actually not technically correct. Like, imagine that, because when you-, when you simplify the world, you're basically compressing it like a compression algorithm. And if you use an unbiased compression algorithm to represent a set of data, then you sample equally from the entire dataset. You don't take all the data, but you sample equally, and then you get a representation of the whole. It's an accurate representation — it's just not as detailed. Well, that's sort of what you want to do as a journalist, to the degree that you can, you know? And partly you understand that you have biases, so you talk to people who have different opinions, or maybe you even figure out what the different opinions are and make them strong and address them while you're-, while you're telling the story. And to say that you can't do that is-, well, I think that's deeply and insanely cynical, because it also means-, if you can't do that, it also means you can't communicate. You know, if there's no truth, why do people talk to each other? What the hell's the point? We wouldn't communicate if there was no way of communicating truth. It would be pointless.

An answer to that could be to create consensus. And you can create a consensus based on falsehoods.

I mean, the postmodernists tend not to admit, in some sense, to the existence of the objective world, you know, and I think that's fundamentally a complexity issue — that there is a world that exists beyond our comprehension of it. And so, that's the simplification problem. But the problem with the consensus theory of reality is that, well, there are obstacles in the world that you bump into regardless of your damn consensus. And so, you can-, you can argue that that's not the case, but it's futile. I mean, because you learn in your own experience that there are elements of reality, even within your subjective experience, that your interpretive structure can't lay a hand on. You can't argue yourself out of being hungry — especially if you're *really* hungry.

Sometimes you can't argue yourself out of being in love — even if you know it's the wrong person. You can't-, and, fundamentally, you can't argue yourself out of pain, you know. That's why I think that the ultimate truth, in some sense, is that life is suffering. It's like, "Good luck laying down an ideological overlay on that." Like, you can adjust your pain to some degree through thought, you know — it is malleable to some degree — but not in the final analysis. And so, arguing that a separate world of constraints beyond your interpretive framework doesn't exist is: A) It's futile — it's not going to work for you, and B) You never act that way.

You know, people who talk about science say — our patriarchal Western construction, you know — they're making observations that the scientific method is, first of all — to some degree, a consequence of the subject of interest of the researcher. Fair enough. And that researchers are subject to ambition like everyone else and, hey, absolutely. But part of the scientific method is the competition of ambitions and-, and the decision through the competing ambitions about what actually constitutes the shared ground of experience. And you might say, "Well, I don't believe in any of that." It's like, yes, you do. You use computers. You fly on airplanes. You drink filtered water. You participate in the technological society and you, by participating in it, you indicate your assent to the ontological presuppositions and the epistemological presuppositions upon which it's based. And you might say, "Well, no I don't." And I would say, "Well, who cares what you say?" I'm going to watch how you act as a better indicator of your fundamental truth, and there's no reason to assume whatsoever that what you say and what you do are in alignment, like, they might be, but often with people they're not in alignment at all.

So...and the postmodernists are a classic example of that. They wouldn't turn to Marxism, otherwise. You know, because the postmodernists say, "Well, there's no grand narrative." In some sense, everything is a matter of contextual interpretation. And then that leaves them with nothing and nowhere to go. So they-, the Marxism comes in as a substitute for that.

Or maybe even the postmodernism was just a rationalization for the Marxism to begin with. It's not obvious from the historical record. But they don't act out their claims, because they can't. So-,

so this "post truth" idea is-, that's a demonic idea, really. I mean, you know, that's strange language to use. But there are some ideas that are so pathological that only archetypal descriptions are appropriate.

Did the media not construct an artificial reality using false facts that people now believe and act upon?

Well, you know, it-, it's always a question, to some degree, which of our partial realities is true and which of them is false. It is, to some degree, context dependent as well, because the environment tends to move around. You know, like, so you might say that there was a set of relatively more radical left-wing ideas that were more appropriate in 1964 than they are now — say, with regards to civil rights — and because the underlying situation has actually changed, and so, the representation should change.

Is it false consciousness? Well, that's a very deep question, because it depends what you mean by *false*. I mean, people have all sorts of motivations that they don't necessarily understand, and sometimes they put forward one set of motivations as a mask for another set of motivations. I mean, one of the things I've been trying to unpack, for example, is there's a Marxist claim that the Marxist theory is predicated on care for either the working class or the oppressed — depending on whether it's classical Marxism or sort of identity politics Marxism. And I read a book by George Orwell called, *The Road to Wigan Pier*, where he questions that assumption. He said, as far as he was concerned, the English socialists that he met — and this was back in the 1930s and '40s — didn't so much like the poor, as they hated the rich. Well, maybe that isn't true of everyone who wants to speak for the working class, but it's certainly true of a substantial number of them.

Often [you] use an ideological mask to-, to shield from yourself what your truc motivations are. Say, well, you look at Marxism and you think, well, are they actually-, are the Marxists actually motivated by compassion and the desire to help the working class? Well, then you allow the Marxist ideas to unfold in society and you watch what happens. What happens is the working class gets slaughtered and so does everyone else.

And so, then there's an indication that the stated motivations and the real motivations aren't the same. And that's a big problem. And you see — because we're polarizing in our society now — you see that sort of thing happening all the time. It's not easy to put your finger on what the-, what the actuality of the situation is.

Media gives a pass to those seeking violence if they're in Antifa. Essentially no better street gang to join right now.

Well, I think, with ideologies like that, often, is that they place a mask of virtue over a dark set of motivations. And I really do think that that's the case with-, well, it tends to be the case with extremist ideologies — period. You know, "I'm standing for the nation." And so, "But, no, I really have a tremendous amount of hatred and I'm going to take it out on anyone who's foreign." Now, that's sort of typical of that-, of the Nazi-type ultranationalists. And then, on the left, it's like, "Well, I like the poor and the oppressed and I stand for them." It's like, "Well, no, you're just resentful and jealous and-, and you don't believe that hard work matters, because you don't work hard and you don't plan to, and so, you can place a mask of virtue over your miserable, destructive resentment and then you can tolerate looking at yourself in the mirror." And so, I mean, this is why I'm no fan of ideologies, generally speaking, because they have exactly that property.

How do we know if we're lying to ourselves?

I don't know how we know, but I do know that we know. You know, like, sometimes you say something and you're not sure whether it's true or not. You have-, it's a complicated question, because you have limits on-, your knowledge is, in fact, limited, so you're limited by your ignorance. And so, you can never necessarily say that what you're saying is true, especially if you think of truth as a complete description of reality. It's like, well, then, never anything you say is true, because it's incomplete. But I don't think that that's in accordance with people's actual-, the actual experience of their reality.

I think that you know perfectly well when you're lying — at least some of the time. And I think that manifests itself physiologically as much as any other way. You know, I've asked my classes, for example, many years in a row — because I think it's an interesting phenomenon — it's like, "How many of you have had the experience of a little voice in your head talking to you, essentially, when you're about to do something that you know to be wrong," and everyone puts up their hand. Now, it isn't a voice for everyone. Sometimes it's a feeling, but people have that capacity, right? Well, we think about that as conscience, what-, whatever that is. It's a-, it's a mor-, it's a form of moral orientation, partly as a consequence of socialization. I think it's biologically instantiated, because it seems so incredibly-, people have been talking about it since the beginning of time. We better have a sense of when we're in alliance with the truth, or when we're spouting falsehoods, because when you act out a falsehood, then something terrible happens. That's the definition of a falsehood, fundamentally. So it's-, it's based on a slightly different notion of what constitutes truth than one that's purely based on the idea of objective reality. It's based more on pragmatic reality, you know? So, if you accept a set of propositions and you're-, you are-, you receive a psycho-physiological signal that that's unreliable, that's an indication that if you acted out in the world, you're going to walk over a cliff and then you'll die and that'll be the end of that.

And so, to think that we have no instinct, so to speak, to help us identify when that's the case is to say that thought is of no utility in relationship to survival. Well, I mean, you can say that if you want, but it's not a very-, it's not a very credible argument.

Regarding cognitive dissonance, aren't we hardwired to lie to ourselves?

We're hardwired to be *tempted* to lie to ourselves, and the lies are very interesting. You know, I've studied that for a very long time trying to figure out exactly that. Now, so, imagine that your belief systems are essentially maps of the world, so, they're maps that you use to orient yourself with, because we move from point to point, right? We're active creatures and then those maps are very complexly structured — they're sort of hierarchically structured. And so, for example, you have some assumptions that are predicates of more of your actions than others.

So, for example, here's a good way of thinking about it: Imagine that you're teaching your child to set the table and they put the fork and the knife on the reverse sides of the plate, and you say, "You're a stupid kid. You've always been a stupid kid, and you're always going to be a stupid kid, and there's nothing that you can do to change that." While you might say, "Well, is the fact that the child made that small mistake an indication that he or she is that kind of stupid kid?"

An answer to that is, "Well, it's some evidence." Now, a sensible person would say, "Look, you've got the knife and fork to the table and you put it near the plate. So, good for you, but you made this local mistake. This tiny local mistake. You just flip these and you got it exactly right." Now, I think everybody who had any sense would realize that the second response is much more reasonable than the first. Now, the first response is one that knocks out the child's whole axiomatic system. Right? You say, "Well, you're stupid, so, you're bad. You've always been that way." So, that covers your entire history. "You can't learn," so, you're destined for that in the future. It's like you-, you've torn apart the orienting map that the child uses in the world.

And that's a very important illustration, because if you have an argument with someone that you love, one of the appropriate tactics is to make the argument about the least that it has to be about, and to specify what you want as precisely as possible, because then you don't take the person apart. Now, there are times when we encounter pieces of information that threaten the integrity of our entire belief system.

So, another example would be: You have a relationship with someone — an intimate relationship — and it's predicated on the idea of fidelity. And so, all of your memories of the relationship have that as an axiom — for the representations, the way that you construe the present has that as an axiom, and the way that you construe the future has that as an axiom — and then you find out that the person has betrayed you and, perhaps, multiple times. Well, your world falls apart. And the reason it falls apart is because that presupposition of fidelity is an axiom for every representation of that relationship you've made, and maybe of every representation of yourself you've made, and maybe of every representation of other people that you've made. And so, it's a-, it's a crucial card in the card house. Right? You pull it out and everything falls. Okay, well, when people encounter information that is like that, they're likely to turn a blind eye to it. While that often happens in the case of betrayal — because it's very rare, it happens sometimes — it's very rare that if someone in an intimate relationship betrays you that you can't go back over the past and think, "You know, there was a hint two years ago. There was another hint eighteen months ago. We weren't holding hands often." You know? "He or she was always distracted. I knew, but I didn't ask any questions." It's willful blindness.

Now, the ancient Egyptians, they represented the state as Osiris. And Osiris was willfully blind. That was one of the characteristics of the state, and it was because of that that his evil brother, Set — who was like a precursor to the idea of Satan — chopped him up and destroyed him. And so, the lies that you're talking about are often sins of omission rather than sins of communism. It's like something threatens our axiomatic system at a very fundamental level.

We get a physiological signal of threat. The physiological signal says, "You should watch this and pay attention and unfold it and unpack it." And we think, no, we're not going there. And no wonder, because, like, do you want your whole house of cards to collapse, and you fall into chaos? It's a terrible thing. So, that's why we're motivated to lie to ourselves. But it's not helpful. It's-, and the more you do it, the more likely a precipitous collapse is to occur, because you're not updating your-, your world models.

And, actually, the neuropsychology of that is reasonably well understood. A guy named, [Vilayanur] Ramachandran, for example, has done some good work on that and Elkhonon

Goldberg as well and-, but that's why, you know, it's very useful to know that our axiomatic systems orient our-, us in the world and regulate our emotions.

And so, if you destabilize someone's fundamental axioms, you-, you dysregulate their negative emotion. That's also why people fight so hard to protect not only their belief systems, but their social systems. So, there is plenty of motivation to falsify it. But it's-, it's a bad idea. You live out the falsifications and-, and the world hits you.

You see this play out on a mass scale — with the election — the cognitive dissonance introduced by Trump's election. Instead of saying, "We were wrong," the media doubled down and invented the Russia narrative. Do you see this as mass cognitive dissonance in action?

Well, people are motivated to do the least amount of damage to their cognitive structures as possible, to correct prediction errors and that-, it's for the reason that I just described, which is that, you know, that the deeper the axiom that you have to adjust, the more you lose of your-, of the map that orients you in the world, and then the more emotional dysregulation you experience. And that's no joke, like, you know, because people think of emotions, in some sense, is just subjective feelings, but they're not just that — they're psychophysiological reactions. Say you're in a rough part of the city and you-, and you lose your map — it's like, well, you're going to be worried. And the reason you're worried is because something bad might happen to you. And so, what your body does is ramp up in to a state of emergency preparedness and emergency preparedness is *a bunch of bad things might happen.*

And so, I better be ready for any and all of them. And so, it's very, very, very physiologically demanding. And you can handle that for short periods of time. But if you're in a state like that and it's chronic with all that stress, that hurts you-, you know, it hurts your brain. It destroys brain tissue. It-, it suppresses immunological function. It enhances insulin production. It increases the probability you'll be obese and you'll develop cancer, heart disease — that you'll age.

It's really no joke, and so, when something axiomatically impossible happens, people are going to scramble to find reasons that don't require retooling of their worldview. And it's-, it's no wonder, because they're avoiding — in architectural terms — they're avoiding an involuntary descent to the underworld and even to hell. You know, like, for example: Let's say that you're betrayed by your partner. You don't want to admit it. Well, no wonder, because all your memories of the past are *wrong*. Your view of your partner is incorrect, and so, maybe your view of human beings and yourself is incorrect, and your future is like, well, okay, it isn't what you thought it was going to be.

So, God only knows what it is. But then, you know, when you dig into that, you might also find that there are reasons your partner was not faithful. Maybe you're a real son of a bitch and you deserved everything you got. And so, when you dig down, and you have to restructure those axioms, not only do you have to encounter the unknown as such — which is no joke — but you may also have to discover your own malevolence. Well, it's no wonder people turn away from that. You know, like, a worldview adjustment is a major revolution and it's-, you may not recover from it. That's the other thing, you know, if you're broken — and you can be broken by betrayal — there's no reason to assume that you're going to pop out at the other end of that sadder, but wiser. It just might do you in. It might kill you, or maybe you're chronically depressed, or maybe you're resentful and hostile and murderous, or...there's no reason to assume that you will recover. So, it's no wonder people are afraid to do that. It's not surprising at all, and everyone is like that. So, you struggle to find the least amount of repair you have to do to keep your pragmatic prediction system intact.

Well it's-, often that means accusing someone else, because then *they* have to change — not *you*. And it means exaggerating one fact, at the cost of another, as you scramble to maintain your ground.

I would say...I don't know if it's the media so much in the U.S. as it is the Democratic Party — you know, the Democratic Party made some big mistakes in that election. They basically lost the election. It isn't so much that Trump won, although there's some of that. And in my view, definitely they lost. And I think they lost for a variety of reasons. There was probably a number of things that tipped the scales, because there wasn't much tipping that had to be done. But the fact that they decided to play identity politics was a big part of it. Now, what that means, perhaps, is that if the Democrats want to get back on track, they have to reexamine the axioms that led them to accept identity politics as a-, as an appropriate mode of being in the world.

That's a big retooling, man. It may not even be possible. It may be that new Democrats have to emerge to replace the old ones, because the old ones are done. They can't learn. It's too late. We'll see.

I'm quite pessimistic about humanity's ability to ascertain truth.

Well, you know, there's a difference between wishing that people would live by truth and wishing that they wouldn't lie. We can do that. You know, if you watch yourself through the day, there are things you don't know about and then maybe you talk about them anyways — and hopefully that isn't what's happening right now — but, you know, now and then, that you're saying something or acting in some manner that isn't in accordance with what you know to be true.

Well, you cannot do that! Living in truth, that's a different issue, because, I mean, that requires — it may not be possible — it would require superhuman effort to never utter a falsehood.

But...and then, maybe you can start seeing what the truth is, so to speak, but at least people cannot lie. Not outright lie. And that's a good start.

I mean, you see this-, well, I've been-, I've had some posters put up in my neighborhood recently, warning the community about me. So, that's actually what they say, "Community Warning," you know, and I don't-, I don't mind that people disagree with me. It's their fate. They'll act out their presuppositions and they'll find out what the consequences are, so, fine. But there is a lie on the poster, you see, and so, the lie is that they put a picture of me up. And I look very aggressive. My mouth is open and I'm yelling — and I am actually *yelling*. But the reason I'm yelling is because I'm at a free speech rally that was shut down by radical leftists and they took the mic and they shut down the P.A. system and they blasted white noise. And so, the reason that I'm yelling and look aggressive is because I'm trying to make my voice heard over their noise. But that's the picture they picked to portray me.

Well, they knew — or they were willfully blind — they knew that that was a trick. Now, they feel the ends justify the means, I suppose. But they didn't have to do that. They could have put up posters about me without lying. I think the posters would have even been more effective, because what's actually happened — I tweeted the posters, for example — is that because they tell people to write the university and tell them what a reprehensible human being I am, as far as I know, they've had the reverse effect. Many people have written the university and told them how reprehensible the poster producers are and that, you know, that I'm not what they claim I am. But the lies didn't help them. They knew they were lying. They did it anyways. Well, when you do that, you-, you-, you corrupt the structure of the world and you corrupt your own soul. And, God help you, so...

So, you know, we're talking about whether there is such a thing as *truth*. I think journalists played this role quite nicely before. I think things started to go south in the '80s, but I think the journalists in the '70s and '60s and '50s, and so on, were-, many of them were trying to lay out an unbiased simplification of the situation and to let the viewers/readers make up their own minds, you know, to the degree that that was possible. Like, if you look at an old *Time* magazine, it's a completely different thing. From the '70s, they're like one hundred pages thick — it's all text, it's dense — it's denser than today's *Economist* by a large margin. And, you know, it's people grappling with ideas. Okay, so now, that isn't how things work now, let's say, in the mainstream media — to use a rather cliched phrase. Well, you know, maybe they say, "Well, it doesn't matter. There's no such thing as truth anyways." It's like, "Yeah, it matters. Nobody under thirty listens to you." Why? Why is that? Why are they going to people like, well, Rogan's a good example — who has no production values and no real editing and it's just, like, a real conversation between two people — why are they listening to that?

Well, there's your evidence. Now, you don't have to pay any attention to it, and I don't really think that the classical media giants are paying attention. I think they're too old, actually. Like, I was looking-, there was an MSNBC clip on YouTube about this robot that has embedded AI and some emotional responses. So I was kind of interested in that, so I went and watched it, and it was like a four-minute clip. Well, it only had like twelve thousand views, which I found peculiar. But, they put a thirty-second ad at the beginning of it and you couldn't skip it. Like, they don't know the conventions. It's like, first of all, an hour of content might justify a fifteen-second ad, and you get to skip it. It's like, "You're going to ask me to pay for your four minutes of professionally edited fluff with thirty seconds of my time?" That's not going to work.

So, they're off in another world and it isn't working out. And-, and they're collapsing. And young people are turning in droves to these alternative media sources. And I think the reason for that is they're not getting an unbiased simplification from the media, which is what they should be getting.

So, consequences...you know, falsehoods have consequences. That's what makes them false. And you cannot believe that, it's fine. You can even get away with it for some period of time. But you're not going to get away with it for very long.

What's the difference between news and propaganda?

What's the difference between news and propaganda? Well, if it's news, it's-, it's kind of like, the question is sort of like, "What constitutes information?" Well, if something is informative, well, it informs you and what that means is that it brings you into alignment better.

There should be an alignment between you and the world. If you're properly informed, you're in a formation, right? And a formation is ordered and sequential and you think, "Well, what does that mean?" Well, I might ask you for directions and you inform me about where I'm going and then I follow your directions and I get there. So, I'm in alignment with the world, all of a sudden, because you've informed me. Well, if it's real news, it informs you, and what that means is it updates your map.

You know, it takes something that's-, you have a journey that you're on, and it isn't fully mapped out, because *what the hell do you know*? And then someone tells you some news, and you think, "Oh, I have to make a slight detour here. I have to change the way I'm looking at the landscape, slightly." That's news.

Now, you might ask, "Well, is much of what is news actually information?" And the answer I have to that is, "No, hardly any of it." I haven't watched television news for thirty years, I would say, because I think, "Well, it's only relevant today — it's not relevant." I don't want to know what's only relevant today. What-, why the hell would I pay any attention to that? So, you know, I've subscribed to *The Economist* for quite a long time, although I haven't renewed it recently for a variety of reasons. But, at least they're talking about things that are going to be relevant conceivably over a month, or a couple of months period, and I believe they were reasonably unbiased...although I'm not so sure about that anymore.

I think the quality of that magazine has actually dropped. News updates your map and then you don't fall into a hole and get eaten by a crocodile. And that's what information is, essentially, too, is that it updates the manner in which you orient yourself in the world — so, that's partly your perceptions and partly your actions. And you'll pay for that, right, because it's cheaper to pay for it than it is to learn it through experience. So I guess that's what news is — news is something that-, it's cheaper to learn than it is to learn by experience than it is to pay for it. And most of it's not *news.*

Where do you get your news?

I scan a lot of different sources. You know, I do look at newspapers a bit. I read a lot online, but I spend most of my time reading books, not-, I read books, mostly. And that's where I get my news. You know, and you might say, "Well, that's not the cutting edge dynamic news." It's not.

And I follow Twitter, and I look online and I glance at the major-, I still glance at the major news front pages, now and then. I like the BBC, so far. But, mostly I'm trying to concentrate on things that have a longer shelf life.

What do you think of Alain de Botton's book, *Status Anxiety*?

I don't know it.

You had mentioned that to stay up-to-date: read a book. And I always recommend people understand status to figure out what's really going on.

Well, status is really important to people. I mean...although I would say, I've had to think through my terminology with regards to that for a long time. Now, I mean, people exist in hierarchies like most animals, right?

Even very ancient animals live in hierarchies. It's not something human beings created. The patriarchy is not a human creation. It's way older than human beings. It's a third of a billion years old. So, and you have a counter in your brain that tells you where you are in the hierarchy, and the higher you are in the hierarchy, the more serotonin your brain produces, and the more your negative emotions are regulated. So, what that means is, that for every unit of uncertainty you encounter, you produce fewer units of *emergency preparedness*. It's a big deal, you know, because if you're at the top of a — let's call it a *hierarchy*, for now — you're pretty secure. Got a lot of allies, right? You've got a lot of influence. You've got a lot of wealth. You've got a good place to live. And so, if something creeps into your life that's not so good, you don't have to panic about it. You've got options. Whereas, if you're at the bottom of the hierarchy, you're barely clinging to the side of the window, you know, with your fingernails. Something that moves one finger might send you plummeting to your death, so you're in a constant state of hyper anxiety. People really care about where they are in the hierarchy, because that old counter, which is a third of a billion years old, tells them how upset to get about uncertainty, as a consequence of their placement in the hierarchy.

Now, the postmodernists would say, "Well, all those hierarchies are predicated on power," which is to say, they're all tyrannies. And that's actually untrue. Not in functional societies. And our society is functional. And you might say, "Well, how do you know that?" And I would say because the electricity is on. You know, I mean, this incredible infrastructure we have works almost all the time, almost for everyone.

And so, that means the hierarchy isn't a hierarchy of power and tyranny — it's a hierarchy of competence. And so, there's no reason to be cynical about that. Now, you might say, "Well, it gets polluted with power and it gets polluted with tyranny." It's like, yeah, yeah...yeah, it's not perfect. You know, and tyrants emerge and psychopaths emerge and, you know, and not everyone is equally well-served by this system ob-, obviously. But, compared to any other system that's ever been, or anyone that exists currently, well, all you have to do is look around. All these people complaining about the tyranny of the system communicate with their iPhones, their Androids, and never think for a second that the only reason those things work is because we live in hierarchies of competence, not hierarchies of power.

So, well...so, status is important, but it's not based on-, in a functioning society, it's not based on power. You know, even Frans de Waal, who's a primatologist, showed quite clearly that even among chimpanzees — they're pretty damn brutal — tyrannical chimpanzee hierarchies are unstable. So, what happens is, you get a big ugly chimp who-, who's, like, all muscle and irritability. He climbs the dominance hierarchy, because he he pounds everyone flat. It's like, "He had a bad day, though." And then two of the people-, two of the chimpanzees that he brutalized gang up and tear him to shreds.

So what de Waal has found among the chimps is that the stable hierarchies are run by males, because chimps are patriarchal in their structure, essentially. But the chimps that stay at the top and produce a stable hierarchy are ones that groom other chimps and have friends and engage in mutual reciprocity and pay positive attention to the females, and also to the infants. So the tyrant chimp just doesn't last. That's even true for chimps.

Well, so, this is the big leftist idea: *All the hierarchies are corrupt. They only serve those who are at the top. It's all power.* It's like, "No, it's-, that's wrong." And the proof is the fact that the hierarchy functions.

Is mainstream media a prestigious hierarchy of status? As opposed to more egalitarian platforms of alternative media?

Well, the prestige of the classic media was predicated on their influence, and so, let's say that *The New York Times* is an influential and prestigious outlet. Okay, why? Well, here's an example: You write a book, it hits *The New York Times* bestseller list. Well, who cares?

Well, the reason you care is because, if you hit the list, your book sales exponentially increase.

And so, the prestige is related to the power of the-, of the institution to change perception and behavior. Well, so it's-, it's-, it's the brand, so you could say the brand is the marker of that prestige that's being stored up across time. Yeah.

But, the thing is that the older media forms are raping their brands. Right? They have value, because they were prestigious... because they did change people's opinions and behavior, but that's evaporating. And it's partly evaporating because-, well, there are new media forms, and it's partly evaporating, because people no longer really trust them to give them that unbiased simplification.

And the thing about the egalitarianism of YouTube is that it's got its pros and its cons — and this is the same with the Web, in general, is that the signal-to-noise ratio...there's a lot of noise. There's a lot of noise and that's what happens under extraordinarily egalitarian circumstances is there might be a lot of signal, but it's damn hard to find it, because you don't have qualified gatekeepers.

Now, that's changing, because even though YouTube is egalitarian, there's a vicious hierarchy that's already developed, like, almost everyone on YouTube has no subscribers, right? You know, a thousand, a hundred...something like that. A tiny proportion has one hundred thousand. An even tinier fraction has half a million and then above a million...it's like vanishingly small. So, the hierarchy emerges and, I would say, it's a hierarchy of competence almost by definition. Let's say we don't know what YouTube does, but whatever it does, the people who have four million subscribers are doing *best*, so it's a hierarchy of competence right away.

What would you say to someone who would claim that media legitimacy is a social construct?

Well, like, everything, to some degree, is a social construct like that. The problem with those sorts of phrases is that they're used as one-phenomena causes for everything. That's how you can tell if you're talking to someone who's an ideologue. It's like, well, "Why is that happening?" "Well, it's the patriarchy." It's like, "Oh, I see! It's happening because of society!" Well, yeah, of course, you know, you can even say that you die because of the inadequacy of the patriarchy. You know, if it just got its act together, it can figure out how to make you immortal. Well, fair enough. You know? That's true, although it's not true in any useful sense. It's like, is it a social construct? You got to be way more specific than that before a comment like that has any utility whatsoever.

You've got to delve into the details, you know, and you also have to define what you mean, to some degree. Because we're social animals. There isn't anything that we do that social-, that society has no influence on. So, but that doesn't mean that everything is a social construct. That's just muddy, muddy thinking.

How can the media regain its public trust and legitimacy?

I don't think it will. I think it's done. You know, Marshall McLuhan in his famous — I don't remember what he said exactly — "The medium is the message." There we go. That's it. What did he mean by that? New technological forms require new forms of perception and behavior. And I used the MSNBC example earlier to show that they don't know the idiom, right? They think, well, "YouTube? Pffft. Low production values." You know, cute cat videos? There's no idiom.

It's like, there is an idiom. There's conventions. They don't know them. They can't make the translation. They don't know how. And so, I don't think they're going to survive. I don't see any evidence that they are, because I don't see any evidence that people under thirty care anything about — or even know, to some degree, about — the old school media organizations. That's not where they live. Now, I don't know where they live is any better. It's different, though. That's for sure. It's not obvious. I don't think very many horse-and-buggy makers turned into auto manufacturers. You know, I mean, I assume *some* did. But my guess is the vast majority of them couldn't make the adjustment, because they thought of the car as a horseless carriage. Well, that's not what it was. We don't even know what it was, but it wasn't a horseless carriage. That's for sure.

So, and YouTube isn't TV by a different form. First of all, it's permanent. That's weird, and unbelievably powerful, because it also means that for the first time in human history, the spoken word or the-, or the received image has as much permanence as a book, but it's faster to market. Way more people attend to it. Like, you know, I can put up a YouTube video that I make in a day, and it'll have fifteen thousand views in a week. I can't do that with a book. That would take me three years and probably it wouldn't happen. I probably wouldn't sell fifteen thousand copies. So, it's a whole new thing and it's-, God only knows how powerful it is. You know, we have no idea. It's a Gutenberg Revolution for the spoken word.

I advised [Anthony] Scaramucci to start his own media company after the CNN fake story fallout, and to do videos on YouTube.

Yeah, well...I mean, it's-, it's a different thing. That's right — it's a different landscape. The old rules that work for television don't work for YouTube, because YouTube isn't television.

Now, that doesn't mean I know what it is, but-, but it likes things *rougher*. You know, you can observe it to some degree. It doesn't like editing very much. It wants to see the mistakes. It wants to see the warts. It trusts it then. It doesn't want everything airbrushed and edited out. It doesn't care as much about attractiveness. You know, like, it isn't as though all the YouTube people who have become influential are the good-looking news anchors that you see on CNN. In fact, I think that's also something that people have come to distrust. So, but you just can't make the lateral move from of an old media to new media — especially if you have contempt for the new media, which is a big mistake. It means you don't know anything about it. So, you're shunted off into irrelevancy before you realize it. And so, you know, maybe the same thing will happen to YouTube, too, in five years, because the new technology will come out and that could easily happen, so...

Do you think people are becoming more forgiving now, because they realize that so much of what we say is edited, and that they're more permissive in terms of being forgiving and redemptive?

I would say, no. I don't think so, but I think that's-, I think maybe that would be the case if they knew the context. You know? But I think-, I think it's very easy, and it's been something I've been absolutely horrified about for the entire last year. It's certainly possible that I've said something in the two hundred and sixty videos that are online — most of my previous courses — that, if taken out of context, would sink me. Right? That hasn't happened. Thank God for that. You know, it means I've either been very fortunate, or I've been very careful about what I've been saying, and I would say both of those are true. It's certainly possible that I'll say something tomorrow and be done. That's the most likely — I've felt that way the whole year — the most likely outcome for me was that I would say something that would sink me. And all the context in the world wouldn't matter.

So, I think it's-, I'm more protected than that now, I would say, because I've been attacked a lot and, you know, it's the crying wolf phenomenon. If you attack-, if you hear a hundred attacks on someone and they all turn out to not be true, you're probably less likely to believe the one hundred and first. But, I have this talk coming up on November 11, that I'm actually very worried about, because I know that the protesters who will be there, in force, have been emboldened by the fact that they got the same talk canceled by Ryerson University about three months ago.

And I'm quite nervous about the possibility that someone who's hypothetically — what would you say, I hate to say — who's-, who hypothetically holds views that are similar to the panelists — even though the panelists are very diverse — will do something fatally stupid and it will be captured. Or-, or even not so stupid, and will be edited to look bad. And, you know, that-, that'll be a catastrophe. Or that there will be agents provocateur placed in the audience to do exactly that. So, the price of a social media mistake is infinite.

I disagree. I would posit that you own your own message now.

Yes. Yes. Look...I mean, maybe it would be appropriate for us to think about the media access that individuals have now as an amplifier, you know, rather than something that's necessarily negative or necessarily positive. This has happened a lot to me in the last year, where something that could have been negative, wasn't. In fact, it turned out to be very positive. And, I do think I'm in a position now so that I have more leeway for error.

But-, but, I don't have-, I still don't have a lot of faith in that. You know, because I can come out, I can make a video and say, "Look, like, as far as I can tell, this is what happened." I take responsibility wherever that was necessary. And now I might-, that might be okay, depend[ing] on the magnitude of the-, of the error, right? So, but...so, fair enough.

A hit piece doesn't land anymore. You can retort.

Yes, well, you certainly have more defense now. You know, so if-, that-, that's exactly right. So, if-, if something is published about me, I can make a video saying, "Well, no, this is what I think..." and-, and that is powerful.

And that works for people who have some influence in YouTube. Like, if you're someone whose channel has very few viewers, and someone takes out a hit piece on you, then you can't defend yourself very well. But certainly someone who is well-positioned on YouTube...like, it's not obvious to me — this is a weird thing — it's not obvious to me that I have less influence than the Canadian Broadcasting Corporation, for example, which is pretty damn weird, you know? It's, like, I say that with-, it might not be true. That might not be true. But we don't know how to measure these things, so, if I get attacked by a major news outlet, it isn't clear that they will have more readers than I will have viewers.

So the easy access to YouTube does give you some defense, but that's also predicated on having a following of some significance so that you have some impact when you speak.

So, I guess it's a consequence of being a media force as an individual, but you can certainly have that now. It's not easy, but it's certainly possible.

There's the example of PewDiePie versus *The Wall Street Journal* and how the issue was viewed differently by different segments of people — two movies/one screen.

Right, right, right, right. Yeah. Well, you can see that-, that power shift occurring. Definitely. And, I mean, I haven't seen any good studies of this, like, I don't know...

You know, if you took your typical twenty-five-year-old — say, American twenty-five-year-old — what proportion of their information they're garnering from — let's say that the YouTube heavy-hitters — and what proportion they're garnering from classical sources. My suspicion is it's more the former than the latter, and certainly the case for a very large number of people, even though it might not be true for the average person yet. I don't know. And it's so new. Like, I would say YouTube's only become a significant cultural force — what? — over the last three years? It's something like that. It's like-, it's completely new. So, we don't know what to make of it yet.

I've had an epiphany about how much power YouTube can give you.

Well, I was just on Jocko Willink's podcast. Jocko has published a book recently and it's had no real media coverage, but it hit *The New York Times* bestseller list. And the only reason for that is because he's been talking about it in his podcast. He has a *million listeners* a day — per podcast! Like, that's a lot of listeners. I think he does one a week — something like that. So, yeah, you can-, you and I...I've got this book coming out in January, called, *12 Rules For Life,* and it's doing very well in pre-sales. And the only reason for that is that I've tweeted about it. A bit. Not much. I haven't even made a video about it, yet, although I talked to Dave Rubin about it yesterday, but we don't-, and I'm trying to work that out with...

It's Penguin Random House that's publishing it, and they have publicists, right? And we're trying to figure out-, it's like, "Okay, how, exactly, do you market this?" Like — and I don't even know — like, is their publicity team any stronger than my publicity team? So, it's not obvious at all. And so-, well, it's new territory. We're all feeling our way.

I was wondering if you could talk about the narrative map of Christianity and whether-, do you believe that that map no longer has the influence that it did, and how that has affected — or influenced — the rise of postmodernism, perhaps?

So you're going to ask an *easy* question — that's the idea.

And, perhaps, also, you know, one of the people we talked to — an historian, on journalism — just mentioned the fact that, you know, there were a lot of Christian journalists, you know, back in the '20s, for instance. And, so, I was curious if you think that he thinks that that might have an influence as well in the way that objectivity and journalism is on the decline. And if you believe that.

I think that we're at a point where, like, Judeo-Christian ethics can't die. Because if they do — or it does — then our civilization is done. Because its foundation blocks are of that ethic. Now, then, the question is, "Well, is there anything to that?" Well, that's partly what I've been exploring in this biblical series, which has been oddly popular, and I think the most popular video I've ever made — the most viewed video — is the first one in a thirteen-part biblical series that I've done so far, called, "An Introduction To The Idea of God." And it's an investigation into the metaphysics of consciousness, I suppose. My proposition is that what is expressed in the story of Genesis, right at the beginning, is the idea that the essential creative element of divinity is expressed in the idea of the Logos — the Word — right?

So, the idea there is-, that there's something about what we're doing here, say, which is the exchange of communicative information that is constitutive of the world. It calls a world into being. And-, and that consciousness plays a role of calling the world into being through language. And that's the image of God in man, as far as I can tell. Now, that may not be all it is, and I'm not claiming that I have an exhaustive account of that story, because it's not possible to have an exhaustive account of it. But there is a really deep idea in there, which is that the individual participates in the creation of being through his/her use of communication.

And that — as a consequence — that's the reason that the individual is of transcendent value. And I think that's true. It's not metaphorically true. It's not symbolically true, although it might be both of those as well. It's just true. And if we lose that, then we're in trouble. And we can't lose it. Now, people act as if it's true, because we treat each other — when we're treating each other properly — as if we're locales of the co-creation of being. That's why your opinion matters. That's why you have a right to it. That's why other people listen to you.

It's important that that happens. Now, unfortunately, our explicit understanding of that, and our implicit understanding of that, aren't in alignment. That's really the death of God, in some sense — in the Nietzschean sense. And that's one of the things that I'm trying to, let's say, rectify. It's one of the things that Carl Jung was trying to rectify. Now, because Nietzsche knew that with the death of God there would come both nihilism and totalitarianism and he knew it would be of the radical leftist sort, most particularly, and he knew that it would result in millions of deaths, he predicted all of that which is unbelievable. And-, and Nietzsche thought, well, human beings would have to become supermen, in some sense, in order to overcome the death of God. To bear it. And that they could do that, in some sense, by voluntarily recreating themselves.

Now, Jung was a student of Nietzsche's. Not technically, but, you know, but intellectually, and he was very interested in that idea of the recreation of the superman, but Jung knew something that

I would say Nietzsche didn't know, which was that we don't get to create ourselves.

We participate in the creation of being, but we're already formed creatures. We have a nature which we cannot override. Well, you know that. You can't just tell yourself what to do. You won't just trot out and obey yourself, which is really weird, you know. It's like, you think, "Well, I'm going to change my diet and I'm going to exercise more," but it's like, *No, you're not!* You can't just-, you just don't follow your own orders. And so, Jung said, "Look, we have a deep, deep nature and it's expressed in symbolic vision and in archetypal reality, essentially, and we have to communicate with that in order to restructure our value systems." And I believe that he was correct.

And so, that means going back into the past. And well, this has almost become an Internet meme: Rescuing your father from the belly of the whale. Rescuing your *dead* father from the belly of the whale. Right? And that's-, that's what needs to be done.

And that means to revivify — particularly, the idea of the Logos — the idea of the divinity of the communicative capacity of the individual, which is the fundamental predicate of our society. Right? Our society says that the individual is sovereign over the community. The community is important, and the individual has responsibilities to the community, but the community has to hold the individual as the sovereign entity. It's like, *Yes, that's right*. And it's taken people — it's not an arbitrary ideological statement — it's taken people hundreds of thousands of years to develop that idea to the point where it can be reasonably articulated. You know, it was expressed in ritual, it was expressed in myth, in image, all of that. We're acting out this dream that represented that.

That's what the Christian drama is about, in essence. It's what the entire Bible is about, in some sense. But it's not like we understand that in an articulated manner. Now, I think Jung went farther than anyone to-, to make that articulated understanding a possibility, and that's the sort of thing that I'm trying to further. And that seems to be working. I mean, one of the things that I've noticed is that — this is a remarkable thing — is that talking to young men, in particular, about responsibility and truth is a highly marketable message. They're half-dead for lack of that message. And that's-, who would have guessed that? You know, it's-, it's...So, I have this theater in Toronto, where I give these lectures and they're sold out every time — which is, you know, if you would have gone to someone with a business plan and said, "Well, I'm going to rent this theater and, I mean, give lectures on the psychological significance of the biblical stories... what do you think? Do you want to lend me some money?" — on that bet, they would have laughed you right out of the office!

It's completely unlikely, but these old ideas, man, they're-, they're *eternal*. That's what they are. And you become dissociated from them at your extreme peril, psychologically and socially. So...

When we were dreaming up some ideas for the film, Jon was inspired to make this, sort of, having the opening of the film being a painting of the Garden of Eden, where Eve was tempted by the serpent. The line had come up that, "Fake News is older than sin." Meaning, deception, and how they are interrelated. I thought it was a little heavy-handed. Yesterday, we saw the painting in a room. So, we filmed that. And then today, we're interviewing you. So, I was wondering if you could speak to that story in terms of, maybe: truth, falsehood, the archetypal resonance of that story?

Oh, so, deception? Yeah, I mean, deception...people — arrogant people, resentful people — believe that deception works and it-, that's just not the case.

You can't bend the structure of reality without it snapping back at you. It might not snap back when you expect it to, but it'll knock you off your feet at some point. You might not even notice the causal connection, but the causal connection is there, because the world is a causal place and things just don't go away. You know? If you introduce an act of deception into the world, it stays in it. It manifests itself until someone fixes it. So, the Adam and Eve story...let's think about that for a minute.

I think I need a more specific question about it, because it's such a complicated story. I don't really know where to begin. Now, you guys said that you were thinking about using that as a-, as a cover image for the film?

An opening for it. Well, basically, you know, that story to me-, that moment the extension of the fruit is predicated on the lie where [the serpent] makes Eve question the Word of God. Right? And that's-, that's where she allows herself to be deceived. So, maybe you can touch on that?

I don't know if I can, you know, because it's such a...I don't-, I don't know if I can. That's such a strange part of that story, because it's too complicated. We'll have to try a different question.

You know when-, when you were speaking with Michael you made this analogy of why-, it wasn't an analogy, but you were talking about the big muscled-up chimp. And, you know, he's not going to last long, because a lot of other people lower than him conspire together to take him out. So, I was wondering if you see that sort of dynamic play out with the mainstream media and...

Okay, okay. Well, that's a question that I can answer. So, you know, the postmodern idea — one of them — is that there's an infinite number of ways to interpret the world. And that actually happens to be true. So, you have to give the devil his due. The world is a very complicated place and there is a very large number of ways of interpreting even a very small set of objects. So, but that's not-, but then-, okay, so fine, so, that's a problem. Then the question arises, "Well, how do you know if your interpretation is canonical or true or valid or valuable?" Well, how can you tell? Maybe you can't. That's the postmodernist claim. And then immediately everything devolves into something approximating a power game. It's all very sketchy in terms of its logic, but the initial presupposition is correct. But the second presupposition is wrong, because actually the range of interpretations that you can successfully apply is unbelievably tightly bounded and it's bounded-, well, it's bounded in the case that we talked about earlier with regards to the chimps. There are levels of brutality that the chimp troop will not tolerate.

So...so, here's-, here's how the constraints work: I mean, first of all, there are the constraints of the world beyond the social. Let's call that, *the natural world*, for lack of a better term. And if the interpretation of the world that you're using doesn't allow you to meet your basic biological requirements, then you die. Now, you might say that, well, just because you die doesn't mean that you were wrong. It's like, okay, you can have a discussion about that. But it certainly does mean that you're dead.

So, if you're not dead and you don't have the right-, a useful, proper interpretation of the world, then you're in extreme agony and you're probably going to want to avoid that, because that's sort of the definition of agony. It's that which you want to avoid.

And so, there's a lot of interpretations of the world that you can have that will produce agony. You can walk into a biker bar and go, like, harass the biggest, ugliest guy in there and then you'll get pounded half to death. And that would be an indication that, unless you were aiming at being pounded to death, that wasn't a good selection from among the infinite number of interpretations applicable in that bar.

Okay, so, those are pretty basic, right? But then there's more complex ones, like, you shouldn't have an interpretation that works today, but that puts you in a worse place tomorrow. That's-, that's a tough constraint, right? That's a really tough one, but then it's even worse. You shouldn't have an interpretation that works today, but puts you in a bad place next week, or next month, or next year, or maybe even ten years from now. So, there's a sequence of temporal extensions across which your action in the present has to function. It's like, *good luck figuring that out!* That's hard. That's really hard. You act now, so that you benefit in the future. But that's not the end of the constraints.

You have to act now, so that other people will either cooperate or compete with you in the present in a sustainable manner across all those timeframes. So, infinite number of interpretations — yes. Finite number of practically applicable interpretations — like, really bounded, tightly bound. That's actually why, in some sense, there are archetypes, because there is a very small universe of functional interpretations, and those-, and those are-, they're ancient and stable. Otherwise, we wouldn't even be able to perceive the world. So the whole postmodernist idea is correct with regards to the infinite number of interpretations, and just wrong beyond belief about the rest of what unfolds as a consequence of that initial presupposition.

Those timeframes can extend into eternity.

That's the thing. Well, and, you know, the fundamental religious claim is that your proper timeframe should extend into eternity. Right? And that's sort of the idea behind acting so that you enter Paradise for eternity. That's — speaking psychologically — that's the idea. You should aim at the eternal good. And that should be the constraint system within which you perceive and act moment-to-moment. And again, I don't-, that's not a metaphor. It's not a symbol. It's none of those things. It's actually, as far as I can tell, it's just *true*. So, and how could it be otherwise? How could it be otherwise than that which you should aim for is the highest good that you could conceive of? How could it-, it's, by definition, that's what you should aim for. The highest good is that which you should aim for. So, you have to aim. You can't even see without aiming. So, you have to have an aim, and that should be the highest aim. What is it going to be? You should aim for the lowest? Well, no, it contradicts the very *idea* of aim.

So, well...so, that's part of the postmodernist critique. Well, then you asked about its relationship with Christianity. Well... so, there's an aim in Christianity — apart from its individuality and its emphasis on the Logos — the truth, right? And the highest aim. There's actually an elaboration of part of what that highest aim is. And it's rough, man. It's a rough one. And it's sort of embedded in the idea of Christ's Passion. And so, two things happen that are archetypal in the Passion story. One is that Christ takes responsibility for the evil of the world onto himself. That's a psychological statement. It's like, you're human, right?

Human beings have the capacity for malevolence. So, the malevolence in the world is your problem. It's partly there because you're not good enough. You haven't put yourself together enough, and you're capable of those things. And you can say, "No, I'm not." It's like, *yes you are!* You just don't know, and it's no wonder you don't know, and it's no wonder you don't *want* to know. But it doesn't matter.

And so, Jung said, "The shadow reaches all the way down to Hell," and what he meant by that — it's no joke, and this is why people don't read Jung, it's like-, it's not fun — he says, "You look into your heart, when you're deceiving and arrogant and resentful, and you go all the way to the bottom of what's there, and you're going to find something that — once you see it — you'll never be the same." Well, so, people don't go there. What Jung said, well, that's a precondition for any form of enlightenment. That's why Christ has to harrow Hell before He can descend into Paradise. And that's a-, that's a terrible idea. Okay?

So, that's the malevolence end of it, but then the other element of the Passion is, well, it's to voluntarily accept your-, your torturous destiny. Voluntarily — that's what acceptance of the cross means, symbolically, the cross is an X, [and] you're at the center of that X. That's the center of suffering. Okay, what are you going to do about that? You're either going to embrace it, or you're going to run from it. Well, what? Are you going embrace it? I mean, that's a hell of a thing to embrace. Well, what happens if you run from it? It gets worse. So, there is a call there. There's a call to accept and-, and attend to the malevolence. To constrain it. And a call to courageous being in the face of ultimate tragedy. And that's part of the highest aim. It's like, that's not symbolic. It's just true.

And so, we can't lose that, because the alternative...like, you think, "Well, what's worse?" Is there anything worse than voluntarily accepting your own crucifixion, so to speak? Yeah! Running from it!

So...you got your poison on the one hand, and you got your poison on the other hand. You get to pick which one.

But there's no pain-free way out. So, you're either going to act nobly in the face of that and try to make things better, or you're going to act in a cowardly, deceitful and resentful fashion, and make everything worse.

Those are your choices and you're making that choice with *every* choice. That's the axis of choice. So...and it's no wonder people don't want to believe that. God, that's a horrible thing to believe.

You know, we think people have meaningless lives because they've abandoned God and they're nihilistic and, *isn't that a catastrophe for them*? It's like, *yeah, it's a catastrophe*. But it's not clear to me that it's more difficult than the alternative, which is to think, "Oh, you're actually responsible for your decisions, and they're decisions between good and evil, and your decisions tilt the world towards Heaven or Hell in a very real way." Directly, it's on you. It's like, *who wants to believe that?* That's meaning. That's meaning. You want meaning? That's meaning. It's like, *no, man! I'll take the nihilism. And the despair. It's easier.*

Can you speak about how your video opposing Bill C-16 — the Canadian anti-free speech law — went viral?

Oh, because it was an — what would you call it? — it was an intrusion on the Logos. That's one way of thinking about it. I'm not going to say other people's words. Period.

Well, I just explained why, to some degree, the words you choose determine the structure of the world that you bring into being.

I'm not going to have my words put in my mouth by anyone other than me.

And so, I don't care what the rationale is. I don't care if the rationale is compassion. I don't care what the rationale is. It's not happening. I have responsibility for my words. I take that responsibility very, very seriously. And I just told you why. Because I believe that this Logos idea is correct, and so, if someone wants to say something, that's fine. If someone wants to believe something, that's fine. But when that belief impinges on my right to determine my words, then that's not all right.

You know what? For a while, it was sort of about the trans community — which isn't a community, by the way. It has just as much diversity as any other group of people. And I've gotten plenty of letters from trans people supporting me — about forty — and none criticizing me, so far. And they're not very happy about being made the poster boy for the latest ideological moves of the radical left. So, the idea that it's compassion, or that it's some sort of community consensus, is absolute nonsense. But, in any case, it wasn't about that. That was a peripheral issue. But the line had to be drawn somewhere. It's like, *compelled speech is wrong, so, I'm not doing it*. And when I made my video — which I made like at 3:00 in the morning one night because I was upset about a variety of things, including this legislation — I think the reason that it went viral-, there was a bunch of reasons, but one was: I actually said that there was something I wouldn't do. It, like, it was really concrete. It brought a vague ideological issue to a very precise point. Right? And so that's how you make things real — you make them into a very precise point. It's like, so when I said, "That's not happening," and I meant it. And I think people could tell that I meant it, and I had my reasons for meaning it, which people more or less figured out when they started watching my other videos — and that also protected me, right? I had all these other-, virtually every word I said to students in the last twenty years has been recorded and is available, unedited, for public consumption.

And so, that lent me some credibility. You know, people realized that I wasn't just flying off the handle — that I had read the legislation properly — that I was serious about my opposition to compelled speech, and that I had very well-thought out reasons for being opposed to it. Like, I think I've thought it-, well, I would never say that-, that anyone-, I think it's a mistake for anyone to claim that they've thought something through all the way to the bottom. But I've thought it through as deeply as I can and I've been thinking about it for thousands of hours for thirty years. So, like, if I've made a mistake, man, I'd love to find it. But-, but-, but I can't find it. So, and then people watch the videos and, like, the question is, "What's going on? What's going on with Bill C-16? What's going on with this trans issue?" Nobody knows. We're moving up and down the levels of analysis. "Is it political? Is it ideological? Is it philosophical? Is it theological? What the hell's going on here?"

Well, the people who opposed me said, "Well, it's all political, and so are you." And I said, "No, it's not political at all. It's philosophical. It's probably even theological, but it's at least philosophical." Well, so, was that true or not? Well, yes it was true, because, otherwise, what should have happened is: I made the video...there was a flurry of interest...it died out in fifteen minutes...it was over.

That's not what happened. So, that means that there was more going on than-, than what was on the surface.

Can you describe what was on the surface?

Well, there was a variety of things. I mean, the legislation itself looked rather harmless. It's not very long. It purports to add gender identity and gender expression to the list of protected groups under the Canadian Human Rights Code, essentially. And there's a bunch of problems with that. One being, gender expression is not a group. So-, and that actually bothers me, because, like, this is fundamental legislation, and you have to get your damn terminology right, because otherwise you haven't thought it through. So, but that piece of legislation was surrounded by a cloud of policies — many of which were elaborated on the Ontario, the website for the Ontario Human Rights Commission — and the federal government stated that, explicitly, although they took that link down, which was not acceptable, because of falsification of the legislative intent. And the media didn't make much of that.

Some people reported, but it was a very bad thing. Anyways, in the legislation, there were a number of things that I objected to. One of them being the instantiation of a social constructionist view of gender into the law. The social constructionist view of gender is incorrect.

Now, social — as we already discussed social viewpoints — society has an impact on everything. It has an effect on gender, but so does biology. And that's-, there aren't credible scientists who don't believe that. *None*. There are wingnut theorists in activist disciplines who push that and have now got it into the law, because they know perfectly well they've lost the battle intellectually, and I think it's terrible that we've instantiated a social constructionist view of human identity into the law.

Now, that's a sophisticated topic, you know, and people don't get it. But I get it. I know why they're doing it. So, that was one. Then there was the compelled speech issue, which is: It's a requirement that I use your preferred pronoun. Well, which one? Well, whichever one you prefer. Well, there's seventy of them, and no one knows how to use them, and no one's picked them up in common parlance, and there's no agreement on what they should be. And why not your preferred adjective, then? And why not your preferred verb? And, like, where does the limit of your control over my language end? Well, as far as I'm concerned, it's like: If I knew you, and you wanted me to call you something and we came to an agreement, I'd probably do it if I thought you were reasonable, that it was good for you, and that you were honest. But, as soon as you tell me that I have to participate in your construction of reality under pain of law, it's like, *no, I don't have to...and I won't.* And so, that was the issue.

How would you characterize the media's coverage of that?

Well, I would say it's the same as the university's reaction, in some sense. Look, if you're a Canadian, and you come out and say, "Look, Canadians, there's something wrong with what's going on in your system," the right response from a Canadian is, "No, there's something wrong with you," because Canada is very stable and our government has been extraordinarily reliable and, like, it's a good country, and you can ignore the politics. You know, we kind of move from a little bit left, to the center, to a little bit right. That's the whole political game in Canada, you know?

So, if anybody comes out and says, "Wake up — something's wrong," you should not believe them. And then you should figure out, well, is there something wrong with this person? And so, that was the initial response. It's like, there's probably something wrong with this person, you know, he's making a fuss, and maybe he's mean and he won't, you know, be nice to the poor, oppressed people. But then they did their homework and found out that I'd actually read the legislation and that I knew what I was talking about. So, and then the press turned very rapidly in my favor and I've stayed that way ever since — the mainstream press.

So, the major journalists in Canada — the print journalists — have virtually, without exception, been on my side. Two hundred newspapers — there is a conglomerate of two hundred newspapers — came out expressly stating that they supported what I was doing. And even the university — which was all thrown up in the air by this to begin with, and sent me two warning letters telling me that I was probably violating the law by making the video complaining about the legislation, which is exactly what I had said in the video, that just making the video was probably violating the law, and so the university's legal experts actually agreed with that — they told me twice to stop, then we had a debate. I said I wasn't going to. They left me the hell alone and they gave me a sabbatical this year, and they've taken steps to strengthen their commitment to free speech, so I would say that the university, you know-, people make mistakes and they didn't know what to do, and it was a weird situation. But, I would say...they did as well as could be expected under the circumstances and maybe better than that. So, the public support has been absolutely overwhelming. You know, within Canada, and then also now internationally. It's absolutely beyond comprehension.

[KIARA'S QUESTION:] So, in my limited experience with the media, I get the impression that, although they know that they are

lying and deceiving people and, you know, making wrongful edits, they still believe that their narrative is true. And I'm curious as to what you think about how you-, how people ought to determine truth from falsehood in the media.

Well, it's tricky, right? Because you are making decisions about what to include and what not to include when you're-, well, when you're making this film, for example. And so, your-, your narrative is going to intrude on the film. So, then, I guess the question is, "Well, what should your narrative be?"

Your narrative should be something like: I'm constantly trying to go beyond the truth that I already hold, because the truth that you're already holding is not enough. Your life isn't what it could be, and everyone knows that. So, you need to know more than you know. And so, the narrative should be, when you're constructing a film, it's like, "Okay, I'm trying to clarify things more. I'm trying to extend what I understand more." Not: "Here's the ideological truth about the structure of reality, and here's how I edit this set of interviews to conform precisely to that." It's dead and sterile. It's propaganda. That's what propaganda is, and that's a propagandistic conversation...can even be that. And you know when you're listening to one, because they're boring as hell.

You know, if you listen to a conversation and there is genuine striving for the truth, it's a compelling conversation. This is partly why I don't script my lectures, because what I'm doing when I'm lecturing isn't telling you what I know to be true. What I'm doing when I'm lecturing is trying to figure out things better. And so, I'm thinking. I don't know what-, what the consequence of the thinking is going to be, but I hope that it will be more clarification of the proper path through life. And the reason that I'm committed to that is because I know what happens when you deviate from the path. It's not good. It's seriously not good. It's-, it's like world-shaking not good. And we know this. If you read who I would regard as the most profound analysts of the totalitarian societies of the twentieth century, they come to the same conclusion, which is that the totalitarian states would not have been possible without the moral corruption of the individuals within that society.

So, it was the degree to which the individuals within that society were willing to falsify their own experience that produced the totalitarian state. And if you think that through, then it should make you quake in your boots, because it means that to the degree that you falsify your own reality to yourself, say, you're contributing to the pathologization of the state — and the state is no joke. And it's-, you think it's powerful now, you wait ten years. So, we better get our acts together, because there's things coming down the pipes that we want to get right, or else. So, artificial intelligence would be one of those things. And we're seeing all that already in places like Google. They're using AI to-, to-, to...what would you call it? Censor. Well, hey, you better have your act together before you design AI systems that regulates people's communication. Because they're going to get unbelievably powerful — and really, really fast.

Just thinking to myself, the majority of those people share a liberal narrative and would regard it as true.

They-, there are many things that everyone does that they-, that each person knows to not be true. Like, they're microdecisions, usually. You know, they may say, "Well, the macronarrative is accurate." The thing about-, you know, there are some circumstances under which a predominantly liberal narrative is accurate. Liberals are high in openness. They're quite creative. They're not very conscientious. So, that's a problem. But they tend to be creative and entrepreneurial. That's extremely useful. Conservatives, they're lower in openness, generally speaking — they're more tradition-bound and they're very good at implementing. And so, both those narratives, so to speak — if you think about them as embodiments or articulations of character — have their place in the world. It's the dialogue between them that keeps the balance right. So, to the degree that what's being shut down is dialogue — genuine dialogue — then that's a big problem. Liberal or conservative - doesn't make any difference.

You spoke earlier of the necessity of logos when framing an issue or debate. It seems on many campuses across the country, currently, students have begun to supplant the notion of logos with that of pathos, in order to invalidate an idea that they may not be able to adequately defend or articulate, and, in such, they've begun to put pathos as the main organizing factor versus logos. What are your observations on that?

It's a good way of thinking about it. I mean, I suppose what that means, in some sense, is that: *I'm correct in proportion to the degree of my suffering.* Something like that. And then the problem with that is you have a competition of suffering under those circumstances. And that's-, that's actually the origin of intersectionality. The oppression narrative was lacking differentiation. And so, that's why intersectionality arose, and that differentiated it, but it has to be infinitely differentiated all the way down to the level of the individual. You know, it's a logical flaw in that issue to begin with, because it's actually the individual that's the locus of suffering. But it isn't because you're suffering that I believe you. It might be that I have some compassion for you because you're suffering. It might depend on why you're suffering. Sometimes

I might think, *well, that serves you exactly right.* And then, unless you're willing to repent, let's say, then your suffering is just fine, because you haven't learned your lesson yet.

So, just because you're suffering doesn't mean that you're right. Then you might say, "Well, what if you've chosen to voluntarily bear your suffering?" Well, then, you know, you have a higher claim to the truth, I would say. You're acting out of your claim to the truth. And people know that, because when you look out in the world and you see people you admire — even if they're not necessarily people who share your ideological presuppositions, but you sort of spontaneously admire them — you see very rapidly, if you investigate why, that it's courage that you respect. Courage in the fact of uncertainty. And maybe the willingness to fight malevolence.

So, it's a natural orientation and it has very little to do with suffering. It has to do with the willingness to bear it and move forward, regardless. So, yeah, it's a bad idea to replace logos with pathos, for any number of reasons. We're not agents of the truth because we suffer. That's not how it works. We're just suffering.

ANTHONY SCARAMUCCI INTERVIEW

I'm Anthony Scaramucci. I'm a serial entrepreneur. I just sold my second business and I spent eleven days as the White House Communications Director. But, prior to that, I was on the president's executive transition team and I worked on his fundraising.

You had been on the media quite a bit. Is that right?

I spent a lot of time in the media and, since the White House, had been the focus of a lot of media intention-, attention, yes.

What's your opinion of the media, generally?

I would say the general impression of the media for me is that there's a lot of pockets of dishonesty. And they have fragmented into a different business model than the one I grew up with as a kid. And so, when I learned about journalism school — there was an objective standard in the front page...[it] was about trying to get the story right and cleansed of any political bias. But, because of what's happened with the advent of social media — Twitter,

Facebook, guys like Mike Cernovich — they have fractured the old media and they've turned this into business models that are trying to get to a certain segment of the population. And so, they are trying to reinforce biases — reinforce opinions — of that segment. So, when people turn on the TV or they go to their website or they pick it up in the hardcopy, they're reading things that they-, like, it's sort of what happened with cable television, too. We've got three hundred channels, but each of us is only watching one or two channels, so the media has destroyed itself in an effort to remain profitable.

It's a massively successful year for the mainstream (CNN, etc.). What's your take on that?

I think-, I think that the business model is working from [how it relates to] the profitability. So with-, the decision was to fragment and segment and go after...if you're CNN liberals or MSNBC liberals, or Fox conservatives, that has been a very good business strategy, because you get a lot of advertising revenue — a lot of advertising dollars — and you're getting a lot of sub fees from the cable operators. But it has destroyed journalism. And so, if you want to bifurcate the two things, great business model... they've got the celebrity president — the Celebrity Apprentice host — as the president, a real estate developer that has had high brand name recognition in the United States for about forty years. And so, he's also a smash-mouth, counterpunching, not going to take any guff from those outlets that are targeting him. And so, that creates the hysteria that's related to these ratings and the profitability.

When I say, "the media," what does that mean to you?

When you say the word "media" to me, my Rorschach Test is: I better get my cup on, protect everything underneath my belt, and put a crash helmet on and wait to see what happens.

Who do you think of — like, specific brands or personalities — when I say, "the media"?

All my favorite people in the media [who] show my bias are guys like Mike Cernovich; Sean Hannity is one of my best friends; Bill O'Reilly, I'm not close to personally, but I respect him as a journalist who is an objective opinion maker. I like Lou Dobbs. Those are the kind of the people that I associate myself with, who I think think the way I do. The flip side is I can't tell you that I disrespect Rachel Maddow. I think Rachel Maddow has a point of view. I think she's honest about it and has high integrity in terms of delivering that point of view. Now, it may be wildly different from my point of view. Lawrence O'Donnell — I think he's a complete piece of shit. And I think you know he's just got really bad karma. So, I expect really bad things to happen to him.

Yeah I'm surprised he hasn't been caught up in all this stuff.

Well, I mean, you know, Lawrence O'Donnell was hitting me when I was in the White House. I'm laughing. I mean, this guy's a joke. I mean, you know, he's probably got a zero-to-negative net worth. And he's obviously unintelligent.

So it's just a matter of time before his show gets cancelled.

A friend of mine says she was on-set one day, right around the time he had that meltdown.

You know, I retweeted that, so, I had a retweet of Lawrence O'Donnell. I mean, in fairness, he said I was the stupidest person that ever worked in the White House, which I thought was funny, because if you divided my IQ by a hundred, you're getting to *four times* his IQ. So, I just think it's funny. But he was, like, upset with me for the-, some of the remarks that I made off the record to a dishonest journalist, and he's out there screaming, "Stop the hammering!" and yelling all these expletives. One of the things about me that I don't like about people like Lawrence O'Donnell, is they treat subordinates very rudely. Okay, my grandmother came to the country — started as a maid. So, anybody that's in a service position for me, I've got to treat with respect and dignity and kindness. They could be my grandmother, circa 1923. So, I find Lawrence O'Donnell, of all the people in the American media, the most despicable person.

Yeah he's one of the only people I think is a bad person. Jake Tapper — I might good on, but he's not fundamentally awful.

Jake Tapper, to me, I think he will give a fair interview. He may not have my point of view, but I bet on his air, he gives a fair interview. Chris Cuomo and I share the same heritage, but we're very different ideologically. But Chris Cuomo will let you talk. He'll give you a fair interview. Brian Stelter, when I had the CNN debacle for me — and just to remind people: Three CNN journalists wrote a Fake News story about me personally. They got it from who they thought was a very good source inside the White House, so they thought it was 100 percent true that I was involved in some kind of Russian hysteria. Of course, that wasn't true.

And, thankfully, I have a deep pocket and a set of you-know-whats. I went right after those guys. I got all three of those guys fired and basically I explained to their bosses that, if you don't fire them, we're going to end up in a fight with the FCC and try to get your license taken away while you're going through the

AT&T-Time Warner merger. So-, so, you have to fight back. If you do not fight back, they'll pitch and roll you and flatten you out. Okay, so, in my experience, leaving the White House is an example of that: I said three curse words on a recorded phone line. They treated it like it was-, I poured hot water on a newborn baby. I mean, it was just ridiculous.

So, for me, I find the faux outrage — the mock outrage — to be reprehensible.

Yeah, that was one thing we wanted to talk about with you, actually. The other thing, more recently, they tried to claim you and your Jewish business partner were Holocaust deniers.

That's the sort of nonsense...so, by the way, I am and I stated up front, you know, my Jewish business partner who lost family members in the Holocaust reacted to an Anne Frank costume that was put up on Amazon.com.

So the 13-year-old young girl that wrote a diary while she was in hiding — and was eventually killed by the Nazis — people are trivializing her by putting out a Halloween costume. And so, this gentleman who grew up as an orthodox-, in the Orthodox Jewish community here in New York, was upset about that. And he was trying to make a point, through the Scaramucci Post, that many Americans and many people in general are not aware of the magnitude of the Holocaust atrocity and so...but I'm a little cross with him, because he put it out as a poll, and immediately got people like Jake Tapper and these other guys — it was like a dog whistle for them and they started going berserk and they were trying to say that we were opening up a scene for Holocaust deniers to slip through, and white supremacists, and so on and so forth. And because of my Trump affiliation, they like to label you that way, the first move for the radical left media is to label you a sexual harasser or a racist or a misogynist, something like that to start the conversation. So, they have to take you and two-dimensionalize you, and characterize you, so that they can prevent you from getting your voice out there. So, guys like me — I got raised in a blue collar family. I went to Tufts and Harvard Law Schools, built two businesses in the United States that I sold for nine figures each, had a television show that I hosted...

And so, I have a pretty strong opinion — pretty strong political philosophy — and I'm also a guy that can deliver that information to people that I grew up with. And so, I've got to be destroyed by these guys. They've got to find something on me. I sort of feel bad for them, because they-, they figured I'm Italian and I got twenty-eight years on Wall Street. I had to do something dishonest. So they spent seven months, like, ripping through my financial records and background, couldn't find anything. So, they got me on three curse words and tried to characterize me like I was, you know, *Gym, Tan, Laundry,* from the Jersey Shore. All fine, I can take it. I'm a big boy. And they're not going to win, because I know how to fight back. But people, they don't know how to fight back, get demolished and they get put into the corner and their little shame box with their dunce cap on. You know, they tried to take Mike Cernovich, as an example, and build him a shame box and stick him in the corner and have him face the corner. And he's a guy that fights his way out of a box like that. And so, that's me, and that's why these guys are going to lose, because I've never seen guys like me or Michael Cernovich in the new media space that can fight back and have the verbal dexterity and also the intellectual data to push back on these bozos.

And here's another thing I will say about the mainstream journalists — and I saw this inside the White House, outside the White House — they don't do a lot of homework. So their information is this-thin. The Holocaust poll comes out on the Scaramucci Post, they go crazy, but they don't even read the tweets related to it or the context that the poll was put into. Here's the Anne Frank thing — it's a disgrace. Thirty-five percent of the American people are not aware of the magnitude of the polling. And then, of course, my Jewish partner — I'm saying the word "Jewish" because obviously [he's] not a Holocaust denier — he pointed out that there were seven or eight polls done recently. No fanfare about those polls, because they were issued by a left-wing organization.

So I'm-, even though I'm a libertarian — which is not really right-wing, because I don't care who marries who, and I don't have a right-wing orthodoxy, I'm more of a Libertarian — because I sided up with Trump, I've got to be demolished and creamed and, you know, good luck is not going to happen as long as I'm aboveground.

That's not going to happen.

The public shaming thing is so important because, for most people, a fake story about you [and] your life is over. For me, they call me everything, I just joke about it. I link to the article.

Well, I mean, I mean so here is the move to discredit people — it's an age-old move, it probably was developed by Socrates: In my first week at Harvard Law School, when I was in the trial advocacy class, what the professor said was, "If you're wrong on the facts, hit the other side in an ad hominem sort of a way to deconstruct the opposing side to the jury. If you disfigure and get the jury to hate that person — even if they're right — the jury will side with you." So get your likability up. It's all these soft things, okay, and destroy the other person. So, the left does a phenomenal job of that. I give them a lot of credit. They write Fake News stories all the time. They try to push people into that shame box. But guys like me — guys like a Michael Cernovich — they're not going to sit-, stand for that. You know, I grew up in a pretty tough neighborhood. I find it laughable that these guys think that a couple of words written about me on the Internet, or the front page of a story, is a big deal. Okay, I mean, I saw, you know, a lot of messy stuff growing up as a kid, so, that doesn't bother me at all. But there's no question that that's the strategy and they ruin a lot of people's lives with that strategy who are not capable of fighting back. So my message to people is, if you're going to be in the arena with these people, they're going to use those nasty nefarious tools against you.

Learn how to be resilient. Learn how to fight back. And remember what your grandmother told you: What other people think of you is none of your business.

Focus on what you think is right and go right at these people.

And on that vein, let's talk about that CNN article. There was a big article — big scoop — that you were under investigation for colluding with Russia. And a few hours later *poof* the story disappears.

So, what basically happened to me with the CNN investigation, and the eventual firing of those journalists and the Fake News story, is that I was in Davos, Switzerland, at the World Economic Forum, and I ran into one of the guys who worked for the Russian Sovereign Wealth Fund. He came over to me in a restaurant and said, "hello." We had a six- to seven-minute conversation, all of which was quite superficial. One of the journalists there took a picture of the two of us talking. [A] Trump soon-to-be administration official talking to Russian Sovereign Wealth Fund. And so, at Steven Mnuchin's nomination hearing two days later, Senator Warren said, "Well, are you going to investigate Anthony Scaramucci for his ties to Russia?" At which point, Steven said — or Secretary Mnuchin said — "Yes, if that's what-," you know, "if he did something, of course, we'd investigate it." There was nothing there. I had a six- to seven-minute conversation with the guy. And so, somebody from inside the White House...this is the problem with the Republicans — they like shooting at each other from inside the tent. Democrats have a way of unifying, you know, they hate each other — you know, like Bill Clinton hates Hillary Clinton, they both hate Barack and Michelle Obama — but they walk hand-in-hand like a chorus line on Broadway. Right? But the Republicans try to kill each other — me and Bannon, or Preibus and me, and all this sort of nonsense — so, somebody inside the White House leaked the story about me saying that I was under Senate and Treasury investigation, both of which was not true.

I told the reporter that called me to please call Mitch McConnell's office or the head of communications at Treasury. They will verify that it's not true, but they don't want to do that. They know my name gets them a lot of clicks and they know that it's just one story and a guy like me would likely not fight back over it. And so, they published the story. And so, I said, "Okay, that's it." I hired an attorney. I got on the phone with senior management at CNN and I said, "This is an absolutely total fake story about me. *The New York Times* versus Sullivan. I took constitutional law at Harvard Law School — you can't write fake stories about a public figure. So I'm going to bury you guys. Okay? This will be a one-hundred-million-dollar lawsuit, and if you don't take the story down immediately, I'm coming after you guys.

"And then the other thing I'm going to do is, I want to go to the FCC, and I'm going to file a claim to make you lose your license, because you do have an integrity obligation to get these FCC licenses."

So, inside of, like, five or six hours, they called me back, and said, "Okay, this story is false." And then they took the steps of firing the people. And now, why did they fire those journalists? They fired those journalists because it did actually bring the lawsuit. They wanted to separate the firm and the organization from the actual journalists, and so, they were-, they were mitigating their damages. They were also mitigating the potential case that I had before the FCC.

But that's not my personality. I'm not that kind of guy. They apologized to me. Within minutes, I put out: "Apology accepted. Let's move on."

And that's-, that's how I am as a person. I'm not looking to fight with people or have a litigation, but I'm looking for *fairness*. I'm no longer looking for objectivity from the mainstream media, because that's not part of their fragmented business model. But I am looking for fairness and integrity. You can't write stories that are full of lies, okay, to mislead the American people, without having people like Mike Cernovich or myself, or other people like us, calling you out on it.

So that's the good news for the American people.

Right. What I thought was interesting is that they didn't mention the lawsuit.

I mean, listen — I want to try to be as super hard-, to be as fair as I can be, to CNN. I do think, from time to time, you can get a story wrong. I know I've had information when I was a host of Wall Street Week that was factually inaccurate, but I *thought* it was accurate. I really thought in my heart I was operating with integrity. But, in fact, they got the story wrong, so I don't want to sit here and say [for] every Fake News story that's out there, the person maliciously knows that it's fake.

I will say that the people at CNN, that I got to, realized the story was fake, [and] they did move quickly and they did move honorably. But I do think that there is also a nefarious element, where there was a group of people inside a scene and said, "Oh, my God, this guy's got a deep enough pocket to sue us. He's a forceful enough media personality where he can hit us hard." And so, they started taking those steps to-, to fire people and to get themselves prepared. So, to me, that was a combination of two things. Let me tell you this: If I was a Joe Schmo of a guy — not saying I'm not a Joe Schmo sorta guy...I sorta am, but I do have a little bit of dough — if I didn't have a little bit of dough to be able to fight them, if I didn't have a little bit of courage and conviction, they woulda rolled me very, very hard. I would have been another casualty of theirs on their-, on the dustbin of their shaming history of people like me. Just not going to happen though.

How do you define Fake News?

Fake News is a purposeful, nefarious lie that's perpetrated by a group of people that want to discredit people that they disagree with. It primarily comes from the left, because what we find on the right is that we're open to the conversation — we're open to the exchange and discourse of ideas. Okay? Even, you know, Anderson Cooper, or one of the CNN guys — maybe it was Brian Stelter — had an issue, and Sean Hannity went and defended him. And Sean basically said, "Hey, you know, they have the right to say what they're saying. So, you can't blow them up or throw them off the air because you don't like what they're saying." And so, I respect that about Sean. I respect that from most of the pundits from the right. The left, however — and this is the truth about the left — they're primarily one hundred percent wrong about their ideas. They have very, very good intentions. I'm not saying they don't, but what you find about left-wing philosophy — it's very well-intended, but the actual application of those policies is a disaster for society. And so, you can't take away the incentives in a human society. So-, so, the left gets that wrong. They *know* it's wrong.

So, [what] they have to do is, they have to silence the right. So, the great irony of the liberal mind is that they're about fascism and silencing the right. And so, one of the things that you learn about fascism is that you have to distort the truth, right? If you read Joe Goebbels'-, Joseph Goebbels' biography: *The bigger the lie, the more impact and the more believable it will be.* And so, that's coming from the left. Now, the left will be super mad at me for saying that. But that's actually the truth. It's just the way it works. And so, us on the right — or us that are libertarians that want a freer society, less government, more empowerment for the individual — we have to fight back against that, because that's organized. That's organized. That's a group of people that think that they're smarter than the other group of people. No good.

I think-, I think that left-wing talk radio and, in general, a lot of left-wing television gets less ratings.

[It] has to do with the fact that it is so mainstream. It's, like, such a big part of the voice and market share, that people are sort of tone-deaf to it. The reason why right-wing talk radio — or right-leaning television — galvanizes a lot of viewers is because the country is primarily center-right, and the country is like, "Whoa! That's so refreshing that there's actually somebody on the TV that I can identify with." I think you find, in the coastal cities, the coastal cities are probably more focused on the left-leaning stuff, but the heartland of America is probably more center-right.

So, I think that's a big difference between left-wing-, why they don't get the ratings that the right-wing gets, so to speak.

The left, being in coastal cities, tend to think that whatever happens in New York or D.C. is all that matters.

Yeah, I think it's a nexus between New York, D.C., San Francisco and L.A — you can say, some elements of Chicago, but not all elements of Chicago — and, perhaps, Miami...those are the cities that are really driving the cultural left-wing [zeitgeist]. And so-, and, by the way, for myself, I'm actually okay with some of that. You know, I view myself as a socially inclusive person and a fiscally responsible one. I don't like saying I'm socially liberal, because we've spent billions of dollars on that word, getting half of America to hate the word *liberal*. I don't like saying I'm fiscally conservative, because we did the same thing. Billions of dollars to hate the word *conservative* and get the American people to hate that word. So, to me, I think the middle mainstream of the country probably wants a smaller, energetic government that's held accountable. We've got to get term limits in there. We got to get these bozos out of there that are permanent ties, themselves, in the artifice of our country. It's just unbelievable.

I think George Washington would be, like, *throwing up* if he knew that there were guys-, men and women staying forty years in Washington. I mean, it's just ridiculous. Since I've-, anything about citizen responsible government, you go, you serve your term, you pick the decisions and policies that are right for the American people, you don't focus on left or right and curry favor for lobbyists. You focus on right or wrong. We're not doing that anymore. Okay, we've got a *cesspool.* I don't even think it's a swamp. I think it's like a gold-plated hot tub at this point. You know, so-, so to me, we've got to crush these guys and I expect that we will.

You went from a media-loved person to a media-hated person. What was it like?

Yeah. I mean-, I mean, so, I mean, when I started out in my media foray, I was mostly a television business commentator. Then I started commentating a little bit on politics. I was helping Governor Romney and his campaign, and I-, and just to state the facts for me: I was with Scott Walker and then Jeb Bush...I eventually got to Mr. Trump — then "Mr." Trump — because of the team nature of-, I played team sports my whole life, he was going to win, I always said I was going to support the nominee, and so I went full-in for the nominee. However, because of President Trump's personality, the left-wing media wants to knock his block off and they want to hate upon every single person in his orbit. So, I started to get tainted with and painted with that brush, so to speak.

And my attitude on this is *fine*. I haven't changed one bit. And so, I am the same exact guy that the media liked five years ago — that, now, sixty or seventy percent of the media hates — and that's fine. What I find ironic about this — and I actually had this conversation with the president on my second day on the job...we were talking about how the negativity in the media perversely is galvanizing — so, I find that there's a direct functionality between the media hitting me and the American people liking me. It's a direct function. And I would say that's probably also true for Mike Cernovich. The more the mainstream media hits you, Mike Cernovich, the more galvanized people are around you. And so-, so, the American people are now in on the joke of the devious manipulation. Just think about what the media was like in their feeding frenzy during the campaign. And Donald J. Trump still won the presidential election. She [Hillary] had seventy-five/eighty percent of the media behind her. She outspent us one point six-to-one. She out-manned and -womened us in terms of personnel. I think she was two-to-one to us on-, on personnel. And she had a voter registration of seven-to-five in terms of Democrats versus Republicans that were eligible to vote in the election, *and she still lost.* Just imagine if we had more balance in the media — less Fake News, less of that garbage — how powerful we would be, because our ideas are right.

It's not about left or right, it's about right or wrong.

You said something actually profound and it's something I thought about: A hit piece is now viewed as a status marker. *The New York Times* wrote a hit piece — doesn't matter what they said...*he must be amazing.*

I think these hit pieces — that fifteen/twenty years ago would have meant character assassination suicide and the person would then have to remove themselves from public life — are no longer, because there's so much disingenuous activity in the media. If I'm getting a hit piece written about me from *The New York Times,* it's like, "Oh, okay, *The New York Times* is super biased, absolutely hate Trump, he's affiliated with Trump, they're hitting him, they must be worried about him." You see the way I was getting hit — one of my buddies said to me, "You're getting hit like that because you can articulate the president's strategy."

I'll tell a very quick story: I'm on BBC Newswatch, and I'm being interviewed by Emily, and it's a live presentation. I've got the White House behind me and we're talking. It's over...I shake her hand. I'm walking to my office in the West Wing. My cell phone's ringing. I pick up the cell phone — I'm not going to tell you who it was, but it was a person in Republican opposition research for thirty years — [and] they say, "Ant, you're in a lot of trouble." I said, "I'm in a lot of trouble? Why?" "Yes, I just watched you on BBC Newswatch. They're trying to disfigure you, and two-dimensionalize you as an Italian street thug. But you just-, you had great verbal dexterity on BBC Newswatch and they're now saying, 'Oh, my God, this guy might be able to have tea with the Queen!' And I've gotten four or five calls on you since you finished that interview, saying, 'What do you got on this guy? We got to take this guy out.'"

Why you going to take me out? Because I'm not part of the permanent political class. You take me out because I'm a business executive and I can smell the rotting cadaver of Washington that sits in the basement of the American Public in the American Community. And I'm ready to help the American people remove the cadaver from the basement, so, they're going to hit me. They're going to disfigure me. They're going to malign guys like

Mike Cernovich and I'm totally cool with it. I wear it as a badge of honor. And I also find that it galvanizes a large group of supporters around me. But I thought it was fascinating. I'm on the BBC. I'm walking back into the West Wing and I'm being told by Republican Party opposition research that they're calling around trying to figure out a way to take me out.

People don't realize how nasty Republicans are to each other.

The Republicans are very, very nasty to each other, and they make a very big mistake with that. That schism inside the party has to end. Even if Steve Bannon is right on some of the stuff that he's saying, look at the way the Founders put the country together. All of us are byproducts of this amazing country. Again, my parents are blue collar people. I was able to rise in class as a result of this country. My life story doesn't happen in any other country. And so the Founders wanted us to collaborate. The Founders wanted us to go for, as Reagan said, eighty percent of what we wanted, recognizing that we could never get one hundred percent of what we want. And so, I find that some of these Republican ideologues are messianic bomb throwers, and they're not going to get the job done for the American people. And whether we like it or not, you know, the Bible says that the poor and the rich will always be among us. Well, so will the left-wing, fellas. Okay? Just the way it works. Okay.

So, we have to figure out a way to collaborate with them and out-man them with our ideas, cause our ideas are *better*. Trump won because his ideas were *better*. Look at how the economy's growing. Look at how people feel about the American society now economically. If-, if-, if a Republican establishment figure won, or Hillary Clinton won, there's no way there would be a five trillion dollar boost in the stock market since the election.

No way.

If you watch the news, you'd think the United States is about to fall into another Depression. But, if you watch the stats, it just said the GDP was up another three percent this quarter.

The big-, the big fallacy about the news now — in addition to fragmenting so they can achieve their business model by attracting a certain genre of viewers — is there is a mass hysteria. "*Breaking news! Breaking news!*" every 15 seconds, and you don't know what the hell is going on. There's a Malaysian airline [missing]. We're going to talk about that for two years. You got, "The economy is going to fall into a cliff," and all this sort of nonsense, but at the end of the day, it's not really what's going on in the real society. Moreover, the media want you to feel that the society is way more polarized than it actually is. And at the end of the day, most people want to get along with each other. They don't really care about it the way these Washingtonians or these media pundits do.

So, the economy is actually doing quite well. The one problem that I have is that the lower and middle class are not getting enough of the piece of the action of our economic opportunity and growth. That's bad policy. That's all it is. You don't have to invoke socialism or communism to spread the wealth. What you have to do is just come up with the right policy, and the right incentives, so that people can get paid more money. Corporations that pay their people more money — maybe you give them a little bit of a tax incentive to do that. And these business executives should know that by paying their employees more money, there's more aggregate demand in the economy, which will lead to more compensation for them. It's just-, it's a longer term strategy.

And we've got to start getting back to that. And that's something I wish the president would talk more about, because he-, he-, he was very good at that at the Trump Organization.

What should the White House be talking about more?

Well, I think, you know, listen — I put a full-, fully blown and Michael Cernovich was great enough to leak it out there for me. Not leak it, but put it out there. I had a seven- or eight-page communication strategy, and I think there were three components to that that were usually important. Number one: The President has to go outside of the beltway into the heartland of the American people and literally activate the American people like it's his Congressional Liaison Office. They have to overwhelm the Capitol Dome with calls and literally tilt the Capitol Dome, because if they don't do that, the permanent political class will reject the President's agenda. They do not want this president to succeed, because he's now opened the door for other billionaire entrepreneurs. It's not just the right-leaning ones. They don't want Mark Zuckerberg to be president. They don't want Jeff Bezos to be president. Jeff Bezos — worth ninety billion dollars — he shows up in the Oval Office. You think he cares about the business model of the swamp? He'll want to break up and disrupt the whole thing and try to serve the American people, so what these guys are trying to do is, they're trying to kill Trump. So, one component of the communication was: *Get outside of the Beltway and activate the American people to tilt the Capitol Dome.*

The second thing I think they have to do is use the presidency as a bully pulpit to explain all of the good things that are going on in our society now, as a direct result of the president's policies. We are eviscerating ISIS. We are going to end up with a positive negotiated deal with North Korea, because of the president's tough stance. We're growing the economy faster now than we were even a year ago. We're unleashing investment in economic opportunity. This society will become fairer as a result of these policies. And so, the president controls the bully pulpit and the daily news cycle. We need more content and rich content related to that.

And the third thing that we need to do is, we need to out-media the media. Okay? And what the president needs, I believe, is almost like a counter-offensive strategy with the media. And one of the things I wrote in my comms plan is that we return every call, we get back to them immediately, we rebut every angle of their attack. Because I do feel that the Bush Administration — in the last two years, 2006 to 2008 — they were steamrolling him, and he took a break, and he basically went to Camp David, or he went down to his ranch, and he didn't fight them every single day. And so, one of my components of my media plan was: 24-hour crisis return, 24-hour flip it back to them, and continue to defend and fight for the president. And so, unfortunately, in my opinion, he's a little weak in there. He needs to fortify that better with more, more! I mean, Hope and Sarah are terrific people. I'm not saying anything bad about them. It just needs *more* of them, to help him on the surrogacy side, etc.

There should be an in-house media production company.

I always thought there should be an in-house media production company in the White House, because it's a new generation now of new media. And so, you know, one of the criticisms would be, well, it would be Pravda. It would be like a state-owned media organization, but I never felt that way. I thought we could have set it up — and I explained this to the president when I was there — that you could set this up and you can put it in place and you could permanentize it for the next president.

And so, whether it's a Democrat or a Republican that enters the office, they have this set up the same way you have the press room set up, and the briefing apparatus set up for a Republican or Democratic president. But I think the world has changed. And the president needs a narrative creating production product every day to help him get his message out there, so that it's not blunted by the ridiculous fragmentation that's going on in the media.

Why do you think they don't do more live streams?

I think-, I think one of the reasons why the White House is reluctant to use live streaming on Facebook and all this other stuff, it has to do with the White House Counsel's office: They're very wary that a piece of confidential information could come out, or something unplugged, which could be a violation of national security. I could have a security clearance and I'm asked something about Korea and I say something, you know, and it's unplugged but there's a Periscope involved. And then, all of a sudden, I've breached the national security protocol, you know, so...

So, I think that's one of the reasons. But again, one of the components of my plan was to even screen for that, and say, "Okay, we're going on Periscope: Here are the dos and don'ts. Let's get some fresh authenticity out there, UNSCRIPTED." I think what the American people like about the media rogues, sometimes represented by the Cernovich clan, etc., is they like the unscripted authenticity of those people. Even my profanity-laced interview, which I really wish wasn't made public. I mean, the guy was very dishonest. Again, I didn't say, "off the record," so I have to own it, but it was just a-, it was outside of the spirit of human relationships, what he did to me. Just shows you how scummy some of these people are. But at least the good news is what I said when people said, "Well, did you say it?" I said, "One hundred percent, I said it." I owned one hundred percent of it and I didn't even know he had a recording of me.

I wasn't going to walk it back, as that's not my personality, and I think the American people want that freshness. They want that authenticity.

And, I think, down deep, they like that from the president.

You could say one sentence wrong and it turns into a news cycle.

I think that's a mistake. If they are making a judgment of not going live on Periscope, because the answers won't be super canned and homogenized — and there won't be one sentence that can get pulled out of there and blown out of proportion — I think that's a huge mistake because, again, what I have found with the media [is]: Let them blow it out of proportion, because when it is blown out of proportion, the average person will look at it and say, "Hmmm, that's been blown out of proportion by the media. I have a soft spot now for the guy that they're blowing out of proportion." I find that when you overly can something like...a group of guys are doing a documentary on me and I gave them complete access, an unrestricted editorial, artistic capability. Some of the stuff is absolutely terrible about me. I'm-, I'm-, I'm looking at it. It's like Ryan Lizza going off on me. I'm like, "Oh, my God, this is terrible." But, in my mind, it's actually the opposite, because at the end of the day, you don't want to be in a position where you're forcing people to like you or you're canning a documentary like an infomercial. You want to offer a balance to people and let the people themselves decide on what is good or bad about the person, or what is good or bad about the policy. And so, I think that unplugged stuff is the future. I mean, we've been living in a reality TV world since like 1999, 2000...unplugged, unscripted is what the millennials are used to.

And let's give them more of that. They'll feel more comfortable and they'll feel a lot more trust and authenticity in their public servants if we go in that direction.

I call it, Reality News. That is what people want.

I think-, I think the inauthentic, overly staged, canned political presentations are over, and thank God for that. I think Donald Trump — some presidential historian fifty years from now will write that President Trump broke the mold and he stopped the digestible sound bite and the overly canned, homogenized BS that comes out of a politician's mouth.

And so, I think that's a positive thing — on both sides, is a positive thing.

The next president will be, like, the GoPro President.

And that was in Dave Eggers' book, *The Circle*. He wrote about what was being referred to as, "the GoPro President," where you have a police camera on you, or the helmet cam, and people who are able to then purvey and look into everything that you're doing. What Dave Eggers said in the book, *The Circle*, is that politicians will either elect for full transparency, or a lack of transparency, and that the voters would shift their mindset to go with the politicians that are offering full transparency. The one issue I had with Dave Eggers' book, *The Circle*, or the notion of the

GoPro presidency, is you've got to be very careful that you don't create a dystopian society. Because, at the end of the day, there is a sacredness to some private conversations. There is a sacredness to a one-on-one interaction with somebody that's held dear to both of those people. So, we just have to manage that, but I do predict that the people that are talking about a GoPro presidency are full transparency for politicians. I do predict that that trend will be there very shortly.

Old media versus new media. What comes to your mind when I talk about that?

Old media, I think, of a 1950s-, 1960s-style paradigm, where there are printing presses and there are large television stations and there are large production control companies and there's magazine layout and seven-color processing, and so this is all remnants of the '50s and the '60s here in 2017 and '18. And so, the big problem with that, since the introduction of the iPad in 2010 and other tablets, we dematerialize the world. We've shrunken down. The iPad represents all fifty of the magazine subscriptions that you want. All twenty of the newspapers that you want. Even your film library, your television shows. So, what we are doing in our society now is, we're dematerializing what used to take lots of space...lots of energy. We're doing it in retail. People that are in the retail industry are suffering because Amazon is such a behemoth you can one-click it through your phone or your iPad and it comes to your house. Why do you need to walk around in a shopping mall? So, other than if you want that cultural interconnectivity. So, what's happening now, old media has not made an ADAP — an adaption — okay? It reminds me of Jerry Yang in the mid '90s, who was the founder of something called, "Yahoo." He marched into Pacific Bell, and he went to those guys, and said, "Hey, look at this cute algorithm. I'm calling it, Yahoo." You typed the name in, and then it comes up on the World Wide Web. Michael Cernovich — there's his phone number. Or Domino's pizzeria — there's the local phone number. "And you can buy this from me for a million dollars." And the Pac Bell executive said, "Why would we do that? We're killing millions of trees and we're building four-pound, yellow-stained phone books that we're delivering to everybody's house. And why would we need this? This is our business model."

And so, I take you to that story, because what's happening now is very, very disruptive to that old style footprint. Mike Cernovich, with an iPhone — he's got a radio communications company, a television studio, a film production company in his hand. It has the processing capability that is two times now what put the men on the moon in the late 1960s/early 1970s. And so that power, that capability, that dematerialization is where the paradigm is.

As an example — and based on a recommendation from Michael Cernovich — I started something called, The Scaramucci Post. It's in an experimental phase, but we realized that we need very few employees before, you know what? We could have an aggregation site that rivals other aggregation sites at a very, very low cost. And so, old media...it's dying. They can't move fast enough. It's literally like they're in the horse-and-buggy era. And there's this thing coming that's called, "horseless carriages," and they don't want to switch gears in time. So, many of these people are going to get melée-d.

You got into a new media company. What are your thoughts on that?

Yeah, it's very experimental right now. But what I have found, I think there was probably a billion, to a billion and a half, dollars of name recognition/free media associated with my firing from the White House. And I think that I've done a reasonably good job of articulating the president's strategy and a really good job of hailing myself on TV and radio. And so, I have a voice. Now, I know that all the bots that hit me on the Internet say that I don't have a voice, and my fifteen minutes are over, and all that sort of nonsense, but I have a voice. And so, I'm going to use this platform to aggregate ideas and themes related to what I think can work for our society — make our society better. So, again, if it's a left-leaning idea, but I think it's applicable, it will be on that site. If it's a right-leaning idea, it'll be on-, on that site. I'm politically — from a philosophical point of view — quite agnostic. I'm just really looking for ideas that will progress the society and make it better. My number one thing at this point in my life — given my relative level of success — is I want to ensure that children that grow up-, that are-, that are growing up in 2017, the way I grew up in 1975, have the same opportunities that I had. I was in a blue collar family. I'm the product of a public school — a very good public school — went on to an Ivy League law school after [Tufts] and made myself a level of financial independence.

I want people that grew up similarly situated to me to have that same opportunity, and I can tell you the data right now is against those people. The schools have gotten way more uneven. The socioeconomic classes have gotten way more stratified. The tax structure is not really benefiting those people. And so, there's a lot that we can do to change it. We can also do things on the trade side globally that will help bolster the lower middle class of the United States. And so, those things are going to be working on.

What's one question you wish somebody would ask you?

I guess the most fascinating question that I've never been asked is: Why are you doing this? Why are you out there? You have a good life. You could hang out in your suburban home and hang out with your kids and, you know, have enough money to travel and sort of do whatever you want. So, why are you doing this? Okay? And so, because there's a lot of negatives to this, okay? I mean, this is the conversation that I've had with the president, you know, the president has given up multiple billions — hundreds of billions — of dollars of opportunities to go run the White House. Why are you doing it? And so, the nefarious people, they would say I'm doing it because I'm "drunk on power," or I have some level of narcissism and all that sort of nonsense. But if someone really asked me, "Hey, Anthony, why are you doing this?" Okay? I would say I'm doing it because I want to cheat history. I want to help the country cheat history. Republics typically last two hundred and forty years.

And if we don't reset the country and reset the social contract, we run the risk of — and, again, am I talking about a revolution — but we run the risk of turning the country into something different than what it was that we grew up in. I grew up in the opportunistic-, I grew up in the aspirational working class. The working class today is desperate. And so, the reason I'm doing it is I want to really help that, because the country's been so good to me. I'm willing to take the hits. You know, so, if there's Holocaust deniers out there, and I want people to know that over six million Jews died in the Holocaust, and somebody is going to accuse me of being a Holocaust denier for that, I'll take the hit. If I think the president has the right economic or regulatory strategy, and they're going to disfigure me and call me a misogynist and a-, and a racist, but I know these are the right strategies to help the American people, no problem. I'll take the hit. But no one's ever asked me why am I doing it. And that's the reason.

Do you think people who interview you want to get to know you, or do they just want a sound bite?

I would say eighty percent of the people that have interviewed me in the media are looking for a sound bite, a news story, click bait, something salacious that they can go to their suits and say, "Look at, you know, I brought this story and led to this level of viewers or this level of eyeballs." I would say there's twenty percent of those people that are actually intellectually curious and are really trying to get to the truth. You know, what I find is, like, I don't like the crowd think in the media. We put out this Holocaust poll. It was absolutely stupid to do it, by the way. I think we didn't offer enough context. But, like the notion of somebody like Stephanie Ruhle, who I considered a friend, lighting me up on Twitter in some, like, maniacal faux rage, I find it very dishonest. You know, it's like, "I'm going to be part of this media cabal and I'm going to run with the pack in a way so that everyone knows that I hate Donald Trump, and I hate this. These are all evil people," and blah, blah, blah...

It's a bunch of BS. You know, nobody — here's a big lesson for people that are watching this documentary. Nobody is the way they are actually portrayed in the media. Everybody is very, very different. I find that when I give these public speeches around the country, I come off the podium and somebody says to me, "Oh, man, I didn't realize you were like this." Because they-, they try to portray you this way, you know.

I was at a college — it's a cute story, I can't give up the name of the college, I signed a confidentiality [agreement] — there was a parent-teacher weekend. Twenty-six students. They got together and they voted on the one person they wanted to come to college to be the keynote speaker for their parent-teacher weekend. And the twenty-six kids picked me.

Very flattering. But the university president was like, "No way will I bring in him," okay? And so, they were like, "No, no, we're bringing him." And so I went, and I gave a one-hour talk and I gave forty-five minutes of questions and answers at the end. When I came off the podium, the university president walked over to me, [and] said, "You know, I was wrong. I should have allowed you to speak. I didn't. They've disfigured you in a way where I thought you were not going to talk with the intellectual gravity and the historical content that you're capable of talking." So that's-, that's one of the nightmares of what I have to live with right now, temporarily.

So they got a-, look. You're-, you're threatening the status quo. You're threatening the establishment. They have to throw a bomb at you. They have to crush you and they have to crush your personality. Otherwise, they don't really have a game. Where are they going to go? Where are they going to debate me? Lawrence O'Donnell — who has, probably has the IQ of a mule — how is *he* going to debate somebody like *me*? What topic do you want to debate on? I'll go all night with you, on any topic that you want. Okay? And so, all he'll do is get super frustrated and call me names and ad hominem attack me, you know? So it's fine...I'm a big boy. I can handle it. I was six-foot-four when I started with Trump. I'm now, like, four-foot-eleven, but I'm okay.

Unedited live stream hedges against that. Surprised there aren't more people doing a Joe Rogan-style podcast.

I totally agree. I think people in the media are making the mistake of still putting on the hairspray and the makeup and scripting, when they are going to galvanize more viewers and a wider berth of viewers ideologically if they unscript and unplug themselves.

Joe Rogan's podcast is a scalable model that should be done in media.

Well I think Joe-, the Joe Rogan model, and the unscripted stuff is great, but I think that the problem is the paradigm in the old media has not shifted enough. You know, I have a hard time getting cell phone service here in midtown Manhattan because the cell phone towers are built in the 1980s. But if I go to a suburb of Beijing, I get pistol-quick cell phone service. Okay, so what happened is, it's the paradox of progress. Okay? They skipped over the copper wires and they skipped over the 1980s cellular technology, and they're installing 2017 cellular technology, and it's pistol-fast. We suffer in the United States from the Paradox of Progress. Our airports were made in the 1930s and the 1940s. And so, that footprint is aging on us while they have these beautiful, gleaming airports in Dubai or Beijing. And so, it's the same thing in the media. The media is suffering from, *they got there first.* They had an operating model that worked in the '50s, '60s...possibly '70s. It's not necessarily working in 2017. And then, someone will push back and say, "Well it is. We're super, super profitable." Yes, you are, but you're losing your integrity and you're losing your voice to the American people, and you're allowing new media — unscripted reality news — to take over and be that voice of honesty and objectivity to the American people.

What advice would you give to people in traditional media?

The first thing I'd do — start new CNN. I would look at Cernovich's model and other new media models and I would start a new CNN and I would fund New CNN, and I would fund it separately, and I would have it compete with Old CNN.

And the best example I can give on that is, in 1994/1995, Bill Gates said that the Internet was a *joke* and it was a "temporary fad." And then it dawned on him, the power of the...at that time it was called Netscape — the browser. He was like, "Oh, my God. All these people that are using this browser...I am completely wrong." And so, he-, he adapted and pivoted, and he went out and he asked the question. He said, "How many people are being employed right now in the Internet?" And they said, "Three thousand." He said, "Okay, that's great. We're going to put this building here in Seattle, Washington — or Redmond, Washington — and we're gonna put three thousand people in it." And he immediately went out and created Internet Explorer, and he made an adaptation and pivoted, even though it was off his business model — it was off his core operating system business model — he literally created New Microsoft alongside of Old Microsoft, and it, frankly, saved the company. And so, if I was sitting with Jeff Zucker at CNN or one of these guys, I'd say, "Go create New CNN right now and allow New CNN to compete with Old CNN." And Steve Jobs would tell you that. You know, Steve Jobs — took a Glock and capped the iPod. "Why'd ya kill the iPod, Steve?" "Well, someone was going to kill it — it might as well have been me." And he embedded all the mechanisms of that iPod into the iPhone. And so, now the iPod is completely obsolete. It was going to happen anyway. You know, look at-, look at what's happened to film. You know, we used to go and get a roll of film — Kodak film — put it in the back of a camera. And that's been an annihilated.

Somebody had to do it.

Kodak actually had the patents on-

They did! They had the patents on the digital technology. But again, you know, you just-, you don't think that CNN with their footprint and their media capability could create an unbelievable fresh, new CNN? They absolutely could, but they don't want to disrupt their existing business model, so they'll end up hurting themselves in the long run. But all the great companies take a Glock to their existing business model and they cap it. And if you don't do that, you're going to end up getting melée-d by, you know, renegades and guerrilla warfare — Gorilla Mindset people like Mike Cernovich.

That's what's going to happen.

What would the New CNN look like?

It would be small.

It would be equipped with iPhones and it would be racy. It would be unscripted. It would be getting the news from places like the White House and traditional content, but also it would be newer sourcing, newer ideas and it would be *rogue*. It would be rogue. It would be a different culture and a different business model and it would galvanize people very quickly. You know, there's-, there was a-, when I was a kid, there was a brewery called, "Red Dog Brewery." Most of the great ironies, most of these microbreweries are owned by Anheuser-Busch or Miller Brewery, and-, but they know that they have to have these microbreweries out there to give taste selectivity and-, and make people feel that they're in an avant-garde [setting] trying something new. CNN should be doing that. So should these other media news outlets.

CNN should be tapping into niche audiences.

I think that-, I think that these-, the older paradigm media companies are making a mistake by not operating a parallel business model to tap the niche markets, and to tap the renegade part of the system. Millennials are going to digest and get their news very differently than the current demography that's watching the CNN appointment television news channel.

What are some of the worst examples of Fake News during the election?

The biggest Fake News story of our generation, in my opinion, is the Russian Collusion/Faux-Fake News story related to the president and his campaign and the Russian government — or whatever they're talking about — Russian hackers or Russian influence. I just think it's totally bogus and unfair. I'm not saying that the Russians aren't hacking into our system or trying to hack our water grid or may have some fake bots out there, that are trying to influence the election. I didn't say-, I don't know if that's true or it isn't true, but I know definitively that we were not colluding with the Russians to try to beat Hillary Clinton. So, there was no sovereign state interference. And, by the way, you know, whatever people say about the president, he is a stand-up guy when it comes to that sort of stuff.

He won the election fair and square. He didn't have to do anything like that.

The campaign didn't even coordinate with social media.

People forget today — I'll make this statement, because I was there. People forget today how disorganized and how entrepreneurially lunatic-oriented we were inside that campaign. And so, it just wasn't that kind of campaign.

And, by the way, let me state this for the record [and] I hope you're really listening, and I do hope this makes the documentary: President Donald J. Trump carried every one of us over the finish line. Steve Bannon didn't make him president. Kellyanne Conway didn't make him president. I didn't make him president. Reince Priebus didn't make him president. Donald J. Trump made *himself* president, and he pulled every single one of us over the finish line with him. And so, I find it very disingenuous when people think that they put him in that office, because it was the very opposite.

Well victory has a thousand masters.

Of course. Exactly right.

Talk a bit about the race wars the media's been fomenting.

So, my-, my opinion of the race-baiting that is going on — and my opinion of the portrayal of social strife and the neo-Nazis, and etc. — is another example of a business model by the mainstream cable news networks and media, to try to gin up controversy and to try to create an environment of discontent.

If you look at the population — and, by the way, I have nothing but disdain for Nazis, I think the whole Charlottesville thing, I think you have a zero tolerance policy on Nazis — but I think that they're a very, very small portion of the population. And if this was the 1960s, '70s, or '80s, objectively they wouldn't be worthy enough of the news standing that they're getting right now. So, the weird thing about it is, like, they're calling me a Holocaust denier, because I'm trying to let people know that five million, six million, six and a half million people died in the Holocaust. But they're fueling the neo-Nazi or the Antifa movement by putting them on the air. Just leave them alone. Get them off the air. Get them off the air and they'll stop protesting. They're paid protesters, anyway, so, I mean, you know...just cut it out.

Charlottesville — everyone in America knew it was happening, but only five hundred people showed up.

Exactly. It's not a big deal, frankly, so I think that they gin this stuff up as part of their business model to get ratings and create hysteria. I think that the media has a tendency to gin up controversy and conflict to stir up ratings.

I think-, I think that the media-, I think that the media will gin up controversy, take things and blow them out of proportion, to gin up ratings. These-, these chyrons and graphics, "Breaking News," and all this sort of hysteria, is part of their business model.

It glues people. It's addictive.

Did media underreport violence against Trump supporters?

Well, I think the media, if some historian really gets a hold of-, if some historian really gets a hold of, objectively, what happened during the campaign, they'll find that a lot of the violence at these Trump rallies was instigated by people that were against Trump. It wasn't really the Trump supporters themselves going after each other. So-, so there's another Fake News thing. The greatest thing that happened from that Fake News situation is the American people *knew* better.

Like, "Okay, there's the media trying to go after Mr. Trump and that's going to doubly make sure that I passionately go out and vote for him." Right, exactly.

Exactly.

HAWK NEWSOME INTERVIEW

PART ONE / LOCATION: CHURCH

What is your name, who are you, and what do you do?

> My name is Hawk Newsome. I'm the president of Black Lives Matter of Greater New York. I'm a freedom fighter. I'm a revolutionary. I'm a Christian. I'm a proud American.

I'm gonna throw a little softball question out to you first: What is truth?

> What is true? Jesus Christ? The Word of God? I don't know... *true*? Meaning, "truth?" Wow...I've never been asked that question. We can call it a "softball," because it is profound. But *truth*...what is truth? Truth, to me, is purity. It's powerful. It's not always popular, but it's what's needed.

And how can we know what truth is? As fallen people.

Finding out truth would require a little bit of work, and I would advise everyone to do it. I would say question the source. Question the method being used to deliver this truth to you and do your own research. Really evaluate the information that's being presented to you, so that you can really determine the truth for yourself.

How did you get involved in BLM?

How did I get involved in Black Lives Matter? And when did I become a revolutionary? I was *born* a revolutionary. I was born on a night, it was April 4th, 1977. It was a storm outside. It was thunder. It was rain. It was, like, a really powerful night. And on that night, my mother would say, "A *force* came into that world." Whether it is good or evil is to be debated, but she always makes a joke about that. But, on April 4th, I was born. That was the day that Martin Luther King, Jr. died — a different year — and also Adam Clayton Powell, Jr., who are, you know, prominent civil rights figures. My parents met at a protest. In the South Bronx. They were protesting for an African-American studies class.

I would say that I was born to walk the path that I'm walking now.

I mean, aren't we all? But yet, I mean-, I mean, realistically and sincerely, I was born to fight this fight, and I'm fighting right now for civil rights — for human rights — whatever that may be, whatever form that may be.

I grew up in a very militant household. People say they are "militant" [and] they think *military*, but when we say, "militant," we mean very pro-black, very "woke" is a word that is used now — a very conscious household, whereas you would say, "Look at the employment rate...why are blacks always suffering? Why do blacks always have the poorest schools?" Like, it's just a heightened level of awareness and a desire — a true desire — to change it by any means necessary. And, for me, that meant getting an education and eventually going to law school.

What did you do after law school?

My last year in law school, Trayvon Martin happened. So, that was the first protest I'd ever organized. And I went to two law schools. I went to Howard University, which is really black. And I went to Touro, which is really Jewish. Right? So just two opposite ends of the spectrum — two completely different perspectives. And I was able to combine the two and and come up with this, I guess, this sense of logic...this way of rationalizing that I have when it comes to the law.

When Trayvon Martin happened, I had a hoodies-up rally, and that was at Touro law school. I had white folks, Muslims, Jews, Christians, Latinos...they all came up. The youngest person there might have been twenty-one. The oldest was a judge in his eighties — a little old Jewish man who wore his hoodie to stand in solidarity to say, "Hey, what happened to Trayvon Martin is wrong," and...

After I graduated from law school, I ran for city council right in my hometown, in the Bronx, and I had a message that was different from your average politician. What I was saying to the people was, "The Republicans don't care about your interests — at least, they don't express care for your interests. The Democrats say that they care about you and they don't do anything for you. So, right now is the time for you to really value your vote, and vote for someone who's going to fight for you." I ran. That message was a little too revolutionary. There's-, there's things that happen in our communities, like, you'll see one face in the news in the media-, you'll see that in a neighborhood, but what you're not seeing is that these people are doing you a disservice. Right? Perfect example: You'll see news coverage of a city council member who's playing with children, fighting for children's rights, fighting for housing. However, if you look at the money they raised, thirty-, forty percent came from real estate developers who want to come into these poor neighborhoods and kick people out. So, I ran, and I told people exactly what was happening. And they didn't want to hear the truth. Right?

They wanted something that was comfortable, and something that was familiar, and to, I guess, to put icing on the cake — my opponent gave out free turkeys. Everybody was like, "How can we vote against *her*? She's giving us turkeys for Thanksgiving." I'm trying to give you freedom, jobs, education. Right? I'm fighting for your lives...your rights as Americans. And, unfortunately, you are voting for free turkeys. It hurt, man. But this is-, this is the world...this is the reality that people live in.

What did you think of the media coverage of that election?

My election was really interesting, because there are issues that I had with the media coverage of my election for city council, and they're really significant. Because I could have a press conference, now, as president of Black Lives Matter Greater New York about those same issues today and you get media coverage. But, back then, as a candidate who was fighting against the Democratic Party in the Bronx, and the system that keeps my people oppressed, I would call a news press conference and they wouldn't show up.

Why?

Because if they covered me, the powers that be — which are the senators, the congressmen, the city council members — they say, "We won't give you a story. The next time we get a great story from one of our constituents, we'll make the call to CBS — and you're NBC. We won't give you this on a local level." Right? And this is the way they work. A lot of times, if I want coverage now, I'll call one of the major networks and say that their "... competitor's on the way. Are you coming out? Yeah. Yeah I'm on my way." Like, this is the way it works now.

So, it's sad, because you have people who are great candidates [who] are not getting media coverage — and the incumbents and people doing a disservice to the community, are always on the news. And the constituents always see their faces. A lot of them don't even have to pay for media ads because they're always in the media.

Do you think that same kind of bias exists against both anti-establishment candidates on both sides?

I think anti-establishment candidates on both sides don't get the media coverage that they should get, because they are anti-establishment.

The establishment is the status quo. And for you to challenge that, you are uprooting the very-, you are destroying the machine that everybody's profiting off of...the politicians [are] profiting, the special interests are profiting, the media companies are profiting — everybody's profiting off of the establishment. Right? It's established. It's, well , and the folks who are suffering are those who are oppressed. My people historically suffer. Right? But then you have poor whites. You have poor Latinos. You have poor Muslims. You have a lot of poor folks who are suffering, because the status quo feeds those at the very top. We at the very bottom are left to suffer. Who owns these media companies? The people at the very top. Right? So it makes sense for them to perpetuate a news cycle that would keep them rich.

How would you characterize the media coverage of the Trayvon Martin shooting and its aftermath?

Although people won't see it, although people won't admit to it, America is a very racist place. It was founded on racial practices and these-, these practices still exist today. Maybe to the extent that they-, not to the extent that they were before, but these racist practices still exist. And if you are Christian, if you are an American, you can look at the facts and say, "Yes, this is true." So, you take Trayvon Martin, and you look at the media coverage of Trayvon Martin's death: Young black man, who is thought to be in the wrong neighborhood, was walking with a hoodie on. And a neighborhood watchman, who was — let's call them, "gung-ho" — a bit too excited, saw Trayvon Martin [and] thought that he was a threat.

Why? Because of the racist stereotype. Right? Thugs — hoodlums — are black, and they wear hoodies. You see this on the news. You see this in movies. You see it all the time. Here you have this man with racist tendencies, who's also trigger-happy, and he sees a young black man walking, so he follows him. He stalks him. He calls the police and, eventually, he approaches Trayvon Martin. Trayvon Martin dies. The biggest, most significant piece of this case that the media missed was the fact that the 911 dispatcher told George Zimmerman to *stop* following Trayvon Martin.

When it came down to it...when it came down to it, they said that it was self-defense. Right? That George Zimmerman was "standing his ground" and he-, he didn't have to run. He just defended himself. However, you-, however, you have a man who is given a direct order by law enforcement. They told him to stop following this young black man, because police were on the way. And what happened? What happened? He kept following Trayvon Martin. He accosted Trayvon Martin. And he murdered Trayvon Martin.

So, it's a tragedy. It's a tragedy. Let's talk about something that's happening right now.

There's the case of Delrawn Small. Right? Delrawn Small was a black man who was driving right here in Brooklyn, and a police officer, who just got off work, cut off his car. Okay...Delrawn Small pulled up next to him. The police officer gave some sort of look to Delrawn's girlfriend. His stepdaughter and his daughter were in the backseat - Delrawn Small. He came to a traffic light. Both cars stopped. He got out of his car and walked over to the car and asked, "What are you doing?"

He got close to the car. The officer fired three times. Pow-pow-pow. Into Delrawn Small's chest. Delrawn died.

We took up the case. We wanted to spread awareness, so we shut down the Franklin Delano Roosevelt Highway here in New York City. Black Lives Matter. FDR...you can research it. It was last July. July, 2016. We shut down the highway.

Why? Because we wanted everybody in New York to hear — everybody in the world to hear — what happened to Delrawn Small.

Shutting down the highway gets you media attention. Media attention goes out to whoever is listening, if they portray the story the right way.

But, the bottom line for us-, they call us "criminals" who are shutting down a highway. The bottom line is: You'll know why we are out on this highway, whether you choose to take it or take away-, you'll know why we're out on this highway, if you choose to pay attention to it or not. So, right now, Delrawn Small's case...jury selection was last week. I walked in there with the Black Lives Matter Greater New York t-shirt, and the judge told the attorney general to tell me to take off my t-shirt or flip it over. The Daily News did a story about this.

So, I filed the complaint with the chief administrative judge here in New York City for these criminal cases. And I said that it's not fair that I have to turn my shirt over. However, on the first day of trial, there were no less than fifteen cops there with either a uniform, a jacket, or some sort of clothing, or a lapel pin, that identified them as cops. This is a problem. I think maybe two articles were published on it. This is what needs to go out, because this thing that I quote, "A judge called the shirt provocative," in the news — *provocative*. This is a civil rights organization. However, you have the defendant — who's been indicted for murder and manslaughter — who's sitting here. You have corrections officers in uniforms in front of him.

Also, another one standing next to the judge. You have a ton of cops behind him, all in uniform, or they have some sort of law enforcement medallion on him. You had the court officers in front of this officer, Wayne Isaacs, who's been convicted of murder and manslaughter.

You have the court officers in front of him, you have the police officers, detectives, and whomever sitting behind him, all showing support for this officer who was convicted of murder. And the judge feels that my shirt would intimidate or influence the jury. But you had all these cops on the other side. How could that not affect the jury? How could that not affect the jury? So I put this story out. Two articles. I sent it to over thirty news agencies. Two articles, right?

But, I imagine if I would've stood up in that court room and said, "Fuck all cops." God forgive me, I'm in a church. Right? But imagine if I would have stood up and said that in a courtroom. Every newspaper: "Murder Trial for Cop - Black Lives Matter leader says, "F- all police." Every news story, like, this is-, this is important.

This is my first-, this is my First Amendment right being trampled upon and no one's talking about it. But, if I do something that's controversial, it will be all over the place.

So, okay, here's another important fact from Delrawn Small's case that the media is not talking about: The officer said that he was struck in the face. However, if you watch the video, Delrawn never was close enough to hit him. The media's not repeating this. Right?

There are officers from the crime scene unit [who] said he had no swelling on his face. You couldn't see any injuries. There's pictures of him with the inside of his mouth where he was allegedly hit. There weren't. I haven't seen him in mainstream news. But the office-, though, the reporters tweeted them. This is a major story. An officer shot a man, lied and said he was hit, and he then inflicted a wound on himself.

Why isn't this story being told?

But, they rather show people, you know, crying. They'll show his lawyer telling the story of Delrawn being some sort of, I don't know, *bad* person, but they won't talk about what's really happening.

The truth. They won't tell the truth, and it's out there. It's on video. It's in statements given by tons of people, but they won't show that.

Why do you think they won't show that?

I think they like to maintain a certain narrative. I'm just telling the truth, because I represent the widow. And, so, the brother was like, "Oh, man, why did you do that? Don't talk to the media," because they want to stay away from him being hit. But the bottom line is, they ignored-, they ignored that aspect in Trayvon Martin. And they just said, "Hey, Trayvon never touched him," which wasn't the truth, right? It was a fight. But there shouldn't have been a fight, if George Zimmerman would have listened. Right?

The media is a weapon. Right? Mainstream media is a weapon, if-, if-, if you say the right thing. But, know this, right? There are people on both sides...when I went out and did that thing in D.C., hardcore black activists were like, "No, you can't be-, you can't talk to them. They are Trump supporters. They're evil." There are people on both sides who just want us to go to war. I'll fight. But, I just-, if I can avoid it, I will. You know what I mean? If I can avoid it, I will. That's crazy.

Media is a weapon. If you say the right things, and they air them, it can help you tremendously. You can reach people. You can convince people. You can have a really, really massive impact.

There are people who made careers at influencing the media. Right? You look at Donald Trump — who I really don't like using as an example, but — everybody talks about how bad of a person he is. We see what his policies are. But separate the man from the campaign he ran — if I'm not mistaken — he was able to stay so relevant that he didn't spend a dime on media advertisement until after the primaries. That's not intelligence? Like, please, if you air this, like, just include me taking a shot of him, because they would crucify me. Right? For complimenting Donald Trump.

But, I mean, realistically, he didn't have to spend any money on paid advertisements, because he said things that the media liked. So, you can use the media.

And what I do with Black Lives Matter is that I've been able to influence certain people — certain elected officials — and kinda sway public perceptions and sentiment through the media, which is why the media is a gift for me, at times. At other times, the media is a curse, because they think of us as thugs.

Thug, by the way, is a new word for *nigger*, right? When certain black people hear folks say, "...and these thugs," we hear, "nigger." It's just-, if you look at the verbiage, in the way that it is used, they just interchange those words.

How do you manipulate the media cycle?

Manipulating the media cycle...it's tough. There has to be a number of factors working in your favor. It's best when it's a slow news day. You should be looking to say something that the media doesn't always hear. You should want to stand out from other people, speaking on your topic. I think that I'm fortunate, in a way, because I like to bring God into what I'm doing. I pray before I give speeches. I pray before marches. I pray before press conferences. So, if you take somebody who's working from — who's being held accountable to a higher power — to someone who is, you know, just saying what needs to be said, and I might have a little bit more of an influence. But, there are times where I go off on my own, and I say things that are ungodly and, you know, I mean, I'm not perfect, but sometimes my emotions take over. But, as far as manipulating the media, it just has to be factors that work in your favor. And, like I said, the media is a weapon. If you are able to get your message out, and these stations are it, and maybe if it goes viral, then there's so many people listening to your message. Our message at the Patriot Rally — the "Mother Of All Rallies" — had forty-eight million views. Like, that's amazing. You know how many people that is listening to what we're saying?

So, how do we harness that energy into legislation? People don't like bad cops. Some people don't like all cops. Some people will just say, "Hey, I don't like bad cops." Well, we're creating anti-bad cop legislation. Okay? That will affect all of us as Americans. Now, you have, I don't know, let's say half of that — twenty million people — who want to hear what our opinion is on that and it's a great place to be.

Can you walk us through the MOAR?

So, the day of the Mother Of All Rallies, we had originally planned to go to Washington, D.C., to protest it, but we heard about another rally in Richmond Virginia — which is an open-carry state — around the statue of Robert E. Lee. So, we decided to go there and protest. We went there, and we linked with local organizers, and it wasn't much of anything happening, right? We outnumbered the, you know, Confederate-type protesters by, I don't know, maybe twenty-to-one? Not too many of them showed up, so it was time to go back home. On the way back home, Angelique Kearse was driving the Black Lives Matter Greater New York van. And her husband, [Andrew], died in police custody. Similar to Eric Garner. He said, "I can't breathe. I feel dizzy." They left him there for fifteen, maybe twenty, minutes and he died.

So right now, [what] we're working on is a law. We call it, "Andrew's Law," that says: *If a person complains of injury at the scene of an accident, police officers must call a paramedic to that spot*, which makes sense. This is something everybody should get behind.

Well, she's driving, and we get to Washington, D.C., and she's like, "Oh, my god, I've never been to D.C." I was sleeping in the passenger seat, and I woke up. Then Jay — another member of our group who's been with us and when we protested the Republican National Convention, Charlottesville, he's a soldier, he's always there with us — he said, "I've never been to Washington, D.C., either." So, we decided to get out. And then there was another voice in the back of the car that said, "Hey, y'all know the Mother Of All Rallies is happening..." So, we took a vote if we would go or not to protest. It was a unanimous decision. Everybody wanted to go and protest the patriots and the white supremacists that were there. So, we walked out. There were people who were cheering for us, like, "Yeah! Just in time!"

But, when we arrived at the scene — at the site — people started booing us/heckling us. They were saying, "USA! USA! This is our country. If you don't like it, then leave!" Newsflash: Black people built the White House and the Washington Monument for free, so, if there's anybody who has a right to be here doing anything, it's black people. It's just common sense, right?

Are you going to tell people to leave a country that they built, that they've been in for three hundred/four hundred years, just because they're dissatisfied? If they weren't dissatisfied people on American soil, there would have never been an American Revolution. If those folks who were peeved at the Brits, or whatever, like, if they were-, if they were-, if they were peeved and just left, there would be no America. There's an America because dissatisfied Americans took control of their destiny, fought back, and won their rights, won their independence, won their freedom. But I digress.

Washington, D.C: We're standing to the right of the stage at the Mother Of All Rallies and we had just stepped up and people just started-, just, I guess, flocking to us. First, there was the militia. Then there were people, who were just there to participate, booing us...haggling us. We stood there defiantly with our fists in the air. So, we're standing there. We're chanting, "Black Lives Matter...Black Lives Matter."

The police are nervous, because they know if this group tried to attack us, we-, it was eight of us, and we were outnumbered about two hundred-to-one. All right? They knew if their group tried to attack us, there was nothing they could do. Okay? We were fine, because we believe in fighting for what's right and taking a stand when necessary. So, they're chanting back, "All lives matter," and making comments. [It] wasn't violent, but it was definitely contentious.

And, you know, we saw a few people who were in Charlottesville, and who we had butted heads with a few weeks prior. And, out of nowhere, one of the guys said, "You guys want to go on stage?" Right?

Out of everything I had expected to hear that day, that was the *last* thing. So, I looked over at some of our members, you know, "You wanna go? I want to go on stage." They were like, "Yeah, whatever." And we went out. But, walking up to the stage — and definitely when I got on the stage — my mindset changed. It wasn't fear. It was God, right? And something said, "Tell them who you are. And make them *understand* who you are." The average person there — what do they know about us? Right? They know what the media tells them. They think that we are anti-white, because that gets covered.

They say that we are terrorist sympathizers, because when people do call us "terrorists," the media doesn't dispel that notion.

They blame the killings in Dallas on us. There were five police officers killed in Dallas covering a Black Lives Matter rally. Was this man who did the shooting a Black Lives Matter member? Was he a member of our organization? No. Was he upset with racism in this country? Yes. Police brutality? Yes. But was he representing Black Lives Matter there? No, he wasn't. However, everyone in America thinks Black Lives Matter caused the death of those five cops in Washington, D.C., which couldn't be any further from the truth. But this is, you know, this is what they allowed to be-, to be put out there.

And I think, realistically, if the media really wanted to cover Black Lives Matter and police killings and the killings of police, then here's what they would say: A black person gets killed by the police under questionable circumstances. Black people rally. The cop goes to court and no matter how questionable, it always seems as though the cop walks away. Does this always happen? No. Sometimes the cops get convicted, but it just seems to be a recurring theme. And then there's someone — who's mentally ill, right? — who is sick of this cycle repeating itself. And he gets a gun, and he goes out and kills police officers.

So they say, "Stop Black Lives Matter." That's what you see in the media. But, what you don't see is, "Stop police brutality." Right? Because this is the common theme in all of these cases. Right? And you can just open your-, open your phone, and you can look at a cop kicking people in the face. However, they say BLM is anti-cop. No, we're anti-*this happening*. Right? And if it's happening with cops across the country, can you blame people for being anti-cop?

I can't. I'm not anti-cop. There are members of my group who are. Right? Because I know-, I know cops who are, as people, decent human beings. But, can you honestly look at-, when does the media say, "Let's look at law enforcement in this country and their engagement with black communities"?

You ever [sic] saw that? Like, you ever [sic] saw that on the news? Like, "Let's look at the history of blacks and black communities and law enforcement, and let's try to figure this thing out." What will you find?

Black people's first interactions with law enforcement were when they were deputized slave catchers, and what did they do? They arrested runaway slaves, but they also arrested free people who had their papers. This isn't a myth. This is a fact. You look at the Thirteenth Amendment, you're a free person in this country, unless what? You're in jail. And then you had folk — black folk — being arrested across the now-free United States, and working for free as slaves again. Why doesn't the media tell us this story? Why? Because people like you and I will sit there and say, "Let's figure this out." And, guess what? It disrupts the establishment.

People make money off racism, hatred, fear — right? This is Big Business. The media companies definitely do. And we just have to figure out how to get our own truth out there. So we don't have to rely on the media as much.

PART TWO / LOCATION: DELI

[Hawk asks deli owner what the store is called.]

Community Deli? Ah, that's perfect!

We're here in Brooklyn — home of Biggie Smalls — at the Community Deli. We are in one of those communities that we fight for all the time.

You have poverty. You have a need for services. A need for programs, and needs that have yet to be fulfilled by politicians — or by wealthy billionaires who call New York "home" — who could have done this before they were actually elected to the presidency.

One of my biggest problems with Donald Trump: With his money and his means, he could have done some really great things for the country, even before becoming president. If he really cared about black folk, he could have helped them before he became president. What place better than New York City? He could have done all of the things in New York City. However, he didn't.

[Hawk invites his friend to stand next to him on camera]

Actually, we're here on Marcus Garvey Boulevard. Marcus Garvey is — where is he? — is that man right there. And he was the father of pan-Africanism. It's a concept that's founded in the fact that all black people are interrelated. So they should come together as one. I don't know if everyone agrees with me or not, but when white people come from anywhere in the world to America, they kind of assimilate easily with the dominant class. But when black people come over, there's these walls that are built up, right? So, whereas we can have bridges built — let's say white folks and building bridges — black people build up *walls*. They say, "Oh, you're from Jamaica...I don't like you." Or, "You're from Africa...I don't like you." And then the Jamaicans will call us, "lazy Americans," and Africans call us, "cotton pickers." Right?

But we need to learn how to work together with one another, because I don't believe that our help is going to come from government assistance or things like that. I believe that our help comes from building a community. Right? Working together, building our infrastructures in our communities, group economics, right? Working together, supporting each other in business ventures and things like that. That's how we get what we want.

What you've been saying, a lot of Trump voters say the same thing. They don't want to be lumped in with the racists and white supremacists. As a result, they've lost faith in the mainstream media, and have turned to the alternative/online media. Do you think there's a chance to build bridges between black Americans and the people that run the alternative media?

I think that the white people who voted for Donald Trump — who don't align themselves with white supremacists and those with hardcore racists beliefs — they have to make some sort of penance, okay? They have to come clean and say, "Hey, I am not affiliated with white supremacists. I am against racism." They have to step up and say that, because, by voting, they put themselves in line with folks who hate Jews, who hate blacks. So they have to make their messaging clear. And if they want to work together on how to do that, then I'm all about it, because it's not just saying in the media, "Hey, we're different..." It's actually doing something about it, right? It's actually helping with programs that will help inner city communities.

It's like, okay, we need trade programs — we need to teach folks how to program computers. We need future programmers, we need folks to — I don't know...doctors, lawyers, engineers — go into those communities and help out. That's something you can do. Right? Or you can stay in your own communities and talk to people about racism. Talk to people about Black Lives Matter and how we are not hate-filled terrorist devils. Right? Talk to them about that. Kind of bring them in out of the wilderness of ignorance.

So, your statement that Trump voters aligned themselves with white supremacists — do you think it could be inversely implied that liberals aligned themselves with violent leftists?

For people who vote for Donald Trump to get lumped in with white supremacists and extremists, it's true in a lot of regards, because you have the KKK who are marching the morning after Trump won the election. You have alt-right groups and groups that call themselves "hate groups" that are holding up Trump signs at their rallies. There were Trump signs in Charlottesville. Right? So, let's look at the flip-side of it. Folks who vote Democrat: Are they aligning themselves with leftist extremists? Are they aligning themselves with people on the left who want to exploit and oppress black people? Yes, they absolutely are. My hat is Malcolm X, right? On my hat there is a sign of Malcolm X.

People don't know how to interpret Malcolm X. They knew early Malcolm X, but did they know Al-Hajj Malik El-Shabazz? Post-Mecca Malcolm X, who came back and said, "Hey, I'm a child of God. I love everyone. And I'll work with anyone and everyone to fight racism." That's not the narrative that the media wants out there. So, what you hear is, "By any means necessary,"-Malcolm. "I hate white people"-Malcolm, with the AK-47 by the window. Drop the hate for certain people, keep the AK-47, and then replace the hate with the love.

And he's saying, "Hey, I'm here to fight for what's right — anyone who wants to." And I agree with that. I'm going to paraphrase a statement by Malcolm X wherein he said that the liberal, the white liberal, is one of the biggest enemies that black America has, because you have these folks who pretend to be your friends and they are truly exploiting you. Me, personally-, personally, right? If you have a Republican conservative who's for programs-, if you have a Republican...to tell you the truth: If you have a Republican who is a racist and not ashamed of it, I'll take him over a Democrat who's a racist who covers it up. Right? Who'll call you "nigger" at home, but won't say it to your fa-, give me the guy that says it to my face. Because he could say, "Screw you, nigger," I'll say, "Screw you, cracker," and we'll say, "Okay, I love America."/"Good. Me, too." "I love the Bible."/"Good. Me, too." Let's look at it for what it is and let's figure out some answers. All right so, "Fuck you."/"Fuck you." How can we work together to fix some of the things neither one of us like? We can work together.

But, if you have somebody who's acting like they're my friends, right, and acting as if they're working against me, but they're really working...if you have a liberal or a progressive — let's liven up the language here, right? — if you have a progressive who pretends to be my friend, however, he is not truly fighting for me, then I have a problem with him, because you are just deceiving me.

There is a great philosopher: His name was Curtis Jackson. And he said, "I'd rather a thief than a liar, because a thief is after my salary, but a liar is after my reality."

So, you have the Republicans, and they just want to keep us oppressed, as a whole, right? And they're saying, "Hey, we're fighting for you. We don't want you to have health care. We don't want you to have good schools."

But, then, you have these progressives — these Democrats — that are lying to us, like, "I'll help you. I'll fight for your schools. I'll give you equal opportunity." However, our schools still suffer. Fifty years later, we're still suffering. There's still crime. There's still so many needs that have yet [to be] met, and they've been our friends and they have been advocating for us for so long.

In 1960, there was a political shift, right? This is around the time of Dr. King. The Republican Party said, "Okay, if we side with Dr. King, we're going to lose our base. So, let's stay here. Let's-, let's-, let's stay...let's be pro-white, keep that agenda intact, and let the Democrats bend and LBJ...let them fall. We're going to stay hardcore true to the south, right?" They staked their flag and they've stayed true to it for decades. Right?

But the Democrats yielded so that they could get the black vote. What have they done with it?

Yeah, we've had some victories. But my people are still suffering. Like, who's really fighting for us? Who's really fighting to help make life better for black folks? Like, you can say, "Oh, pull yourself up by the bootstraps." Yeah, there are some that can do that. However, poor, underfunded schools, drug-infested communities, homes that are devastated by mass incarceration — how can you fix that? You don't fix that by throwing everyone in jail, and not giving them therapy. You fix that by really looking at what's going on and seeking answers, and really doing something about it. And no one's done it yet. Right?

When living in America as a black man, I'm constantly traumatized. I'm traumatized by the statistics that I see. I'm traumatized by what I watch on the news when black people are choked to death. I'm traumatized by what I see on social media. Black men being shot in front of their families by the police and nothing happening. Black men with full-carry weapons permits. I'm traumatized. Where's the help for my trauma? Who's addressing my need psychologically?

These are things we don't look at. I see schools with old books and teachers that don't really care. This is what I see day-to-day.

And you tell me it's not institutionalized? You tell me, "Pull yourself up by the bootstraps and make it work"? How can you, when you face so many disadvantages that our government sanctioned?

Talk about the coverage of the opioid crisis.

Man, he stole that from my post! You know how good I felt? No, but, go ahead. Talk about it.

Speak about the media's coverage of crack cocaine with Reagan in the '80s, versus media's coverage of the opioid crisis today.

This is the meat. This is the meat. We're getting to the meat of this thing. I like that. I like real conversation.

Okay. So, when we think about media coverage, and how they portray these issues affecting communities, they say that everything is separate and equal, but the coverage of black cases is very different from the coverage of white cases.

You look at victims and why we fight in the Black Lives Matter movement. There was a killing of a white woman by two police officers. She was in her pajamas. She may have been mentally ill. Both officers shot her. And one officer shot her. The next day, the news reports said, "Yoga instructor shot dead by police officers," and it talked about the whole situation and who she was, her friends...

However, when a black person is killed by the police, it lists that they were arrested for smoking a joint twenty years ago. Right? If they're arrested for unpaid parking tickets. But, like, understand, sometimes it's even worse, but when a black person is killed, they're villainized, right? And when a white person is killed, they are victimized. Villainized/victimized. And that's no one else but the media.

The first thing you hear when a cop kills someone of color is their criminal history. If they're an alcoholic, they were a woman beater, they were...who knows? You only hear the negative. They may have been suspended from school or fired from a job. You always hear that. But when it's the inverse, when it's a white person, you hear from their friends how great of a person they were. We have to launch campaigns to prove to society that-, social media campaigns to prove to society that they were actually good people, that they didn't deserve to die, or that just because a man was selling loose cigarettes — or because a male was having an argument — he didn't deserve to be murdered by the police.

We talk about the Constitution — the Eighth Amendment protects against cruel and unusual punishment. So, should a man yelling at a cop be shot to death? That's cruel and unusual. Why do we have to fight this? Why isn't it that the media is portraying this for what it is? That's a problem.

We look at the opioid crisis in America. Right? White people: Opioid crisis / Public health emergency. Black people: Crack cocaine problem. / War on Drugs. Give the white people assistance in treatment that they need. Give the black people — victims and dealers — jail time. There's a problem.

And I was watching Fox News the other night. I watch both. I want to know what everyone's saying. I was watching Fox News the other night and there was a father — a white man of means — he was on the news, and he was like, "My son didn't deserve to die as a victim of his addiction. And what America has to know is these are real people dying from these drug problems." What does that imply? That the blacks who died — that the black mothers who overdosed, that the black fathers who overdosed, that the black kids who overdosed — they weren't *real* people. But this is what the media allows out there.

Now, I watched Fox after our appearance at the MOAR rally, right? — The Mother Of All Rallies. They said that we stood on stage and that we said we loved the police. I'm not anti-cop, but I don't love the police at all. Okay? I do not approve of the way they treat my people.

And I know that they are the gatekeepers. I know how to fix the problem with policing, and that's through legislation. All right? That's through pressure on politicians. That's how we change the police. With that being said, this is what Fox News said. They said you-, they said we love police. We don't love police officers. Like, you know. Really?

What about me says that I love police? People who arrest my folks for no reason, who treat them differently than other Americans — how can I love you? Right? I understand that you have a job to do and I understand that in their profession there are people who are bad. Okay? And all I'm saying is that when they are-, when they break laws, when they will behave in an illegal fashion, that they are subject to the same sort of prosecution as everyone else in this country. That's it. It doesn't make me anti-cop. That makes me pro-justice.

With Twitter and social media bubbles, how can we communicate with one another?

We need to-, it's kind of cool. We need to find a credible, non-biased news source that will report the news from both sides, equally, right? Both sides of the race card, of-, of the political spectrum, equally. Because you have Dylann Roof — who identified with white supremacist groups, alt-right groups — and he went into this church, and he killed nine black people. Right? And then you have this black man, who was — who we imagine is unaffiliated with anyone — who goes and targets six white people. Both crimes. Right? Both, equally like, heinous, but what takes it to another level with Dylann Roof is the KKK has been killing people in this country for two centuries. For two centuries, and nothing has been done about it. Right? Some folks went to jail but nothing has been done about it.

And you read a report from the media that says that the FBI released a report that the KKK infiltrated law enforcement, and you see reports of police officers in the South who resigned because they were discovered to have been in the KKK. This is a serious issue. And then you have a person who's running for president, and he's endorsed by Klansmen, and he doesn't reject those endorsements. This is where it's a problem, right? Because you have a hate group who has carried out terrorist acts. No one can deny it. I mean, by definition, they are a hate group. By definition, they have carried out terrorist attacks and threats.

Why isn't the media showing people all over the country denouncing the KKK, saying that they're wrong? I just-, I don't understand, like, why the media has a problem with denouncing white supremacy, right? This is some-, this is a problem. This has been a problem for five hundred years. Like, why don't they have a problem denouncing white supremacy? I just don't get it.

What do we need? We need truth. We need truth in media. We need to open up our eyes...to both sides. Like I told you, I watch Fox News. I also watch CNN. I've been on CNN before. Fox hasn't invited me up for obvious reasons. But, to be perfectly honest, you need to see what's coming from both sides, so that you can understand what's really going on. Like, I have conservatives who are my friends. And I read their timelines and they come in and they comment in my timeline, and it's good to know what the other side is thinking.

Some folks are trolls. They don't want to know the truth. You can present them with fact after fact and each time they'll find a reason to destroy your logic. Some things are infallible. I mean, some things are just absolute truth. Certain things you just cannot deny. However, they will deny them. That's the problem with the individual. We don't need those people, right? Those folks who are that against the truth, who are against equality, who are against peace, love...I'd say they're even against God. If you don't want to hear the truth about what's causing a certain-, if you won't accept empirical data, absolute truths on what's causing harm to a certain group, then you have a serious problem within yourself.

And I don't know who can help you.

I don't care to deal with those people. Those people are the enemies of all things that are good. There's just something evil about them. But the folks who have an open heart...you don't have to share my politics. You don't have to agree with everything that I say. But if you-, if you could just look at this and say, "Hey, that's right/that's wrong." Then you might be on your way to solving some of society's greatest problems.

We talked about Trayvon Martin earlier...this is perfect. Because this is politics in America. I was running for office. I was running for office and my campaign mana-, I was running for office in maybe 2012 — I was running for city council in New York City and it was a Trayvon Martin rally led by Al Sharpton. Jay-Z was there. Beyonce was there. Trayvon Martin's family was there. Everyone was there. And I got there a little bit late. So, people were standing around taking pictures and my campaign manager said, "Come over here. We're taking pictures with all of these celebrities. You need to be here."

However, I saw a few people walking away, and I'm like, "We're not marching? We're not doing anything?" And it was like, "I'll march." They had a banner. It was four people on my staff and maybe six of them. So, I said, "Let's march. Let's take the Brooklyn Bridge." The whole time we're marching, my campaign manager is on my ph-, on my phone like, "You need to be here with these politicians and celebrities." I was with the people. Where I-, where I belonged. Right? And we led that march across the Brooklyn Bridge. About midway through, there were cops to my left and my right, and there were cops on scooters, right? I look up — there's a police helicopter and there's photographers everywhere. And I looked behind me. What started out as ten people was now three thousand people on the Brooklyn Bridge and it was just amazing. Right? So we marched across the Brooklyn Bridge — we marched at the Barclays Center. We gave speeches there and the *Daily News* — I like the *New York Daily News*, right — I was-, I was in the paper. It was, like, "Jay-Z, Beyonce," and then it was me — this big page, this big picture — my fist up, marching across the bridge, and it read: "It's not about black or white. It's about justice." Maybe I was onto something.

Maybe I was onto something in D.C. Maybe if I talked about it in the forms of justice only, that might be common ground for people...where they join the fight.

But it's hard for me not to talk about centuries of oppression and racism. Right? Like, why do I have to disarm my message to get other people to join in? Why can't they just say, "You know what? Five centuries of racism and oppression. They built this country. They still don't have rights. That's wrong. That's an injustice. Let's help them fight for justice. Let's uphold the Constitution. Let's really make America great."

All right.

WHAT'S NEXT?

If you've made it this far into the book, I hope you've enjoyed it.

While the book has ended, our conversation has only just begun. You can visit www.HoaxedMovie.com for all the latest news and information about this project.

I also write thousands of words each week and have over 100 podcasts for you to listen to.

You can read my ongoing writing at www.Cernovich.com

You can listen to the Mike Cernovich Podcast on iTunes and Android: www.soundcloud.com/cernovich

If you enjoyed this book, please give it an honest review on Amazon. It helps others learn the backdrop behind the Fake News Media, allowing all of us to navigate the competing stories more effectively.

ABOUT THE AUTHOR

Mike Cernovich is an author, filmmaker, and journalist. He is the producer of the 2018 film *Hoaxed: Everything They Told You Is A Lie.* His first film, *Silenced: Our War On Free Speech*, featured Alan Dershowitz, Candace Owens, and a diverse cast featuring rabbis, adherent Muslims, Christians, and offensive comedians discussing the state of free speech in America.

His first book *Gorilla Mindset* is an international best-seller, and has sold nearly 100,000 copies. Its mindset techniques have helped countless people improve their health and fitness, develop deeper personal and romantic relationships, and take control of anxiety and fear.

37684350R00259

Made in the USA
Columbia, SC
30 November 2018